Murder By The Bay

Murder By The Bay

Historic Homicide
In and About the
City of San Francisco

By Charles F. Adams

Word
Dancer
Press

Sanger, Californa

Published by Quill Driver Books/Word Dancer Press, Inc.
1831 Industrial Way #101
Sanger, California 93657
559-876-2170 • 1-800-497-4909 • FAX 559-876-2180
QuillDriverBooks.com
Info@QuillDriverBooks.com

Quill Driver Books' titles may be purchased in quantity at special discounts for educational, fund-raising, business, or promotional use. Please contact Special Markets, Quill Driver Books/Word Dancer Press, Inc. at the above address or at **1-800-497-4909**.

Quill Driver Books/Word Dancer Press, Inc. project cadre:
Kathy A. Chillemi, Michelle Doland, Doris Hall,
Dave Marion, Stephen Blake Mettee
Printed in the United States of America

To order another copy of this book, please call
1-800-497-4909

Library of Congress Cataloging-in-Publication Data

Adams, Charles F. (Charles Francis), 1927-
  Murder by the bay : historic homicide in and about the city of San Francisco / by Charles F. Adams.
     p. cm.
  ISBN 1-884995-46-2 (trade pbk.)
  1. Homicide—California—San Francisco—History—Case studies. 2. San Francisco (Calif.)—History—Case studies. 3. San Francisco (Calif.)—Social conditions—Case studies. I. Title.

HV6534.S3A63 2004
364.152'3'0979461—dc22

                                                    2004014146

Contents

Introduction

Murder has a long and distinguished history in San Francisco and the Bay Area. In fact, there is reason to believe that murder was a fashionable and fascinating crime even before modern history began to record acts of homicide in the City of Saint Francis.

Before the Gold Rush, when the population of the area consisted of native Indians, some Mexican settlers, and a few courageous missionaries, killing a longtime rival or an adversary of the moment was considered by many to be a reasonable and acceptable way of righting a wrong or advancing a cause. The mission fathers were more than willing to overlook a murder if the perpetrator could be converted. And there is more than one murder included in the early military events at the Presidio.

But murder in San Francisco didn't really make its way into the history books until the discovery of gold in the Sierra foothills, when settlers by the tens of thousands came to stake their claims in a territory that had few laws and even fewer scruples. During the first half of the decade of that era—from 1849 to 1855—the historian Herbert H. Bancroft estimates that there were 4,200 murders in Northern California and that at least 1,200 of these took place in San Francisco. For the large part, these went virtually unnoticed and unpunished. It would be unfair, however, to say that local justice was totally ineffective: Over the period, there was one—just one—official conviction for the crime.

In 1853, the government of the State of California announced that it would cease what it described as "the hopeless task of recording murder in California." It was a rare morning when a body was not found lying in the mud outside a San Francisco saloon—or a corpse was not washed up on the shore by the San Francisco tides.

It is little wonder that murder—and crime generally—went largely unpunished. In 1851, for example, San Francisco's population had swollen to 30,000, yet the city had only twelve constables, who answered to no particular organization. Of course, as the area became more populated and more civilized, as families and institutions were established, as more and more laws were enacted, murder became more thoroughly investigated and its prosecution more frequent. The early vigilante groups were the first real, if clumsy, attempts at establishing law and order. And, eventually, the more traditional forces of justice were invigorated. Police arrested, judges adjudicated, lawyers argued, and juries pondered. Yet, it all seemed to have little effect on San Francisco's appetite for crime. Murders by the Bay may have declined in number, but what they lacked in quantity they made up for in character.

Not all murders are created equal, and San Francisco has had more than its share of truly fascinating and historic homicides. Comparatively young at a hundred and fifty years, San Francisco and its Bay Area can stand proudly with Paris, London, and New York in the splendor of its misdeeds—with murders that have suspense, horror, audacity and flair. Perhaps it has something to do with the violent origins of the city, or the willingness of Franciscans to endure outrage, or even the geography of the place itself: the hills and valleys that seem to give everything a disquieting slant.

The murders that you will read about in this book have been selected not only for their shock value or for the mysteries they present, but also because they seem peculiarly San Franciscan. It doesn't seem likely that they would have occurred anywhere else. They all contain a convergence of personality, circumstance, character, and, yes, geography that pin them exclusively to San Francisco and its environs.

These murders have also been chosen for their historic importance. Each of these murders had some impact on its times, on the course or application of the law, or in the manner in which it revealed a shortcoming in society that begged resolution. They range from murders in the earliest days of San Francisco to murders in relatively recent times. Most of these murders were solved; some were not. They are murders that fascinated the city, sometimes for weeks, often for years.

It is the author's hope that you will find them fascinating as well. Violent crime can never be amusing, but, as I hope you will soon discover, it can make for very good reading.

Charles F. Adams

Chapter One

The Doomed Editor—1856

By the mid 1850s, San Francisco was in a state of explosive growth. It had been just a handful of years since the scruffy village of Yerba Buena had taken on its more imposing name, and the population had swollen from less than five hundred to more than fifty thousand. With this awesome growth came a great deal of crime and not a little chaos. Just several years earlier, the Vigilante Committee of 1851, a group of San Francisco's leading citizens who usurped the rights of the constituted authorities, had restored a semblance of order to the city. But within several years, criminality was once again on the rise. Burglaries increased beyond all precedent. Groups of squatters held buildings and land illegally. There was political graft and jury tampering. It would take an historic event to bring things to the point where the citizenry would once

San Francisco in 1856, Yerba Buena Island in the background.

James King of William, crusading editor of the *San Francisco Bulletin.*

again decide to take matters into its own hands. That event was the murder of a remarkable man with an unusual name. He was James King of William, and his murder would change the course of the city's history.

In the summer of 1848, a small band of travelers made its way across the narrow isthmus of Panama, en route from the ship that had brought them from the Eastern seaboard of the United States to another ship that would carry them up the coast of California to the fledgling town of San Francisco. Among them was a bearded man of twenty-six, less than average in height but nonetheless imposing in his carriage. His large, piercing eyes were framed by black side-whiskers and a clump of dark, unruly hair. His straight-lined lips were almost hidden by a mustache, which was in serious need of trimming.[1] He was generally quiet as he walked, but his step was firm and decisive. When he did speak, his voice was commanding and confident. It was a voice that would be heard often over the next seven years on the streets of San Francisco and in that city's halls of power. And, after that voice was stilled, it nonetheless echoed down the hallways of history.

He was born James King in Georgetown in 1822, in the District of Columbia. He was born with a restless nature and a great sense of curiosity. Unhappy with the ordinariness of his name and the fact that he was often confused with several other James Kings in the area, he appended the name of his father, William, to that of his own. As James King of William, he spent his early manhood in a number of places and occupations. He served as a business clerk in Pittsburgh and Michigan. Returning to his native area, he helped publish a Democratic campaign sheet called *Kendall's Expositor* in Washington, D.C. Later, he entered banking with the firm of Corcoran and Riggs, and he also worked as a reporter for the *Washington Globe*.[2] He married and began to raise a family.

But the hot, humid summers of the nation's capital were not to his liking, and he decided to make the arduous journey to California in the name of health and adventure. King's brother had already traveled to that remote area of the country and it was he who recommended the sea and land route through Panama.

As King and his fellow travelers sailed up the coast of California, word reached them of the discovery of gold in the foothills of the Sierra Nevada mountains. The news was electrifying and irresistible, and when King landed in San Francisco, he immediately purchased supplies and struck out for the mines and streams where he expected to make his fortune. Fate and fortune, however, were not with him, and so he journeyed down to Sacramento and worked in a banking firm until he had earned enough money to return to civilization in Washington. However, once back in the East, he missed the rough-and-tumble life of the West, and he decided his future lay in banking in San Francisco. He established lines of credit between that city and the nation's capital, journeyed once again to California through Panama, and on December 5, 1849, he opened the banking house of James King of William in San Francisco.[3]

His bank grew quickly and profitably, and by the following year he was able to send for his wife and four children. King's profits continued to mount, and by 1851, his fortune was estimated at $125,000[4], a tremendous sum in that era. He became a man of importance and influence in the city's civic and political circles. He played an important role in the establishment of the first Committee of Vigilance, and is formally listed as member number 186.[5] On occasion, he took on the defense of accused prisoners, declaring that "none but the vicious should be accused and none but the guilty punished."[6]

King's prospects continued to improve and his wealth to grow. By 1853, his fortune had grown to more than half a million dollars.[7] More important, his reputation as a person of honesty and integrity seemed clearly established. The *San Francisco Alta* described him as a "quiet, dignified and honorable gentleman" who "sustained a reputation for uprightness, fair dealing and superior business qualifications."[8]

Unhappily, King's success would not last long, nor would his reputation. Nothing seemed permanent in this land where fortunes were won and lost overnight and where success seemed all too frequently to be followed by disaster. Due to the treachery of one of his own employees who misused a large sum of money with which he had been entrusted, King suddenly found himself in a precarious financial position. Admitted King, "I am prey to the most agonizing doubts and fears. For the first time in my life I am unexpectedly placed in a position where in the event of a run (on my bank) I could not possibly meet my engagements."[9]

Desperate, King persuaded the banking house of Adams and Company to take over his assets and the responsibility for his financial obligations. The price to King was high. He surrendered all of his personally held real estate and stocks, his home, his furniture, and even his horses. Then he humbly accepted a position at Adams and Company, as a cashier. Still, his humiliation was not complete. Adams and Company shortly thereafter went into default through mismanagement, costing King not only his modest new job but the remainder of his reputation as well.

With a large number of customers of the collapsed Adams bank looking for a scapegoat, attention turned on King himself. A rumor ran through the city that King had attempted to restore his fortunes by creating risky ventures for the bank and that he had profited hugely from its failure. King was enraged at this new attack on his reputation and he retaliated vigorously, claiming that Adams and Company had failed to listen to his own alarms about the bank's methods. He further accused the receiver, a man named Cohen, of misusing the bank's remaining funds. Cohen was, in turn, enraged by King's accusations and challenged him to a duel. King declined on moral grounds.

King was now completely adrift. With the failure of his own bank, the loss of his home and property, and the subsequent failure of the bank that employed him, King's prospects were bleak indeed. But King was nothing if not resilient. Within weeks he emerged, to the astonishment of both his friends and his detractors, not as a banker, but as a newspaperman. On October 8, 1855, the first issue of the *San Francisco Daily Evening Bulletin* appeared on the city's streets. The masthead proudly proclaimed that its editor was James King of William.[10]

In truth, King was not a complete stranger to the fourth estate. As a young man, he had worked briefly for the *Washington Globe*, and he had frequently bombarded San Francisco's papers with letters and correspondence, defending himself against attack and rumor. In fact, it was through the vehicle of an elaborately argued and passionate letter to the *Alta California* that he had declined the opportunity to fight the duel with Cohen.

The *Bulletin* began life modestly as a four-page sheet, just ten by fifteen inches in size, but it would soon bring King state-wide celebrity, and it would enable King to etch his name in the history of the West. King had obtained a firm agreement from the owners of the new paper that he would have complete editorial control and that the *Bulletin* would be willing to tackle the corruption and crime in the city head on. King quickly made it clear that he had little to lose: King declared in the first edition, "Necessity, not choice, had driven us to this experiment. No one can be more fully sensible than ourselves of the folly of newspaper enterprise as an investment of money. But we have no (invested) money of our own (for we have none), and a few hundred dollars, generously advanced by friends, is all that we have risked in the enterprise." King then made a firm declaration of his independence: "Whatever may be our political bias individually, as conductor of the *Evening Bulletin* we shall act independently of either political party that now divides the State. By being independent of either party, however, we by no means intend a neutrality or indifference to public affairs.... We shall advocate such measures as may seem to us best for the public good."[11]

From that point on, King used the *Bulletin* to deliver clearly stated sermons on what he believed to be the outrages taking place in the city: municipal corruption, unprosecuted crime, public apathy. He railed against the amounts that city, county and state governments were spending. He cried out for better schools and improved roadways. Of greater significance, however, was his rhetorical style. His paper and his writing were clearly a reflection of his own character—reckless, extravagant, flamboyant, often wrong, but seldom dull. Nor was he hesitant to name names: Palmer, Cook, and Company were the "Uriah Heeps of San Francisco"; David Broderick was "as unblushing as the darkest fiend"; Mayor Van Ness was "the tool and abettor of thieves and ruffians and a malignant misanthrope."

As the months wore on, King's editorials became the scourge of the city's malefactors, as well as the bane of its leading citizens. King attacked gambling, houses of ill repute, the city's harbor master (principally for being a friend of Broderick's), and even a dinner honoring Tom Paine.

King's editorial style and his eagerness to attack almost any target he could find, however grand or trivial, soon made the *Bulletin* "must reading" in San Francisco.

From its modest first issue of several hundred copies, it grew within a month to 2,500 copies, and within just two more months it passed 3,500 in circulation to make it the best read journal in the city.[12]

King not infrequently called for public action in the streets when the normal processes of the law seemed ponderous. Having been a member of the first Vigilance Committee, he often cried out for another such committee for crimes not properly punished by the authorities. One such occasion was the shooting of United States marshal William Richardson by a gambler named Charles Cora. Following an incident at a theatre during which Richardson's wife had quarreled with a lady who accompanied Cora, there had been a brief argument between the two men. The dispute seemed to have been settled quickly, but several days later Cora encountered Richardson on the street and drew a pistol. Richardson cried out, "You would not shoot me, would you? I am not armed!" But Cora calmly aimed his pistol at Richardson's chest and fired. Richardson staggered several steps and fell dead. Cora, according to witnesses, then coolly pocketed his weapon and strolled calmly on his way. The citizenry, not unaccustomed to disputes settled by gunfire, was quick to express its outrage at the dastardly nature of this particular killing. Richardson had been a respected enforcer of the law; Cora was a known gambler and plunderer. Richardson had been unarmed and pleaded for his life. Cora had coolly dispatched him and then strolled away with disturbing nonchalance.

Cora was duly arrested and eventually placed on trial. The case seemed cut-and-dried to most onlookers, but it droned on and on through the weeks. Cora's improbable tale was that he had acted in self-defense, that Richardson had threatened him with a knife. Numerous witnesses testified that they had seen no such occurrence, but a carefully bribed jury deliberated for several days and then announced that they were unable to reach a verdict. The hung jury was dismissed by the judge and the defendant was remanded into the custody of a Cora confederate.

King and his *Bulletin* went into a frenzy of rhetorical outrage. "Hung be the heavens with black," he railed. "The money of the gambler and the prostitute has succeeded, and Cora has another respite…. Rejoice, ye gamblers! Rejoice with exceeding gladness! You…have triumphed over everything that is holy and virtuous and good; and triumphed legally— yes, legally." Furthermore, King claimed that the princely sum of $40,000 had been raised by Cora's fellow gamblers for the specific purpose of bribing the jurors.[13] King hinted again at the need for street justice. "While we want no Vigilance Committee, if it can be avoided; but we do want to see the murderer punished for his crime."[14]

Also festering in King's mind at this time were the activities of a politician named James P. Casey. Casey had a long history of fixing San Francisco elections. His activities reached their zenith in one election for city supervisor in which Casey had himself proclaimed the victor by a margin greater than the number of registered voters in the district. This was exactly the kind of outrageous behavior that drove King to a fury, and his pen was once again equal to the task. After Casey's defeated opponent had taken a pistol shot at him, King wrote the following editorial, dripping with acid sarcasm.

> "Our impression at the time was that Bagley was the aggressor. It docs not matter how bad a man Casey had been, nor how much benefit it might be to the public to have him out of the way.... The fact that Casey has been an inmate of Sing Sing prison in New York is no offense to the laws of this State; nor is the fact of his having stuffed himself through the ballot box as elected to the Board of Supervisors any justification for Mr. Bagley to shoot Mr. Casey, however richly the latter may deserve to have his neck stretched for such fraud."[15]

Needless to say, this editorial inflamed the redoubtable Mr. Casey, and he hastened to the offices of the *Bulletin* to register his outrage, particularly concerning the reference to Sing Sing. King simply ordered Casey out of his office without any suspicion that his action portended dire consequences.

Shortly after five o'clock, King left his office and hastened up Montgomery Street toward his home. When he reached the Pacific Press Building, he was astonished to see Casey suddenly blocking his way. Some later maintained that Casey yelled, "Arm yourself!"—but others testified he did not. Casey threw off his cloak and aimed a revolver at King. There was the sound of a shot and a puff of smoke; King reeled at the impact of the bullet which struck him in the left breast, passed through his lung and exited under his shoulder blade. "Oh, God!" he yelled, "I am shot!" With blood flowing from his left side, King staggered toward the Express office. Several passersby helped him into a chair, then later to a bed, where he lay in great pain and bleeding profusely.

Almost immediately, pandemonium broke loose in the streets of San Francisco. This was a crime of such magnitude—so brazenly carried out in broad daylight—that even the somewhat numbed consciences of San Franciscans, accustomed as they were to a high level of entrenched lawlessness, were truly shocked. Within five minutes, a throng of men

The shooting of James King of William by James Casey. *Frank Leslie's Illustrated Daily*

Montgomery Street in 1856, site of the murder. *Bancroft Library*

gathered in the streets; within ten minutes, it reached almost as far as the eye could see. "Hang him," they yelled. "Hang the wretch from a lamp-post!" Casey, fearing for his own life, rushed to the nearby jailhouse and demanded protection from the jailor and the sheriff. The crowd rushed to the jailhouse and demanded Casey, and they began to batter the jailhouse door. Casey was rushed into a carriage in the back and hurried to the stronger county jail, located only a few blocks away. The angry crowd pursued the carriage yelling, "Kill him! Kill him!" When the carriage reached the county jail, the mob was astonished to see it protected by dozens of armed men, many of them known to be, like Casey, gamblers and men of bad repute.

The scene that followed was pure chaos. Men churning and screaming; the victim's brother, Thomas King, exhorting the crowd to take the jail by force; the arrival of an armed militia to protect the jail; Mayor Van Ness pleading for order; more men arriving from all comers of the city. Now not only were the streets filled with screaming, yelling men, but every roof, window, and balcony in sight was jammed with people yelling, cheering, and demanding retribution. A second squad of militia appeared on the scene, attempting to restore order, but only adding to the confusion. All evening the restless, surging mob jammed the streets in front of the jail. More police and soldiers arrived with every hour, but the crowd only grew louder and more dangerous. But finally, lacking any real leadership, the crowd's fury ebbed and at about midnight it began to disperse.

Throughout San Francisco that night, rumors abounded: that Casey and his cell mate, Cora, had been spirited away; that the jail would be taken in the morning; that King would actually recover from his wounds; that he would not. But the most exciting rumor of all was that there would be a revival of popular justice to take the place of the elected authorities, that there would be another Vigilance Committee.

Two of these rumors would prove to be correct. The formation of another Vigilance Committee was already underway. Early that evening, several members of the Committee of 1851 had asked William T. Coleman, a leader of the earlier group, to form a new Vigilance Committee. He eventually and reluctantly agreed, demanding absolute authority over its actions in order to preclude any of the excesses of the earlier group. Within twenty-four hours, it had enrolled more than fifteen hundred members, including General William T. Sherman and most of the city's civic and financial luminaries.

Meeting of the Vigilance Committee in Portsmouth Square.

Commandeering a building on Sacramento Street near Montgomery, it met in a solemn, if sometimes boisterous, session and issued the following proclamation:

> "We do bind ourselves to perform every just and lawful act for the maintenance of law and order...but we are determined that no thief, burglar, assassin, ballot stuffer, or other disturber of the peace shall escape punishment by quibbles of the law, the carelessness or corruption of the police force, or the laxity of those who pretend to administer justice."[16]

And what, in the meantime, was happening to James King of William? Casey's victim lay mortally wounded in his bedchamber, attended by a host of friends and doctors. Outside stood a crowd so vast that ropes had to be placed around the building to protect it. People milled about day after day demanding news of his condition. King clung to life, feverish and in pain and attended by a score of doctors (enough, the historian Bancroft noted, to kill any man!). Finally, King expired, and the news of his death ignited a city already in ferment.

The demand for retribution could now not be denied. The Vigilance Committee swung into action. Meeting in Twin Verein Hall at Bush and Stockton, the committee began to assume a markedly military character, with men organized into companies of a hundred each. And there was no shortage of available manpower. Registration of men joining the committee continued at a rapid pace, and the committee soon numbered more than eight thousand.[17]

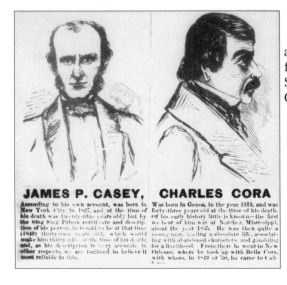

James Casey and Charles Cora, focus of the Second Vigilance Committee.

Hour after hour, the companies drilled. Money raised from the city's merchants provided guns and weaponry in abundance, and on Sunday morning, May 18, the Vigilance companies began their march to the jail. The main body proceeded westward along Sacramento Street toward Montgomery, marching row after row, with steely blue bayonets flashing. Within minutes they surrounded the jail, and their leader, Marshall Doane, strode to the prison door and presented the sheriff the following message: "Sir: You are hereby requested to surrender forthwith the possession of the county jail now under your charge to the citizens who present this demand, and to prevent the effusion of blood by instant compliance. By order of the Committee of Vigilance."

The sheriff estimated that his thirty men were outnumbered by approximately three thousand vigilantes. It was an easy decision. He surrendered Cora and Casey without a fight.

The two men were accorded the benefit of a trial. It was perhaps not the trial they would have received from the established authorities. They were denied the advantages of outside counsel, and the jury was selected from members of the Vigilance Committee. But it was a trial nevertheless, and both Cora and Casey were permitted to make a brief defense. Casey's was the most imaginative, claiming that King had died not from the wound inflicted by the defendant but rather from the incompetent ministrations of his doctors. Nor was their case helped by the fact that the trial was interrupted several times by the tolling of the bells signifying King's departure from the earth. The verdict was unavoidable: guilty of murder; death by hanging.

The two men were taken with reasonable haste back to jail, and they arrived to see that construction was already underway on gallows extending from the windows of the upper floor. Vigilante troops surrounded the platform to hold back the crowd, as Cora and Casey were brought out. The nooses were adjusted about their necks, and a priest gave a final benediction. Cora stood silent and erect, presenting a certain image of courage and nobility. Casey, on the other hand, came completely unglued. Trembling and somewhat hysterical, he began a long and largely incoherent speech. The crowd grew impatient, as did the hangman. He interrupted Casey's babbling by cutting the rope that held the platform and both men went suddenly to their deaths.

That essentially ended the work of the second Vigilance Committee, and after dispatching a few other minor criminals, it eventually surrendered its powers back to the vested authorities. The events provoked much chest puffing and pontificating on the part of the citizenry and the

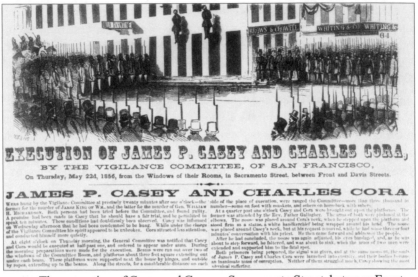

The execution of Casey and Cora on Sacramento Street, between Front and Davis streets. *Bancroft Library*

San Francisco journals. The committee itself left the scene with soaring oratory:

> "Our single heartfelt aim has been the public good; the purging, from our community of those abandoned characters whose actions have been evil continually…. Our labors have been arduous, our deliberations have been cautions, our determinations firm, our counsels prudent, our motives pure. The Committee of Vigilance (finds) great pleasure in resigning their power into the hands of the people, from who it was received."[18]

But the truth is that these events actually involved four separate murders: First was the killing of U.S. Marshal Richardson by the gambler Cora. Second was the shooting of James King of William by the politician Casey. And, if those who claim the Vigilance Committee was nothing but organized mob rule are correct, the third and fourth murders were the hangings of Cora and Casey. Clearly, the official history of murder in San Francisco was off to an energetic start!

Chapter Two

The Senator and the Justice—1859

The custom of fighting duels to settle disputes and to determine right and wrong is as old as history itself. David and Goliath probably fought the first recorded duel. The French refined dueling to the point of fine art in the sixteenth century when King Francis I challenged Emperor Charles V to single combat with pistols at a pre-arranged site.[1] In America, the duel in which Aaron Burr, the vice president of the United States, killed Alexander Hamilton, the first treasurer of the United States, ranks as one of the country's most historic events. In early California, innumerable duels were fought to settle even the most minor disputes, although the intent was rarely to kill, but rather to achieve "satisfaction." Typical of these early duels was the contest in the early 1850s between George P.

San Francisco's
Portsmouth
Square in 1859.

*Johnston and William Ferguson. A quarrel over the slavery issue esca-
lated into a duel with pistols at ten paces on Clugel Island. The agreed-
upon rules of engagement stated that if the first bullets did not result in
satisfaction, the distance was to be halved. The original shots both missed,
so the combatants moved closer. Nothing much happened on the second or
third volleys, whereupon Johnston demanded an apology. It was not forthcoming, so they banged away again. This time Ferguson was hit in the
right thigh and Johnston on the left wrist. This seemed to do the job, so
both parties then retired, having been "satisfied."[2]*

*But another, far more serious duel was about to be fought in
San Francisco—one which would alter the entire course of California politics. It would also bring an effective end to combat on what
was euphemistically called "the field of honor."*

Some said it was a clear case of murder. Others said at least it was
honorable murder. Still others swore that it was not murder at all. The
truth is that no one, to this day, knows for certain which it really was.

It involved two men as different as men can be; one a man of recognized integrity and a rigid moral code; the other a man of dubious character, given to great fits of temper. And their fatal encounter involved a
custom almost as old as murder itself: dueling.

James C. Broderick was born in relative obscurity, the first son of a
stonemason who, in that year of 1820, was at work on the construction of
the National Capitol building.[3] In search of a better life, the family moved
to New York City while James was still an infant, and there he grew to
manhood following his father's trade. Unhappily, fate put him on his
own at an early age. Both of his parents and a younger brother died while
he still a teenager. James developed rapidly into a tall, strong young man,
quick of mind and wit and keen to succeed. He took on the task of edu-
cating himself, reading every book he could lay his hands on, and devel-
oping special interests in law and history. One childhood friend remembered James perfecting his grammar "by writing in full parsing lessons
from all his textbooks."[4] All of his life, contemporaries would be amazed
at the depth and breadth of his knowledge.

Broderick was also a man of action, and at a young age he joined a
volunteer fire department, where he impressed his companions with his
willingness to face both risk and death. Eager to succeed financially, he
opened his own tavern in Washington Square when he was just twenty
years old. Called "The Subterranean," his tavern soon became a favorite
gathering place for politicians, especially Democrats of the local ward.

Senator David C. Broderick at the time of the duel. *The Bancroft Library*

Through friendships made in his tavern, Broderick soon found himself deeply interested in the politics of the day. Broderick's political instincts—and his great ambition—came quickly into evidence. It wasn't long before he became a prominent figure in the fifth congressional district of the city, and a voice worth listening to in the local Democratic Party. He was soon appointed customhouse inspector, and later he became a delegate to the convention that rewrote the state constitution. However, his self-assertiveness was an occasional irritant to his fellow politicians. When President Tyler visited the city in 1843, Broderick completely disregarded the minor role he had been assigned and personally took over the task of welcoming the president.[5]

In 1846, the Democratic Party, recognizing Broderick's potential as a leader, nominated him to be its candidate to Congress from the fifth district. This was exactly the springboard to greatness that Broderick had been looking for—movement into the big-time politics of the nation's capital. But despite an energetic and exhausting campaign, Broderick suffered a heart-breaking defeat when the party splintered and a rival Democratic candidate ran on a reform ticket. Broderick was narrowly defeated, and at the age of twenty-six, he found himself shattered both politically and financially. He had risked everything on the campaign, neglecting his personal affairs and his business in the bargain. For the next several years, he brooded about his future and his prospects. Then one day it dawned on him how he could make a completely fresh start and renew his prospects: by doing what so many other young men were doing. Gold had just been discovered in the West, and thousands were headed for San Francisco! Within days, James Broderick booked himself on the steamer *Crescent City*, bound for Panama.[6]

After an arduous land trip across the isthmus, Broderick and eleven other New Yorkers boarded a steamer named *Stella* and headed up the west coast of California for San Francisco.[7] The ship landed in the summer of 1849, exactly as gold fever reached its zenith. Most of his associates immediately headed inland for the gold fields, but Broderick had suffered tropical fever in the crossing, and his poor health made it impossible for him to join the trek. Thus, he stayed behind, a stranger and a virtual prisoner of the city.

Broderick soon regained his health and vigor and set about making a career and a name for himself in San Francisco, just as he had done in New York. He renewed a friendship with an old political associate from the East, Frederick D. Kohler, who offered him a partnership in a minting and assaying business. Sparked by Broderick's industry, the firm achieved considerable success casting gold coins to the order of its customers, always being sure that the coins contained a slightly smaller amount of gold than the value stamped on them.[7] Using his profits, Broderick began investing in real estate, and he soon had sufficient funds to turn his attention to his first love: politics. In 1850, he stood for election to the state senate and won with an overwhelming majority over a handful of other candidates.

In Sacramento, Broderick established himself as a hard-working politician, a supporter of popular causes, and a man of strong principle. He worked diligently at creating a body of laws to implement the new California constitution and to provide a legal foundation for the state. He fought against laws that would discriminate against immigrants. But it was on the subject of slavery that he made his biggest mark. The defenders of slavery in California were called "the Chivalry," and they became one of the most powerful political forces in state politics. Broderick fought them at every turn, becoming one of California's most effective spokesmen for the anti-slavery position.

In 1851, the governor of the state, Peter H. Burnett, unexpectedly resigned, and the vacancy was automatically filled by Lieutenant Governor John McDougal, who had also been serving as the presiding officer of the state senate. Broderick's colleagues quickly elected him to replace McDougal. Thus, within just two years of arriving in California, James C. Broderick became the second highest official in the state.[6]

This honor, however, did not weaken Broderick's great ambition for high office and political greatness. He quickly set his sights on the position of United States senator for California. Broderick wanted to go to Washington and make his mark on the national scene. John C. Fremont's term was coming to an end, and his successor would be chosen by the legislature. Broderick fought hard to be named Fremont's successor, but he had made too many enemies with his strong stands of principle, including his opposition to San Francisco's Vigilance Committee. After five ballots in the Democratic caucus, Broderick was narrowly defeated in his effort to succeed the West's great pathfinder. The defeat made him all the more determined. Confided Broderick to a friend, "I tell you, sir, by God, that for one hour's seat in the Senate of the United States, I would roast before a slow fire in the Plaza!"[10]

Such overwhelming ambition was not to be denied. In 1857, he was poised to succeed Senator William M. Gwin, a stately Southerner who was retiring, but again he was thwarted. Then just two years later, after an intensive battle and shrewd political maneuvering, the state legislature at last elected Broderick to a six-year term, beginning in March of 1857 and ending March 1863.[11] Broderick would start his term on the date designated, but miscalculation and tragedy would end his time as a United States senator long before its expiration date.

David C. Terry would see to that, as he would see to the quick end of a number of lives and careers over his own lifetime. Terry was a born troublemaker, and whether you approved of him or not depended on whether he was making trouble for your friends or your enemies.

The life of David Terry was fueled by a unique brand of jealousy and a false sense of heroism. He was a strong believer in all the wrong things and an avid supporter of losing causes: making California a slave state; advocating that the Chinese must be deported; struggling against the California Democratic Party. With these core beliefs, it was perhaps inevitable that he would come into conflict with the strong-principled Broderick.

17

David S. Terry at the height of his political powers. *The Bancroft Library*

Terry began life in 1822 in Todd County, Kentucky. His parents separated while he was still a young boy, and he moved to Texas with his mother. He loved conflict even as a youngster, and at the age of thirteen he joined Sam Houston's troops and fought in the battle of San Jacinto. By the time he was twenty, David Terry stood six feet, six inches tall and was strong as an ox. He had a quick mind, a flashing temper, and an urge to be feared and famous. Eventually, he became a pupil in his uncle's law office and, after just two years of apprenticeship, he declared himself to be a lawyer. He looked like most lawyers of the time, except that he carried a Bowie knife with him wherever he went.

When war with Mexico was declared in 1846, Terry, then twenty-three, marched off in search of glory, joined the Texas Rangers and fought under Zachary Taylor. When the war was over, he returned to Galveston, a self-proclaimed hero, and offered himself for the office of district attorney. Galveston declined the honor, and Terry departed hastily for California.

Terry settled in the frontier town of Stockton, a good day's journey from San Francisco, set himself up in a law practice, and promptly picked a few fights. In one recorded encounter, Terry quarreled with a litigant and made his point by slashing him with his Bowie knife. Frontier justice being what it was at the time, Terry was fined fifty dollars for his profligacy.[12]

Soon, Terry once again offered himself to the voters, this time as the Whig candidate for mayor. The citizenry of Stockton preferred his opponent, so Terry turned his attentions back to lawyering and brawling.

Terry, however, refused to believe that the voters of two cities had done the right thing, and he continued to immerse himself in California politics. As an outspoken Southerner and a strong believer in slavery, he defected from the Democratic Party and joined the Know-Nothing Party, a radical group that believed in the supremacy of the white race.[13] In 1855, the Know-Nothings briefly disguised themselves by mutating into something called the American Party. When the American Party nominated its slate for statewide elections that year, Terry was selected for a post on the supreme court of California. To everyone's amazement and to the general consternation of the political establishment, the American Party swept the elections, and David Terry became a supreme court justice.[14] He was suddenly an imposing figure on the California political landscape, and he was the only supreme court justice who wore a Bowie knife in his belt.

As Judge Terry, he quickly put his stamp on the court and the politics of California. Along with J. Neely Johnson, the twenty-seven-year-old governor of California, Terry took control of the forces attempting to turn California into a slave state. The anti-slavery forces were led by David C. Broderick, and it soon became apparent that a confrontation between Terry and Broderick was inevitable.

In 1856, Terry became outraged that San Francisco's Vigilance Committee had usurped the legitimate power of the courts. He took it upon himself to stop the Vigilantes and to embarrass Broderick in the bargain. With constitutional law on his side, Terry issued a writ to the committee to surrender a certain prisoner to the authorities. When his writ was ignored, Terry entered San Francisco with a scruffy little band of pseudo-warriors, which he proclaimed to be a militia, and when a deputy refused to surrender the prisoner, Terry, in "a towering rage,"[15] stabbed him with his Bowie knife.

JUDGE DAVID S. TERRY, STABBING S. A. HOPKINS, OF THE VIGILANCE COMMITTEE, SAN FRANCISCO, CAL.

Terry stabbing S. A. Hopkins of the Vigilance Committee. *Frank Leslie's Illustrated Weekly*

Terry was then promptly arrested by the Vigilance Committee, and he expressed his outrage by saying that he was being detained "merely for sticking a knife into a damn little Yankee well-borer."[16] San Franciscans were scarcely intimidated. One newspaper put the proposition quite simply: "If Hopkins (the deputy) dies, Terry will and must be hung!"[17]

Fortunately for everyone involved, the deputy lived and Terry, after a fifteen-day trial, was found guilty only of resisting arrest and assaulting a deputy. Terry was spirited out the back door of the jail in the dead of night and returned to the friendlier environs of Stockton.

Terry was enraged at, among others, Senator Broderick, whom he felt should have come to his aid as a fellow elected official of the state. Terry was now, mostly by default, nothing less than the chief justice of the Supreme Court of California, but his new, exalted position seemed only to make it easier for him to offend people and make enemies. At the American Party convention in 1859, Terry was denied re-nomination to the Court by the party members, and, in a rage, he took the convention floor and made a rambling, vituperative speech. When he came to speak of Senator Broderick, he threw caution to the winds: "Who have we opposed to us? A party based on no principle, except the abusing of one section of the country against another in a miserable remnant of a faction flying under false colors, trying to obtain votes under false pretenses. They are the followers of one man, the personal chattels of a single individual whom they are ashamed of. They belong heart and soul, body and breeches, to David C. Broderick."[18]

The next morning, at the International Hotel, Broderick read the words Terry had spoken the day before. He threw the newspaper down and turned to a friend of Terry's, saying, "The damned, miserable wretch. I have hitherto spoken of him as an honest man, but now I find I am mistaken. I take it all back. He is just as bad as the others."[19]

Thus began a sad and seemingly inevitable confrontation between Broderick and Terry, a drama that resembled a Greek tragedy. It was not long before Terry fired off a note to Broderick: "Some two months ago, you saw fit to indulge in certain remarks concerning me, which were offensive in their nature. I now take the earliest opportunity to require of you a retraction of these remarks."[20]

After some delay, Broderick sent back a letter that said: "The remarks used by me in the conversation referred to may be the subject of future misrepresentation and for obvious reasons I have to desire you to state what the remarks were that you designate in your note as offensive, and which you require from me a retraction."[21]

Terry continued the ritual dance:

> "In reply to your note I have to say that the offensive remarks to which I alluded in my communication of yesterday are the following: 'I heretofore considered him as the only honest man in the Supreme court bench, but now—take it all back'— thus by implication reflecting on my personal and official integrity. What I require is the retraction of any words which were calculated to reflect on my character as an officer and a gentleman."[22]

This time Broderick was quick to reply: "The remarks made by me were occasioned by certain offensive allusions of yours concerning me made in the convention. My language, as far as my recollection serves me, was as follows, 'I considered him the only honest man on the Supreme Bench—but I take it all back.' "[23]

Terry could stand it no more! He sent Broderick an immediate letter of challenge:

"Some months ago you used language concerning me offensive in its nature…(and are) not making the retraction required. This course on your part leaves me no alternative but to demand satisfaction usual among gentlemen, which I accordingly do. Mr. Benham will make the necessary arrangements."[24]

Broderick took the bait: "Your note has been received…in response to the same I refer you to my friend, Hon J. C. McGibbon, who will make the satisfactory arrangements demanded in your letter."[25]

And there it was, the unthinkable: a duel between the chief justice of the Supreme Court of California and the United States senator from California. It was difficult to believe that it could actually happen, but happen it did.

At first, fortune seemed to favor Broderick in the duel. Although it was Terry who provoked the event, he was celebrated for his skill with a Bowie knife, not a pistol. Broderick, on the other hand, had had some experience with firearms and had even survived a duel.

In 1852, in the early days of his political career in New York, Broderick had been challenged by Celeb C. Smith, the son of a former governor, who had taken offense at some comments Broderick made concerning Smith's father. The two men met on "the field of honor," with revolvers as the choice of weapon. When the word was given, the two adversaries were to commence walking toward each other firing until their weapons were emptied. Broderick's gun jammed and, as he desperately fiddled with it, Smith marched forward with his gun blazing. He was evidently a poor shot, for only one bullet found its mark, and, fortunately for Broderick, it struck his pocket watch, shattering it and inflicting only a minor flesh wound. Broderick then emptied his restored revolver at the disarmed Smith, and either by accident or design, he missed Smith completely. After this clumsy exchange, both men declared themselves satisfied.[26]

The later duel, however, had more ominous prospects. Terry was clearly a hothead, out for vengeance. The seconds met to draw up the terms of the encounter. They designed a frightening document, specifying all the agreed upon arrangements in almost macabre details. Each principal would be attended by two seconds and a surgeon. They would meet on a farm adjoining the Lake Ranch, near Lake Merced. The weapons would be dueling pistols, fired at a distance of ten paces. Weapons would be loaded with a single shot in the presence of the seconds. Choice of pistol would be by the flip of a coin. The contestants were to hold their pistols downward, until these words were spoken, "Gentleman are you ready? Fire one. Fire two."[27] At that point, the shots were to be exchanged. Time: Monday, September 12, 1859, at 5:30 in the morning.

The prospect of an exchange of shots between two of California's highest ranking officials titillated the populace. Eager spectators tied up almost every conveyance in San Francisco. The police, fearing the incident was getting out of hand, issued warrants for the arrest of Terry and Broderick, charging them with intent to fight with deadly weapons. To avoid arrest and the prospect of a carnival, the time of the meeting was changed at the last minute to Tuesday morning at 7:00 A.M. on a plot of land just south of the county line.

There, at the appointed hour, the two parties met. While a few sleepy and chilled onlookers stood about on the adjoining hillside, the adversaries and their associates advanced to the scene in two hostile groups. Broderick appeared to be somewhat nervous, while Terry was seen to glower at his opponent with a sullen calmness. The coin was flipped and Terry won the choice of weapons. He designated pistols supplied by an ex-clerk of the supreme court. They had been used in a previous duel, and one of them was known to have a hair-trigger. The weapons were loaded, at which point there was to be another coin toss to determine

Judge Terry shooting Senator Broderick in the duel. *Harper's Weekly*

which adversary took which pistol. This did not happen. One of Terry's companions simply handed Terry his revolver. It was not the one with the hair trigger. The principals were told to take their places. Both had discarded their overcoats and were attired in simple, black frock coats. Broderick was now noticeably agitated and he examined his pistol with uncertain curiosity. Terry stood with the rising sun behind his back and Broderick seemed to blink into the early light. Now both men stood, ten paces apart, with their weapons at their sides.

"Gentlemen, are you ready?" boomed the voice of David Colon, a follower of Broderick. Both men assented.

"Fire one…"

Broderick began to raise his pistol, but it fired prematurely and the ball buried itself in the ground just a few feet in front of him. Terry raised his weapon, aimed it at Broderick, and fired his shot directly into Broderick's chest. Broderick threw up his arms, shuddered, and sank to the ground, as his pistol slipped from his hand.

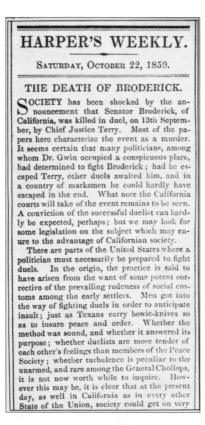

Editorial declaring Broderick's death to be a murder.

One newspaper's version of the event, describing "the scene of the murder."

Broderick lying in state in San Francisco.

One of the spectators yelled out in a voice that echoed across the meadow, "That's murder, by God!"[28]

In the chaos that followed, Terry was spirited away from the scene. Broderick's friends quickly bandaged his wound, lifted him onto a wagon, and drove to a house near the ocean. There he lingered for three days in fever and pain, as San Franciscans prayed for his recovery. It was to no avail. Senator Broderick died shortly before midnight on September 16. The sentiment against Terry in the city was overwhelming. *Harper's Weekly* reported that the "papers here characterize the event as murder."[29] The *Alta* and *Call* mourned Broderick's death and shrieked for revenge.[30]

Broderick's body was brought back to San Francisco. The corpse was placed into a metal casket and put on display at the Union Hotel at Kearny and Merchant streets. An inquest was held to determine the cause of death. The jury quickly reached its verdict: "Death from a pistol ball fired intentionally by David C. Terry."[31] The funeral ceremony that followed was a major spectacle. Tens of thousands of spectators lined the streets as the hearse, drawn by four black stallions, wound its way to Lone Mountain Cemetery. Fire bells at engine houses throughout the city wailed a lamentation. The mile-long procession took two and a half hours to reach its destination, where David C. Broderick was lowered into his grave, as he was eulogized as "the trusted and most unselfish of friends, the most moral of public men."[32] In Washington, D.C., President Abraham Lincoln praised him as "a man devoted to human rights and a man of true character."[33]

25

Terry, in the meantime, had fled to Stockton, and later, sensing the climate for revenge on the part of Broderick's followers, considered flight to Nevada. But when Terry's friends in the legislature passed a bill making dueling an offense to be tried in the district court, Terry decided to brave it out. He was brought back to San Francisco to stand for trial and later released on $10,000 bail. Eventually, Terry applied for a change of venue and the trial was moved to Marin County. On the day of the trial, San Francisco's prosecution witnesses failed to appear at the appointed hour because their boat became becalmed on the Bay. The judge, a personal and political friend of Terry, thereupon directed a verdict of acquittal, and Terry declared himself to be completely exonerated.

The remainder of Terry's life was filled with tumult and controversy. He attempted to organize a secessionist movement in California. Failing that, he secured an officer's commission from Jefferson Davis and fought for the South at Chickamauga. He later led a militia into Mexico in an attempt to overthrow Emporer Maximilian. In 1868, he returned to San Francisco, hoping his duel with Broderick would be forgotten. It had not been. As he made his way through the streets of the city, there were shouts of "Traitor!" and "Rebel" and also "Murderer!"[32]

Plaque marking the site of the celebrated Broderick-Terry duel.

In 1884, he defended the infamous Sarah Althea Hall in her suit against former Senator William Sharon, a case that grew out of a supposed marriage contract which the beautiful Sarah claimed the wealthy Sharon had made with her. Terry originally won the case, but it was later overturned by Stephen J. Field, a justice of the supreme court. When a distraught Terry later accosted Field in a railway station, he was shot dead by Field's bodyguard. Many regarded the manner of his death entirely suitable for a man who, so many years earlier, had shot and killed the respected Senator Broderick.

Whether it was intentional murder, murder by accident, murder by ritual, or technically no murder at all, the killing of David Broderick resulted, for all practical purposes, in the end of dueling in California. The results were so terrible—the slaying of a United States Senator—that the idea of dueling quickly became abhorrent. Over time, dueling became the relic of an age that had passed.

Chapter Three

The Misused Mistress—1870

It is probably impossible to exaggerate the importance of the Bay's ferryboats to the development and well-being of San Francisco. Tens of thousands of people lived in the communities across the Bay, but worked in San Francisco. More thousands lived in San Francisco but worked, shopped, or visited family members across the Bay. Twice a day, the commuters climbed abroad the dozens of ferries that plied their way to and from Oakland, Berkeley, Richmond, Alameda, Tiburon, Sausalito, and San Francisco.

The ferries meant much more to their passengers than just a means of transportation. They also served as restaurants, cocktail bars, living rooms, and clubhouses. Their regular passengers became members of well-defined groups with their own habits, customs, folkways, and friendships. Some poker games on board continued twice daily for years. Vocal groups organized and sang on a regular basis on trips across the Bay. Romances developed and often ended in marriages officiated by ferryboat captains. Longtime passengers had their own seats and newcomers who attempted to usurp them would be admonished by other veteran passengers. Before the bridges were built, the Bay ferries were an indispensable part of life for San Franciscans, the lifelines of Bay business and commerce and the ties that held many families together.

Some of the ferryboats became legends in their own right. A special place in history is reserved for a propeller-driven steamer called

Kangaroo, *which made the first regularly scheduled trips across the Bay, from the San Antonio Creek, now the Oakland Estuary, to San Francisco. A sadder place in history is held by the* San Raphael, *which was rammed in the fog off Alcatraz, resulting in the only fatal ferry collision on record. Other ferryboats are memorable for their style and beauty, including the dazzlingly decorated* Berkeley, *which featured, among other luxuries, stained-glass windows.*

But no ferryboat has a stronger claim on history than the El Capitain, *the pride of the Central Pacific's transbay fleet, which, starting in 1869, shuttled passengers between the Oakland pier, the terminus of the Bay Area's first overland train, and San Francisco. But the* El Capitain *is remembered not for its beauty, its grace, or its speed, but for an extraordinary incident that took place on its upper deck on the evening of November 3, 1870. It was an event that stunned San Francisco, transfixed most of California, and enthralled much of America. It also changed the legal landscape of the state and even altered the geographic boundaries of the City of San Francisco.*

El Capitain, the Oakland-San Francisco ferry boat that was the scene of Crittenden's murder. *San Francisco Maritime National Historical Park*

Dusk was just settling over the early November evening as the train from Sacramento pulled to a stop at the Oakland Mole, terminus of the Central Pacific rail line and home port of the Oakland-San Francisco ferries. Passengers spilled out onto the wharf, followed by carts filled with luggage. More than four hundred people surged toward the ferryboat, the *El Capitain*, which waited to take them on the last leg of their journey to the City. First to board was Leland Stanford, former governor of California, owner of the Central Pacific and one of San Francisco's "Big Four" of power magnates. He and his party were welcomed by Captain Bill Bushnell into his private quarters in the wheelhouse. The other passengers quickly filled the boat's four decks and gathered in its saloons, as the *El Capitain* made preparations to depart.

On the upper deck, enjoying the night air, three passengers sat down on a deck bench near the ferry's wheel. One was a tall, well-dressed man in his mid-fifties. Next to him, on his right, was a somewhat plump woman in a dark dress, and on his left was a young lad of fourteen, dressed in the uniform of a military academy. These were two parents and their young son, who had just been reunited on the wharf, and they chatted amiably about the joys of being together again after being apart for so long. In their happiness, they were oblivious to a fourth figure on that part of the deck. About fifteen feet away stood a woman, who stared at the reunited family, although her eyes were not visible behind the dark veil that covered her face. She was dressed entirely in black, from the broad-brimmed hat on her head to her coal-black shoes. A black waterproof cloak covered her shoulders and her hands were hidden in the folds of her dress. She continued to stare at the three people seated on the bench as the ferry whistle sounded the notes that signaled the time of departure.

Just before 6:00 P.M., the engines of the ferryboat throbbed into action and the boat shuddered slightly as the ropes were thrown off. As the *El Capitain* began to move away from the dock, a cold breeze blew across the deck. The distant lights of San Francisco twinkled through the gloom over the Bay. The plump lady on the bench took her husband's hand and moved her arm through his in a thoughtful embrace.

The lady in black stiffened at the sight of this brief intimacy and then, suddenly and with quick steps, she walked toward the bench. The man on the bench looked up just in time to see the lady standing directly in front of him. She brought her right hand out from the folds of her dress and pointed a revolver directly at the man's chest. A shot rang out that could be heard throughout the boat. The man leaped up, clutching his chest, and staggered forward. "I am shot!" he moaned, and he fell to the deck in a graceless heap. The lady dropped the pistol and stepped backward, and then she disappeared around the corner of the saloon. The man's wife cried out and dropped to her knees next to her fallen husband. She knew in an instant that he had been fatally wounded. Their young son yelled out, "I know who did this! I knew it would come to this."[1]

Thus ended one of the most bewildering and tortured love affairs ever chronicled in California. And, thus began a search for justice that would eventually outrage much of the city's citizenry, that would frustrate the workings of the courts, and that would lay bare the moral standards of fashionable San Francisco.

The two protagonists were Alexander Parker Crittenden, one of the great stars of the state's legal establishment, a distinguished legislator and an admired family man, and Laura D. Fair, a beautiful and often-married woman, mother of a lovely daughter and the keeper of a rooming house. They were as unlikely a pair as anyone could imagine, but that seemed to make no difference to either of them. As Laura herself later stated under oath, "God married me to him when we were both born. God made me for him, and he for me."[2]

So it's possible that there was nothing the two of them could do about the relationship—even though they tried, over and over again. Perhaps it was, after all, just a matter of fate.

Fate, however, did lend a helping hand when silver was found in the great Comstock Lode, for it brought both Laura and Alexander to Virginia City at the same time. And, fate gave another nudge when Crittenden just happened to find lodgings in a rooming house owned by the fair Mrs. Fair. The trails that led them to that particular place at that particular time were as different as they themselves.

She was born Laura Hunt in 1837 in the small town of Holly Springs, Mississippi. Her family was nomadic, as her father hopscotched through the South seeking employment. The family finally settled in New Orleans, where Laura blossomed into a lovely young lady, and where she caught the eye of a liquor dealer named William Stone. Stone was twenty years her senior, but that did not keep them from marrying when Laura turned sixteen. The union was cut short when Stone, an ardent user of his own products, died just a year later of cirrhosis of the liver.

The young widow quickly used up her meager inheritance and joined a convent to forget her worldly problems. However, she left after just a few months and took on still another worldly problem, a man named Thomas J. Grayson. That marriage was also short-lived, as Grayson quickly displayed tendencies toward both drink and violence. He had

Laura D. Fair, hotel proprietor, aggrieved mistress, and perpetrator of the shocking murder. *S.F. Historical Society*

Alexander P. Crittenden, distinguished member of the California bar, recording secretary of the State Supreme Court, and murder victim.

one other conspicuous talent: marksmanship. Once, in a drunken rage, he fired a number of bullets into the headboard under which Laura was sleeping. On another occasion, he demonstrated his skill by opening a window and ceremoniously picking off some fifty chickens as they ran frantically around the yard looking for shelter. Laura beheld the heaps of bloody feathers twitching on the ground and decided that, after just six months of less than connubial bliss, time was running out. She fled town with her mother in tow and headed for California.

After a brief stay in San Francisco, Laura and her mother traveled north to Shasta, where Laura soon met an older man named William D. Fair. Fair was a lawyer of modest means, but also a man of great personal charm. Within weeks, Laura became Mrs. Fair, having previously received a somewhat dubious divorce from Grayson by means of an exchange of legal documents through the mail. Laura gave birth to a beautiful baby girl, to whom she gave the theatrical name of Lillian Lorraine. Eventually, the Fairs drifted down to San Francisco, where Mr. Fair proved unable to establish himself and to properly support Laura and his daughter. Despondent, he went to his office one afternoon, put a pistol to his head, pulled the trigger, and brought Laura's third marriage to a sudden and unhappy end.

With a small inheritance in hand, Laura, along with her daughter and her mother, moved to Sacramento, where Laura bought a boarding house. Her timing was unfortunate, as the legislature had just adjourned and the city was quickly abandoned for the season by most of its monied citizens. Laura soon found herself hopelessly in debt and decided to try her hand at a career on the stage, in an effort to earn some quick money. She secured an acting job as Lady Teazle in Sheridan's *School for Scandal*. She demonstrated great charm and acting ability and was soon booked for a major role at McGuire's Theatre in San Francisco. There, she played two performances in a popular melodrama called *The Octoroon*. She received a rave review in the *San Francisco Alta:*

> "The lady is a debutante unused to the stage, but she was cool and self-possessed, read well and intelligently, and pointedly and by her truly excellent conception and rendition of her part, put to shame many of the professionals who were associated with her."[3]

Good reviews did not go to Laura Fair's head. In fact, she didn't really enjoy her brief acting career. She took the $200 she had earned and headed for Virginia City, Nevada, where she had been told that silver was making everyone rich and that there was a boarding house for sale. She soon found herself the owner and proprietor of Tahoe House, a thirty-seven-room establishment on the main street of town. This time her timing was good.

Virginia City was booming and Laura herself quickly became one of its chief ornaments. With her handsome figure, her lovely face, and her now legendary charm, she became a celebrated hostess, and Tahoe House was soon filled with many of the wealthiest and most important men in town.

The path Alexander P. Crittenden took to arrive at Tahoe House was far more traditional and predictable. He was a Kentuckian, born into a proud and patrician family that claimed famed politicians and successful lawyers. At the age of sixteen, he was admitted to West Point, where he quickly distinguished himself with a prank of some kind that got him expelled. However, his family was so well connected that they were able to successfully appeal to President Jackson to have him readmitted. Crittenden graduated in the middle of his class and was commissioned as a second lieutenant. He soon quit the military, however, found employment in the railroad industry, married, and moved to Texas, where he studied law and was admitted to the bar. Then, like so many ambitious young men of the time, he moved his family to California.

He found success in California as a lawyer, then decided to run for the state legislature. He was elected and spent four years in Sacramento, eventually achieving the post of chairman of the judiciary committee. With a successful political career behind him, he moved to San Jose, where he established his own law firm, later transferring himself and his business north to San Francisco in 1852. By this time, Crittenden had a

Tahoe House in Virginia City. It was in the second floor guest rooms that the Fair-Crittenden trysts occured.

large family to support, including four sons and three daughters, and so, like so many others who hoped to gather rapid wealth, he traveled to Virginia City to seek his fortune. It was only natural that he left his family behind in the comfort and convenience of the big city while he sought to establish himself in the booming silver town. The first thing he needed was a place to stay. Someone recommended Tahoe House.

It is not exactly clear when the two began keeping company, but it was perhaps inevitable that the tall, impressive lawyer, alone in town, and the lovely and charming Laura Fair, now between husbands, would gravitate toward each other soon after they began living under the same roof. It is known that shortly after Crittenden took a room, he began paying regular late night visits to Laura's quarters. Within months, they were pledging their undying love to each other, and Laura pressed her new suitor on the subject of marriage. Crittenden soon gave in to her entreaties and proposed marriage, despite the obvious problem posed by his existing wife. This was not a concern of Laura's, for she had been led to believe that the first Mrs. Crittenden was dead.

The torrid romance continued into the early months of 1865, while Crittenden corresponded with his wife in San Francisco during the day and read love poems to Laura Fair at night. Finally, however, the time came when Crittenden had to announce his wife's existence to Laura. Mrs. Crittenden, it seems, was on her way to Virginia City.

History does not record Laura's reaction to this stunning news, but there were no doubt tears and recriminations, accusations and apologies, break-up and make-up. However, at the end of whatever histrionics took place, Crittenden again pledged his troth to Mrs. Fair and promised to divorce his wife at the first opportunity.

On February 4, Clara Crittenden arrived in Virginia City with several of her children and moved into a house that her husband had rented for her. Conveniently, the house was very near Tahoe House. For the next several months, Crittenden worked hard to perfect the juggling act that he would perform for the next five years—shuttling back and forth between the rented home where he pretended to reside and the room he kept at Tahoe House "for business reasons." Unwilling to separate himself from his wife and family, but also unable to give up the delicious Laura, he would spend the next half decade contriving elaborate schemes, making extraordinary promises, and telling outrageous lies. Over that same time period, Laura would veer between hope and despair, belief and denial, serenity and outrage. Clara, on the other hand, simply lived in her own world of obliviousness. It all seemed to work for Alexander Crittenden until the day that Laura Fair fired a bullet into his chest.

The Occidental Hotel, where Crittenden attempted to show off both his wife and his mistress to San Francisco society.

During the time that Crittenden was not spending with either Laura or Clara, he continued to enhance his reputation as a skilled and distinguished lawyer, settling complex mining claims, forming new corporate structures, and defending wealthy clients in court. When he became aware of rumors that he was keeping a mistress, rumors he feared might besmirch his professional reputation, he concocted a bizarre scheme to show the world, and also his wife, that his relationship with Laura Fair was one only of friendship. His persuaded both Laura and Clara to travel with him to San Francisco, where he installed Laura in a room at the Occidental Hotel, right next to the room he shared with his wife. We will never know what contorted logic he used to persuade Laura to go along with this bizarre scheme, or what exactly he had in mind when, on the evening of their first day in the city, he flamboyantly entered the hotel's dining room with his wife on one arm and his mistress on the other. Perhaps he thought it would disarm the assemblage of friends and associates who were dining there that night—and that it would put an end to speculation about his relationship with Laura. It is also difficult to imagine how Clara and Laura felt about it. At any rate, it didn't work out exactly as Crittenden had hoped. Halfway through dinner, Clara fled the room and Alexander dashed after her, leaving Laura spectacularly alone. The next day, Laura left the hotel and hurried back to Virginia City.

It wasn't long before Crittenden was also back in Virginia City, imploring Laura to move into the house he had rented for his family. She gave in and the two began living together as man and wife. Their bliss came to an end when Clara announced she was once again on her way there from San Francisco. Laura quickly high-tailed it back to Tahoe House, which was now being run by her mother. Soon, however, Crittenden and Laura were desperate at being apart, and Crittenden happened upon a seemingly logical solution. He persuaded his wife that Laura would be good company for her during his business trips and that Laura should therefore be moved into the spare room in their home. He then promised Laura that, if she would move in, he would spend his nights at Tahoe House as proof of his love for her. A typical night apparently went as follows: Crittenden would pretend to leave for Tahoe House for Laura's edification, then he would go to Clara's room and stay there until she went to sleep, whereupon he would sneak into Laura's room for several hours of romance; then he would leave Laura with regret at the necessity of returning to Tahoe House, and then he would sneak back to his regular bedroom and spend the remainder of the night with the slumbering Clara.[4] That he succeeded in this bizarre adventure is a tribute to his own inventiveness and the naivete of the two ladies involved.

Eventually, Laura wearied of this tomfoolery and pressed Crittenden again on the subject of divorce. He told Laura that if she would go to San Francisco for an extended visit, he would confront Clara about divorce and he would then come to her in the City, where they could be married. Laura left, confident that all was well, and while she was in San Francisco, she carried on an elaborate correspondence with her lover, a correspondence which would later be made public as court testimony. Their letters were filled with pledges of love, faithfulness, and the destiny of their being together.

Crittenden, of course, had no intention of divorcing Clara and losing his family, and when Laura began to complain again, Crittenden tried a new tactic. Laura should go East and wait for him there. He would join her and they would go to Indiana together, where he would obtain his divorce, since he knew a legal trick that could be employed in that state to obtain an instant divorce. Laura dutifully traveled to New York and waited. And waited. Finally, she received a letter from Crittenden saying that financial reverses kept him from traveling. Laura hit the roof and replied that she was heading off to Havana for the sole purpose of having a good time. That upset Crittenden so much that he decided he had sufficient funds to meet her in White Sulphur Springs, Virginia, where they had a joyous reunion and where they once again pledged their lives and their futures to each other.

However, when they returned to San Francisco, Crittenden again returned to Clara and the bosom of his family. Laura went out and bought a gun, a Colt five-shooter.

Laura was now living with her mother on Bush Street, and Crittenden came to see her almost every evening on his way home. One night, they had a fiercesome quarrel, which climaxed with Laura taking her gun and blazing away at her lover as he fled down the stairs. Crittenden convinced himself that she had deliberately missed him, which he interpreted as an act of true love.

Laura then moved into a flat of her own on Sutter Street, and Crittenden sent her a letter saying that, if she would not see him, he would kill himself. Laura relented and their affair now reached new peaks of devotion and ardor. Crittenden frequently visited Laura three times a day, renewing his promise to wed her as soon as possible. He encouraged her to buy a trousseau of light clothing because it would be warm in the summer in Indiana, where they would be seeking his divorce. But when summer came, Crittenden once again claimed financial reverses. This time, however, Laura was ready for him. She had sold Tahoe House and successfully invested the funds in Comstock Lode stocks.

"Take the forty-five thousand dollars I have and give it to your family," she wrote Crittenden. "Then, penniless, we will seek our happiness in some distant land."[5] Crittenden carefully explained that no true gentleman would take money from a lady. Besides, he explained, Mrs. Crittenden and the family were now in the East and might never return to San Francisco. Therefore, he said, they could go on as usual.

Then one night Crittenden called on Laura and found her in the company of a Mr. Snyder. The years had flown by, and Laura was beginning to despair of her relationship with Crittenden. The sight of Laura with another man sent Crittenden into spasms of outrage. He demanded that Laura dismiss her new suitor. She refused and told Crittenden not to come back unless he had his divorce papers in his hand. Crittenden left in a rage, mumbling about Laura's lack of faith. But Laura had seen and heard enough. Within weeks, she became Mrs. Jesse M. Snyder.

When Crittenden heard of Laura's marriage, he became almost incoherent. The thought of his beautiful mistress in bed with another man drove him to near insanity. He sent a letter to Laura describing his state of mind.

> "No—I cannot—cannot be content. You are to me sun—air—life—everything; and without you—as we now are—there can be no existence. I am wretched, insufferably, infinitely wretched. I have no heart or mind for anything—can think of nothing but you. Day and night I wander about like a ghost...."[6]

On reading the letter, Laura dissolved. Crittenden's love now seemed overwhelming. They would see each other again, and this time she had leverage: She would also need a divorce. They were on equal footing at last.

They met at Laura's mother's house on Bush Street and fell into each other's arms. Love engulfed them both and they made a solemn agreement that each would proceed immediately to obtain a divorce so that they could be together forever. Quite naturally, Laura began divorce proceedings right away. Predictably, Crittenden did not.

Laura's divorce became final on October 5, and in anticipation of her coming marriage to Crittenden, she ridded herself of all encumbrances. She instructed her mother not to interfere. She sent her daughter to a school down the Peninsula. She sold all of her furniture. Then she heard the news that sent her over the top.

She was making arrangements for the remainder of her furniture to be removed when the transporter casually mentioned that he had another job later that afternoon. "What is it?" Laura asked. "The Crittendens," replied the man. "I'm moving new furniture into the house for Mrs. Crittenden's return from the East."

We don't know exactly what level of rage that news provoked in Laura Fair, but we do know that she went to a gunsmith on Kearny Street and traded in her five-shot Colt revolver for a Sharp four-barrel pistol, a smaller gun that could be concealed more easily. Then Laura bought the afternoon paper and searched the passenger list of the Union Pacific train due in that evening. Prominent among the arriving San Franciscans was Mrs. Alexander P. Crittenden.

Laura changed her clothes, putting on a black silk dress, a dark shawl, and a dark waterproof cloak. She then put on a black hat with a heavy veil that covered her face. She placed her pistol in her handbag. Then she summoned a carriage. It was now a little after four in the afternoon, and the ferry that would meet the Union Pacific left San Francisco at 5:15 P.M.

Laura boarded the ferry just before its departure. Within minutes, she spotted Crittenden sitting on a deck bench with his son, Parker. Laura adjusted the veil over her face and took a seat in the cabin where she could watch her lover. The trip across the Bay was smooth and uneventful. When the ferryboat docked, the commuters swarmed off the boat. Laura stayed on board, anxious to see how Crittenden greeted his wife, to see if there was any demonstration of love or emotion. But now she was distressed to see that Crittenden was also leaving the boat. Desperately, she rushed to follow him in the hope of witnessing their meeting, but she lost him in the swirling crowd. Eventually, she gave up and followed the others who were re-boarding the ferry. She walked the decks, looking for Crittenden, and finally she found him sitting outside on the bench on the side of the wheelhouse facing the stern rail. Seated to his right was his newly arrived wife, Clara. His son, Tommie, on leave from his military academy, was on his left. Laura stepped past them and took a seat where she could see them clearly.

The ferry whistle sounded shrilly in the chilled November air, and the *El Capitain* slipped its mooring and began to move out into the Bay. Laura studied the re-united couple carefully for any signs of affection. The Crittendens alternately looked at each other and then out over the water, as they spoke softly with one another. Their voices were muffled by the pulse of the engines and Laura could not hear what they were saying. Then, suddenly, the couple looked into each other's eyes, Crittenden smiled at his wife, and Clara affectionately took his hand, interlocking her arm with his. Laura stiffened and stood up. She moved quickly across the short expanse of deck and removed the pistol from beneath the folds of her cloak. She fired a single shot directly into Crittenden's chest.

The shot was heard throughout the ferryboat, despite the noise of the engines and the slap of the water on the hull. The Crittendens' older son, Parker, who had been helping with bags on the deck below, rushed up the flight of stairs to find his father lying in his mother's arms. Parker shouted that he knew who the culprit was. Seeing that his father was already being attended by a doctor who happened to be on board, he went searching for Mrs. Fair. Within minutes, he found her in the wheelhouse. When Parker confronted her, she said forthrightly, "I did it certainly. Yes. I did it. I was looking for the clerk on the boat to give myself up. He has ruined me and my child, and I meant to kill him."[8]

One newspaper's diagram of the murder event. *San Francisco Call*

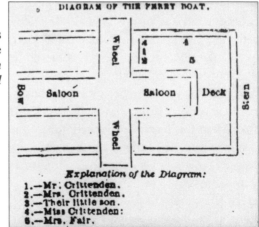

Leland Stanford, former California governor, who shared the boat ride and hurried to the murder scene.

Laura was immediately placed under arrest by Captain Rentzell of the Harbor Police, who happened to be on the boat. The *El Capitain* slowly made its way across the Bay, as a curious crowd circled the victim. None other than Leland Stanford himself comforted the family and directed the crew in controlling the confusion that swirled about them.

Alexander Crittenden did not die quickly or easily. The bullet had entered his chest just below the right nipple and had wound up in a chamber of his heart. Yet, he remained alive and barely conscious. When the boat docked, he was immediately taken by a horse-drawn express wagon to the Crittenden home. There he was laid carefully in his own bed and attended by two physicians. It was clearly a death watch, and the doctors marveled at his stamina and the way he clung to life. An autopsy would later reveal the startling fact that the bullet had carried with it a piece of cloth from Crittenden's vest and that the cloth had actually served to plug up the wound in his heart and had staunched the bleeding. Alexander Crittenden finally died at eight o'clock on Saturday evening, some forty-eight hours after being shot.[9] Laura Fair, in the meantime, was languishing in the San Francisco City prison, alternately lapsing in and out of consciousness. Her speech was rambling and incoherent. At one point, she was offered a glass of water, and she bit off a piece of the glass and attempted unsuccessfully to swallow it. On the third day of confinement, she rallied enough to give a rambling interview to a newspaper reporter, then lapsed once again into a kind of trance.

Crittenden's death stunned and fascinated San Francisco. He had become one of the most important legal figures in Northern California. One of the newspapers rhapsodized: "Mr. Crittenden possessed high le-

Laura Fair, her Sharp
four-barrel pistol, and
A.P. Crittenden, an
artist's montage of the
celebrated event.

gal and literary attainments, and was considered one of the ablest members of the Bar on this coast. He was honored and respected by the judiciary for his learning and manly deportment. Nothing could sway him from his path of duty and what he considered to be the right."[10] Only days before he was shot, Crittenden had been named the official recorder of the Supreme Court of California.[11]

Editorial writers were equally outspoken on the subject of Laura Fair:

> "The mental workings which prompted this bold, bad woman to shoot down a fellow being in the presence of his wife and children we shall not attempt to fathom. She is now in the hands of the law, and if her guilty conscience suffers her to live and retain her reason, she must answer at the bar of offended justice for the deep damnation of this taking off. Let us hope that this is the last victim of her unbridled passions."[12]

There were several matters that postponed the trial of Laura Fair for the murder of Alexander Crittenden. One was the question of jurisdiction. It was unclear exactly where the crime had been committed. The district attorney originally ruled that Alameda County had jurisdiction in the case, quoting California law which stated, "If the injury be inflicted in one county, and the party dies within another county, the accused shall be tried in the county where the act was done or the cause of death administered."[13] There was a spirited debate amongst the authorities of San Francisco and Alameda counties as to exactly where the ferryboat had been when the fatal shot was fired. The California state surveyor-general quickly put the argument to rest by ruling that the end of the long Oakland pier extended so far out into the water that it was actually in San Francisco! The city's cartographers quickly rushed to their maps to take advantage of this remarkable ruling.

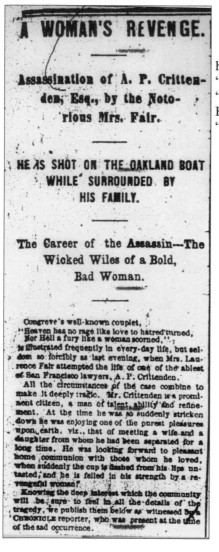

The *Chronicle* headlines the "assassination" by "the notorious Mrs. Fair" and salutes her "wicked wiles."

The trial eventually got underway in late March of 1871. It would last for twenty-six long and contentious days and it would be followed in the most minute detail by the city's avid newspaper readers. Laura pled not guilty at her arraignment, and it was apparent to all involved that she would plead temporary insanity, claiming that she had been driven to the deed by the inhuman treatment inflicted on her by the deceased. There was some speculation that it would be almost impossible to find a sufficient number of impartial jurors, but within a day and a half, a jury of twelve San Francisco businessmen and tradesmen were seated in the jury box, and the trial was underway.

Laura was defended by Elisha Cook, one of the foremost criminal lawyers in the West and an eloquent speechifier, and also by Leader Quint, a lawyer of lesser repute whose primary role was to assist Cook, who was in deteriorating health. The prosecution was handled by Alexander Campbell, an attorney famed by his prosecutorial skills, and by District Attorney Henry H. Bryne, an attorney admired for his tenacity and verbal brilliance. It was clear from the outset that this trial would be a contest not only between law and justice, but also of eloquence and oratory.

It was also clear that a way of life would be on trial. Immorality in the upper echelons of San Francisco society was the larger subject that engulfed the trial of Laura Fair. It was a little discussed but universally accepted fact that men of wealth and prominence would have mistresses and lovers. One editorial writer laid it on the line even before the trial began:

"There is a great lesson deductible from this misfortune that the welfare of society imperatively demands should be conveyed to all whom it may concern. The relations which existed between Mr. Crittenden and Mrs. Fair, the woman who shot him, were of a peculiar nature. They were no secret, but were well known to all his acquaintances. Although blessed with an affectionate wife and beautiful children, surrounded by a family of which any man might be proud, he contracted an immoral intimacy with this woman, who was notoriously of bad antecedents and violent dispositions. Thereby he committed a grievous infraction of Christian morality—one which by its nature destroys the sacredness of family ties and challenges the very foundation of civilized society. Yet civilized society readily condoned the offense. Mr. Crittenden was received in public and private life as though not a stain rested upon his character. There are not many of his peers in San Francisco who could point the finger

An artist's sketch of Laura Fair at her trial. *San Francisco Examinar*

Elisha Cook, Mrs. Fair's defense attorney, whose summation to the jury went on for days. *San Francisco Examiner*

of reproach at him with a safe conscience. It is high time that the false and unjust code of morals which modern society has set up for its own judgement should be openly denounced. We have not the least desire to palliate the horrible crime of Mrs. Fair, but we must say that we can very well understand how she might have been driven to desperation by contrasting her own outlawed and abandoned state with the happiness and respect enjoyed by him who was an equal sharer in the wrongdoing. We want a more general acknowledgment of the cardinal truth that a sin is equally a sin, whether committed by a man or a woman."[14]

This subtext of the trial was underscored by the arrival in town of several of the nation's leaders in the fight for women's rights, including Elizabeth Cady Stanton and Susan B. Anthony. The suffragettes, as they were called, were in regular attendance at the trial, and even though their actions were treated with contempt by the press, their presence in the courtroom re-enforced the sentiment that society itself was in the dock.

Every day, citizens from all walks of life, street people and millionaires, judges and rum-runners, gamblers and housewives, fought at the door and then scrambled for seats in the courtroom. They got their money's worth—for this was one of the most fascinating and lurid trials they would ever see. Laura was a show in herself, always dressed in black, always rocking back and forth in a special chair provided for her by the court, usually with her shoes on a foot warmer provided by her counsel. Her face was pale and worn, her eyes were often downcast and sad. She was still lovely, despite the toll that events and prison had taken on her. Occasionally, she would rise slowly and dramatically and walk over to a reclining couch which a thoughtful court had provided her because of her claims of delicacy. There, she would recline for a period of time before she had gained sufficient strength to go on.

The prosecutors laid out the clear and unmistakable facts in the case—that Laura Fair had followed her lover on the boat—tracked him until she found him seated with his family—then gunned him down without mercy. There were numerous witnesses to the crime, and Laura herself had confessed on more than one occasion.

Laura's defense was not easy to grasp, but it basically amounted to emotional insanity brought on by a variety of factors, including the trauma of her affair with Crittenden, compounded by the emotional abuse she had suffered over a period of seven years. This was further complicated, her lawyers said, by physical ailments and sexual maladies that would have turned any sane person into a raving maniac not responsible for her actions. No fewer than three different doctors testified that Laura was no doubt unconscious at the time of the crime, and Laura herself claimed that she had no memory of the actual event.

When Laura finally took the stand, an eerie hush fell over the courtroom. Under gentle prodding by her attorney she told her story in a calm, sweet voice. "The first thing I remember after being on the boat was Mrs. Crittenden's voice. She has a peculiar voice and it was disagreeable, the sound of it. I looked to see where it came from or what it was, and I know I must have put my hand…I remember seeing, as I turned and put my hand on the glass, or whatever it was, I saw her and him together…The glass seemed to be wet, and I can remember nothing else after that."[14]

Laura's testimony on the stand had an electrifying effect on the audience of court loungers, as well as on the lawyers themselves. Asked by Campbell if she had seen Crittenden during her brief marriage to Snyder, she replied, "I did, sir, I was Crittenden's wife."

"I beg your pardon," blurted the prosecutor. "You were?"

"Yes, sir."

"When were you married to him?"

"Well, God married me to him when we were both born. God made me for him, sir, and he for me. My standing up before the preacher did not make me Mr. Snyder's wife. That was adultery when I married Mr. Snyder. I mean by that I believe there is but one person born for another in this world, because I felt so differently toward Mr. Crittenden than I did toward any other person on earth. I do not believe God put such feelings for a man into a woman's heart if that man is not intended for her husband."[16]

The prosecuting attorney was simply nonplussed and was scarcely able to continue with his interrogation. the next day, the newspapers howled with indignation of Laura's "declaration of free love."

The absolute highlight of the trial, however, was the admission of the love letters exchanged between Mrs. Fair and Mr. Crittenden over the years. They contained the kind of steamy eroticism that prurient followers of the trial had been hoping for, and they made everything preceding their exposure seem tame by comparison. The contents of the letters were eagerly read in court and eagerly reprinted in the daily newspapers. Laura's letters were especially edifying:

> "Now answer me candidly, darling—do you think your dear body will or can ever seem so purely and entirely mine as before it rested upon the same bed with another?"

"You shall kiss me in every corner of the room, hold me in your arms in each chair, lie by me on the sofa, hang over me at the piano, and sleep with me in the bed."

"In the dead of night I have called you—as if you could hear me—as if my voice could reach you over the many cruel miles that separate us. By all the agony of these days—by all the love which I have given you—the devotion, the worship of a lifetime, for I have loved you all my life. You are mine. Say you are mine, my own darling—and then I shall live again."

"When you tell me she is gone and I may come again— oh! How I will make my poor darling happy again. Let her take it all—the dear old bed, the chairs in which you held me in your arms. She can't take your heart and she shan't take your happiness. We will consecrate the new furniture as only we can."[17]

It didn't require students of the ongoing trial to use too much imagination to envision what Laura and her lover did to "consecrate" the furniture. And then, there was the matter of Laura's "tilted womb."

Laura's lawyer Cook had led a veritable parade of physicians to the stand in an effort to persuade the jury that Laura's many physical ailments were of such a nature that they sometimes rendered her incapable of sound judgment, maladies that would turn even a shy maiden into a raving maniac. In the course of these presentations, Dr. John B. Trask, one of Laura's personal physicians, mentioned that Laura suffered from "anteversion of the womb." When pressed to put this into non-medical words, he said that Laura had a "tilted womb." That night in the city's bars and clubs, there was ribald speculation on what might cause a tilted womb. The next day, prosecuting attorney Campbell asked the question directly: Could that particular malady be caused by "excessive indulgence in sexual passion?" Dr. Trask hemmed and hawed, then finally said that he guessed it might be. That was exactly what the court loungers wanted to hear.

Judge Samuel Dwinelle did his best to maintain a sense of decorum in the courtroom, sometimes against daunting odds. The court audience tended to be restive and participative. Laura herself was given to heavy sighs, and more than once cried out, "That's a lie!" The suffragettes were also inclined to demonstrations and were frequently fined by the judge. On one occasion, Laura offered to pay one of their fines personally. Judge Dwinelle admonished, "You will have to draw heavily on your bank if you pay the fines for all of them"[19]

Some three weeks after the opening gavel, the testimony finally dragged to a close, and it was time for the final closing arguments. This, however, did not mean that the trial itself was coming to a swift conclusion. The closing arguments themselves would last for ten full days.

Prosecutor Campbell regaled the jury for two days. Stalking the floor in front of the jury box, pausing only for an occasional drink of water, taking time out only when he could see the jurors needed a break, he railed at the defenses presented in Laura's behalf. He referred scornfully to the defense portrayal of Laura as a weak, worn out, feeble, dying woman, and asked if the jurors had ever beheld a stronger, more ardent, more intelligent, more controlled witness. Roared Campbell,

> "I have endeavored to show you that she is a bold, bad, vicious, malignant, passionate woman whose whole heart was a magazine of malice, that she entertained the most deep and malignant hatred to a married woman simply because she was an honest and true wife. It is for you to determine whether any woman who takes a fancy to another woman's husband may drag him forth from his home, or murder him if he refuses to go."[20]

Attorney Quint opened the defense summation by reading all of Mrs. Fair's and Mr. Crittenden's one hundred and twenty-five love letters into the record. It seemed endless, and by the time he finished, three days had passed and the courtroom was almost cleared of spectators. Both Quint and the jurors seemed on the point of collapse. Laura herself seemed almost asleep before it was over, her head falling on her chest, her eyes half-closed.

Then her other lawyer, Elisha Cook, took over and began what was perhaps the most eloquent and moving summation of his career. He reviewed Laura's entire life, defended her morals, depicted her as the unhappy victim of Crittenden's lust, portrayed her as not being responsible for her actions, and made an eloquent plea for simple mercy. Day after day, he paced in front of the jury, making his case for leniency.

This was not, however, the longest final summation of Cook's career. That had been several years earlier when he harangued a jury for eight straight days. Now frail and in ill health, he had only enough stamina for four days. His final words were evocative: "I implore Heaven, the Great I Am, the Great Architect of the Universe, as to my honest belief, and the sincerity of it as to this woman's condition of mind—that she

Prosecutor Henry H. Byrne, whose eloquence finally carried the day. *San Francisco Examiner*

was unconscious. I implore Him to throw light into your minds, and ask it, gentlemen of the jury, that you season justice with mercy."[21]

Still the trial was not over. Prosecutor Henry Byrne had one last crack at the jury and he made the most of it—for two more days. In an attempt to trump the elocution of Cook, he included in his oratory quotations from Byron's *Don Juan* and *Childe Harold*, Rousseau's *Confessions*, from Sappho, Milton, Shakespeare, Aesculapius, Hippocrates, Locke, Kant, Aristotle, Thackeray, Dickens, Michelet, Mark Anthony, Cleopatra, Lord Nelson, Lady Hamilton, Brigham Young, Telemachus, Julius Caesar, Lucrezia Borgia, Daniel Webster, and Abraham Lincoln. After these final two days of erudition, the trial was finally over. The lawyers and the jury were thoroughly exhausted. Laura, for her part, appeared to be only semi-conscious.

No one could guess long how long the jurors might take to reach their decision, but some feared that after being submitted to twenty-six days of mind-numbing testimony and oratory, they might get revenge on the court with an extended deliberation. They were wrong. In less than an hour, the jurors returned with their verdict. They found Laura Fair guilty of murder in the first degree.

As the city's newspapers trumpeted the wisdom of the decision and heralded the fact that society had been saved, Laura, now a sad, forlorn, and lonely figure, was returned to her cell in the county jail at the base of Telegraph Hill to await her sentence.

It came on June 2, when Judge Dwinelle pronounced the first death sentence on a woman in the young history of California: "The judgement of the Court is that on Friday, the 28th day of July next, you, by the sheriff appointed, shall be hung by the neck until you are dead, and may God have mercy on your soul."[23]

The *Chronicle* announces the verdict to an enthralled citizenry.

[handwritten: Chron Thurs, April 27, 71. P.3. m.]

GUILTY

Close of the Most Remarkable Criminal Trial in the United States.

A Verdict of "Guilty of Murder in the First Degree" on the First Ballot.

ELOQUENT ADDRESS OF DISTRICT ATTORNEY H. H. BYRNE.

FAIR AND IMPARTIAL CHARGE BY JUDGE DWINELLE.

Proceedings of the Jury and How They Arrived at Their Verdict.

Appearance of Mrs. Fair, Her Mother and Daughter.

A FLOOD OF TEARS AND STATUESQUE SILENCE.

Large Crowds in Attendance—Closing Scenes in the Grand Criminal Drama —Points Upon a Motion for a New Trial—Appeal to the Supreme Court—Circulation of the Daily Chronicle.

The trial of Laura D. Fair for the murder of A. P. Crittenden results, on the twenty-sixth day, in her conviction by the jury, on the first ballot, of murder in the first degree, punishable by death. A new trial is to be asked for by the defense, and an appeal to the Supreme Court

One result of the death sentence was a surge of feminist sentiment throughout the state. Susan B. Anthony and her associates immediately undertook a series of lectures in the Bay Area during which they railed against institutions that were created by men that passed laws created by men and that were enforced and adjudicated by men. Said Ms. Anthony, "If all men had protected all women as they would have their own wives and daughters protected, you would have no Laura Fair in your jail to-night."[24] Her speeches were usually met by intermingled cheers and jeers.

The true course of justice continued, as appeals in the case wound their way through the courts. The superior court rejected the first appeal, but in February of 1870, the Supreme Court of the State of California reversed the decision on technical grounds and ordered a new trial for Laura Fair. For most of San Francisco's newspapers, this decision signaled the approaching end of civilization. Bellowed the *Daily Alta Californian*, "The State is disgraced by this reversal of judgement. No future action by the Supreme Court can ever wipe away the stain, the shame, the disgrace."[25]

Laura's second trial did not get underway until September. The cast that assembled at the courthouse was now dramatically different. Laura's lawyers in the first trial, Cook and Bryne, had both died during the winter. Campbell, the lead prosecutor, had returned to private practice. Judge Dwinelle was replaced by Judge T. B. Riordan. The character of the re-trial was also different. Whereas the first trial had been wearisomely long and the deliberation shockingly short, this time the trial itself would be relatively brief while the preliminaries and the deliberation would be boringly long.

The selection of the jury alone took more than a week. The problem was finding San Franciscans who didn't have an opinion about Laura Fair. More than four hundred prospective jurors were interviewed before twelve men qualified. One observer commented, "They must be the dullest collection of badly informed men ever assembled to sit on a case anywhere."[26]

The trial itself was essentially a replay of the first trial, telescoped into a much shorter time period. The defense again claimed that Laura was suffering from emotional insanity at the time of the shooting. The prosecution again painted the defendant as an evil, licentious, lust-filled assassin. Just ten days after the trial began, the case was in the hands of the jury.

This time the jurors spent three days trying to make up their minds. The first vote was ten to two for acquittal. In order to lubricate the minds of the holdouts, the foreman of the jury sent out for a gallon of whiskey, and eventually the dissidents came around.

Just seventeen days after the trial opened, Laura Fair sat demurely in the courtroom and heard the words she had dreamed about for the past two years. As the phrase "not guilty" echoed through the chamber, Laura bounded across the room and leaped straight into the arms of a startled Judge Riordan.

Laura was, however, scarcely welcomed back into the arms of a forgiving community after her acquittal. The newspapers went into spasms of vitriol: "An outrage to humanity"…"A jury composed of twelve idiots"…"License to kill"…"Carte blanche to burn gunpowder"…were only a few of the phrases used to protest the verdict.[27]

Laura became something of a pariah in the community. Women shunned her. San Francisco's usually chivalrous men pointedly refused to surrender their seats to her whenever Laura entered a streetcar. Nor was Laura finished in the courts. She sued her mother for mishandling her funds while she was in prison. Laura, in turn, was sued by her lawyers for not paying their fees. But that was not the worst of it. Parker Crittenden, son of Laura's deceased lover, began stalking her, following her whenever she left her house. When word reached Laura that Parker had purchased a revolver, she decided she would be better off somewhere else. She quickly packed her bags and fled to Sacramento with her young daughter.

While in that city, it occurred to Laura that there might be some way to capitalize on her notoriety. Accordingly, she announced that she would give a lecture in which she would tell her own story in her own words. The venue she selected was Platt's Music Hall and the price was a modest one dollar. But when advance ticket sales were slow, she announced that the lecture would be free to all comers. At that price, the hall was packed. In a talk she entitled, "Wolves in the Fold," Laura really tore into her tormentors. The editors of San Francisco newspapers were "snakes in the grass." Judge Dwinelle was a "judicial pettifogger." The jury that convicted her consisted of "twelve Iagos." Nevertheless, her restatement of what had happened to her was both cogent and persuasive. And at the end of her talk there was sustained applause. Laura returned to San Francisco with renewed confidence.

The remainder of her life is largely unchronicled, and with the passing of the years, she seems to have melded quietly into the mainstream of the city's life. She did have to endure one more tragedy, however. Her daughter, Lillie, grew into beautiful womanhood and was actually named the prettiest woman in California in the state's first beauty contest. With this credential, Lillie went to New York in search of a stage career. It was unsuccessful, and many years later she was found dead in a tenement house. When Laura received this tragic news, she tried to kill herself, but, as in so many other things in her life, she was unsuccessful.

The incident did, however, rouse the newspapers to dredge up the old stories about Laura, her lovers, and her trials. When Laura read them, she once again found herself aggrieved. She sued the papers for the many inaccuracies the stories contained, including the statement that Lillie had been her love-child with Crittenden. She sued and she won. The papers printed elaborate retractions, including statements that they never meant to imply that Laura Fair and Alexander Crittenden had been anything but good friends!

Then, once again, Laura Fair seemed to disappear into history. She continued to live quietly in San Francisco, moving from residence to residence, usually in the less desirable neighborhoods in town. As an elderly lady, she took long walks into town once a week to do her shopping, rarely running into anyone who recognized her. The people who noticed her at all probably had no idea that she had once been the notorious woman who for years dominated conversations throughout the western United States. Laura made news one more time in October of 1919 when her body was discovered in a flat above a store in the Mission District. Laura Fair had lived a full life and died at the age of eighty-two.

Laura was buried in Woodland Cemetery, far from the place on Lone Mountain where her lover had already rested for forty-five years. Alexander P. Crittenden had been given one of the largest and most spectacular funerals in the city's memory. Laura Fair was buried with little ceremony and lies today in an unmarked grave.

It is impossible to conclude the story of the Fair-Crittenden affair without pondering the question of why so many men found Laura Fair so irresistible. She was usually described by contemporaries as "fair" and "handsome," but seldom as "beautiful." She was tall and slender, but she was also somewhat awkward. She was poorly educated and always in need of money. Yet, she was a veritable magnet for men. She married three times. One husband took his life at the possibility of losing her. Alexander Crittenden risked both his reputation and his life to be with her.

Perhaps an answer can be found in a description of Laura by a young man who encountered her when Laura was middle-aged. The noted painter Edward Simmons, having just graduated from college, was clerking at a paint store in San Francisco when he was introduced to Laura as a customer. She looked, said Simmons, like someone's elderly aunt. He was then asked one day to deliver something to her house. Wrote Simmons many years later:

> "The same thin, sallow, worn-looking woman greeted me at the door. She showed, contrary to my expectation, not the slightest impropriety or dissipation, but wonder of wonders—

when this woman spoke, the sound was liquid music, and the words were followed by a smile so dazzling that one could imagine a withered bud suddenly opening into a beautiful flower. She bade me to sit down and have a glass of sherry, then she questioned me about my life. I will always think of her that day, calm and beautiful by some expression within, sitting in the quiet of her drawing room, and showing the most enthusiastic interest in the absurd aspirations of a callow youth. Laura Fair was one of the few superwomen I have ever met."[28]

Chapter Four

The Preacher and
the Publisher—1880

From the earliest days of San Francisco, newspapering has been a high-risk business. Ever since Sam Brannan published the first edition of his California Star in 1847, newspapers have started up and gone under with amazing regularity, and their publishers and editors have not fared much better.

San Francisco, booming in its growth and commerce, lusty in its politics, and rich in its social and cultural pretensions, was, from its beginning, a gold mine of news. A wide assortment of journals were created to keep the city's citizens posted on the latest doings, gossip, scandals, and shootings. Just a dozen years after its founding, San Francisco boasted twelve daily newspapers, including the Alta, The Herald, The Call, and the Bulletin. There were seventeen weeklies, among them The Pacific, The Monitor, and the Weekly Times. There were also four semi-monthlies and thirteen foreign language papers. All of them eventually failed, costing their owners fortunes of varying size.

Financial failure was not the only danger these journalistic pioneers faced: They also risked life and limb. Outraged readers and insulted competitors were all too eager to settle their scores with knife or gun. In 1855, James King of William, editor of the San Francisco Bulletin, was famously gunned down on Montgomery Street by an offended politician. A few years later, C. A. Russell, editor of the California Police Gazette, *was murdered by a printer in his office, as a way of settling a wage dispute. The publisher of the* Evening Picaune *engaged in a pistol duel with Captain Joseph Folsom, who felt aggrieved by an editorial comment. When both missed with their pistols, they went at each other with Bowie knives to their mutual detriment. One editor received so many threats that he put a sign over his door reading, "Subscriptions received from 9 to 4; challenges from 11 to 12 only."*

None of these incidents, however, ever achieved the notoriety of the assassination Charles deYoung of the Chronicle. *The manner in which deYoung met his demise in 1880 set a completely new standard for irresponsible journalism, outrageous behavior, civic malfeasance, and judicial mayhem. It also involved two of the most unforgettable characters ever to stride the streets of San Francisco.*

Many of those who made the arduous journey to early San Francisco came not only in the hope of finding their future but also in the hope of losing their past. Among them was a preacher named Isaac Smith Kalloch, who came to the city in 1875, leaving behind him a trail of scandal and a reputation for lechery. He brought with him a magnetic presence and an eloquent oratorical style that would eventually win him the largest church audience in the city.

Kalloch was born some forty-five years before his arrival in San Francisco in Rockland, Maine, where he grew to splendid manhood. By the time he entered Maine's Colby College, Kalloch stood six feet, three inches tall and weighed a well-muscled two hundred and thirty pounds. Broad-shouldered and slim-waisted, with a full head of shockingly red hair and sporting a spectacular pink beard, Kalloch caught the eyes of women wherever he went. That was apparently all right with Kalloch, for at the end of his freshman year at Colby, he was expelled from the college for "sexual proclivity."

In 1857, while in his mid-twenties, Kalloch's way with words secured him a position as pastor of Boston's Tremont Temple. It was here that he discovered and developed his ability to entertain, enthrall, and move audiences. Gifted with a deep, resonant voice, an amazing vocabulary, and an emotional speaking style, he became a celebrated orator. But once again he ran afoul of the moralists and was accused of "sexual exploits" and "adulterous behavior."

A long and lurid adultery trial ensued, which was widely reported in newspapers throughout the East. Kalloch was eventually freed as a

The Rev. Isaac Kalloch, who survived de Young's assassination attempt and became San Francisco's eighteenth mayor. *Bancroft Library*

result of a mistrial, but not before reporters had dubbed him "The Snorting Sorrell Stallion of Kaw Bottom."[1] With his reputation in tatters, Kalloch abandoned both his pulpit and his home territory, "leaving in his wake, riot, tumult, rape, swindle, perjury, blackmail and shootings."[2] Kalloch eventually surfaced in Kansas City, where he undertook a number of new careers, all of which eventually failed. Over the next fifteen years, he started a newspaper, helped found a university, tried his hand as a farmer and breeder, and ran for the state legislature. For all his efforts, he wound up dead broke—and with a reputation for drinking, gambling and womanizing. When he moved on to a ministry in Lawrence, Kansas, the local newspaper warned its readers to "keep your wives and daughters locked up."[3] Apparently, Kalloch found a few who were not sufficiently closeted, and before long and by popular request he left town and headed for San Francisco. His reason for choosing San Francisco is the stuff of legend: "There are more wicked people of both sexes in San Francisco and I feel compelled of God to go and convert them."[4]

Once in San Francisco, Isaac Kalloch, despite his past problems, had no trouble establishing himself as an eloquent man of God. Within months, he was named pastor of a Baptist congregation at the Metropolitan Temple at Fifth and Mission streets. His reputation as a carouser and a womanizer seemed a dim and distant memory. It might have remained that way if it had not been for Charles deYoung.

Twenty years earlier, the deYoung family had also arrived in San Francisco with a background shrouded in mystery. The favored deYoung story was that the family was the descendant of a French family of royal blood that settled in New Orleans. But there were other stories. One was that the deYoungs were the offspring of Alsatian shopkeepers who came to California to avoid military service. Another was that they came from Baltimore, the children of a Dutch Jewish mother. The most scandalous story, spoken only in hushed tones, was that they were the issue of a Saint Louis prostitute who journeyed to San Francisco during the Civil War.

Some things were certain. There were three children, all boys. They came to San Francisco during the Civil War with a mother, but without a father. Their names were Charles, Michael, and Gustavus, and all three were teenagers. The deYoung family established residence at No. 15 Fifth Street, joined Temple Emmanuel, and entered into the mainstream of San Francisco life.

The brothers secured jobs in the office where the synagogue's weekly newspaper, *The Weekly Gleaner*, was published, and over the next several years they learned how to write for the paper, set type for it, and print it. It wasn't long before Charles decided they could put their new skills to better use.

Charles de Young, co-founder and editor of the *San Francisco Chronicle. Bancroft Library*

Charles borrowed twenty-five dollars, rented some printing equipment, a desk, and a small office on Montgomery Street, and the brothers began publishing a free handout theatre guide called the *Daily Dramatic Chronicle*. While most newspapers of the time claimed lofty principles, the deYoungs' new paper was intended to be a scandal sheet from the outset. Charles announced in the first issue that his paper would chronicle "the actions, intentions, sayings, doings, movements, successes, failures, oddities, peculiarities and speculations of us poor mortals."[5]

It was clear from the beginning that Charles was the leader of the enterprise as well as its taskmaster. He was the paper's proprietary editor, business manager, proofreader, and money collector. To get the first edition of the paper out, Charles worked like a man possessed. He slept only thirteen hours over a five-day period, writing articles, setting type, soliciting advertisements, and running the press. He borrowed money to buy coffee to keep everyone awake. When the first edition was finally out, Charles fell to the floor exhausted.

Propelled by Charles' penchant for searching out the seamy side of life, and his flair for flamboyant reportage, the paper soon became one of the best read and most feared journals in the city. It also developed a reputation for blackmail, bribery, and chicanery. No scandal was too outrageous, no rumor too preposterous to be featured in the deYoungs' paper. One particularly meaty story featured an affair between a rival publisher and a young woman reporter, a scandal compounded by the fact that the publisher was a well-known family man. The story resulted in a lurid divorce trial, a lawsuit against the paper, a celebrated divorce, and greatly increased readership for the deYoungs.

Michael deYoung, popularly known as M. A., was the paper's co-proprietor and assistant publisher. Gustavus had a variety of duties, mostly on the financial side. But it was clearly Charles who was the paper's heart and soul. A dark, smallish man with boundless energy and ambition, he ranged over the city like a predator, stalking its salons and saloons, haunting its halls of power. Competitors claimed that he invented many of his stories. Businesses hinted that he blackmailed advertisers into supporting his paper. Society matrons whispered that he was willing to accept a bribe to keep stories off the front page. But whatever he did, Charles deYoung kept his newspaper growing and prospering.

The *Daily Dramatic Chronicle* was quick to print the gossip and scandal of the day, but it also frequently beat its competitors to the important news. When dispatches came into the telegraph office, deYoung's men were usually on hand to rush the news back to the paper. In April of

1865, the paper scored a true journalistic coup. When news of Lincoln's assassination crackled over the wire, one of deYoung's reporters read the dispatch over the shoulder of the telegrapher. He then ran all the way back to the paper, where the story was rewritten with imaginative details, and an artist drew a sketch of what he believed must have been the scene of the murder at Ford's Theatre. The next morning, San Franciscans saw and read about the crime of the century, giving the deYoungs' newspaper the scoop of the decade.

When circulation reached 10,000 readers, Charles decided the paper's name should be changed to reflect its true and more impressive character. It became simply *The Daily Morning Chronicle*, and with the new name came a new editorial proclamation of independence: "We shall support no party, no clique, no faction…Neither the Republican Party, nor the Democratic Party, nor the Pacific Railroad, nor the Bank of California are great enough to frighten us or rich enough to buy us."[6] Charles deYoung, the courageous, un-buyable, crusading editor was nineteen years old.

Charles wanted only the best for his paper and he retained Mark Twain, Bret Harte, and Warren Stoddard as regular contributors. Though Charles was not an educated man, he had a keen eye for talent and had excellent judgment as to what would appeal to his readers. He continued to be a stern taskmaster, pushing himself and his employees to work long hours and heaping criticism on anyone whose work he deemed inadequate. One who buckled under the pressure was his brother, Gustavus. Suffering from depression and dementia, he was declared incompetent and dispatched to an insane asylum. Charles quickly removed Gustavus' name from the *Chronicle* masthead.

The *Chronicle* continued to prosper, constantly finding new readers, new wealth and new power. By 1875, the paper had a circulation of more than 25,000. More important, the ability of the *Chronicle* to influence affairs in San Francisco was giving Charles deYoung and, to a lesser extent his brother, unusual clout in dictating the political direction of the city. Charles set about making himself the kingmaker of San Francisco, selecting favorites to run for office and then backing them to the hilt, while doing his best to editorially demean their opponents.

Eager to slander others, Charles was outraged when he was slandered himself and he was quick to take revenge. It was widely known that he carried a revolver, although he was also known as a remarkably bad shot. Only his lack of talent at aiming a gun kept him from seriously wounding several competitors whom he felt had wronged him.

The editor of *The Sun*, Ben Napthaly, ran a series of stories in his paper accusing the deYoungs of a series of alleged misdeeds. Charles endured these indignities for a while, but when word reached him that a forthcoming article would mention a rumor concerning his mother's involvement in prostitution, he could take it no more.

At this time, Charles was solidly in league with I. W. Lees, the San Francisco chief of police, and together they hatched a scheme to put *The Sun* out of business. Lees led a dawn raid on the paper's offices, during which the presses were stopped, six printers were arrested, and the plates of the offending story on the deYoungs' mother were destroyed. Napthaly fled out the back door as Lee's men rushed in the front, but Charles was waiting for him and tracked him to the corner of Washington and Battery. A clumsy gunfight ensued in which Napthaly missed altogether, and Charles succeeded only in wounding a messenger boy who happened to be passing by. Charles' reputation as a marksman sank to a new low.

San Francisco politics in the 1870s had become a messy proposition. The city was rife with class bitterness and demagogic politicians. Paramount among the issues was the "Chinese problem"—the popular theory that immigrants from the Orient were depriving the city's longtime citizens of jobs. In the election of 1875, Andrew J. Bryant defeated James Hallidie, the inventor of the cable car. The *Chronicle* had supported Bryant, but a slumping economy had made him unpopular. By the middle of 1877, 30,000 San Franciscans were out of work, and it was obvious that some new political force would be needed to bring the city out of its recession. The Workingman's Party, an organization that preached hatred of the rich and of the Chinese, felt the time had come for it to reach for power. It looked around for a candidate to represent the party in the forthcoming elections, and eventually its eyes fell upon a relative newcomer to the city: Isaac Kalloch, dynamic preacher of the Baptist Metropolitan Temple.

Kalloch had taken the city by storm. His personal magnetism and his dazzling oratory attracted so many followers that it had been necessary to enlarge the church on Mission Street. Every Sunday, Kalloch now harangued, exhorted, and inspired an audience of five thousand parishioners, by far the largest congregation in San Francisco. Kalloch had also deeply immersed himself in city politics and had become a strong supporter of the Workingman's Party. In 1879, the party decided it needed a strong and dynamic leader, and it overwhelmingly selected Isaac Kalloch to be its candidate for the office of mayor of San Francisco.

Charles deYoung had been an early supporter of the Workingman's Party, and the *Chronicle* was alone among the city's newspapers to back the party. But when Charles heard that the party had nominated Kalloch, he became an instant disbeliever. He couldn't stomach Kalloch and his distasteful background. More important, he had no control over Kalloch. Charles and the *Chronicle* immediately went on the attack. In issue after issue, the *Chronicle* railed and wailed against Kalloch's candidacy, and its prose left little to the imagination.

As an opening salvo, the *Chronicle* featured the following cascade of headlines on August 23, 1979:

> "Depraved Kalloch—The Vilest Fraud of the Kansas Jayhawkers—Disclosure of His Crowning Exploit of Mean-ness—He Swindles A Poor Widow Out Of Her Last Dollar—Refusing to Pay Her and Boasting of His Rascality—A Crime Punishable by Penitentiary Imprisonment—Wearing the Livery of Heaven to Serve The Devil In—The Black Record of the In-famous Ike Kalloch." [7.]

Another *Chronicle* diatribe stated, "At the head of the list of com-munist tyrants stands Kalloch, the mock minister, travelling mounte-bank and carpet-bag demagogue, who wants to be mayor, not because he is fit but because he knows himself to be unfit for the pulpit, and is probably an atheist and a blasphemer at heart!"[8]

Charles deYoung was just warming up. In a subsequent issue he referred to Kalloch as "a burlesque divine whose aspiration to high office is in the nature of a public shame."[9] The *Chronicle* also stated Kalloch had been observed seducing dozens of women and drinking great quantities of gin in the city's saloons.

Kalloch was scarcely intimidated. He roared back from his pulpit that deYoung had offered him a deal if he would split the political spoils. But, said Kalloch, he had told the *Chronicle* man to "give Mr. deYoung my compliments and tell him to go to hell." He further proclaimed:

> "I pledge to you that the day after the election I will pros-ecute for libel that venal, corrupt blackmailer sheet. I promise you if you will elect me I will kill the *San Francisco Chronicle!*"[10]

DeYoung didn't let up. His next front-page headline read:

> "Kalloch: The Record of a Misspent Life—Driven Forth from Boston Like an Unclean Leper—His Trial for Adultery—His Escapade With One of the Tremont Temple Choristers."[11]

Once again, Kalloch felt a response was in order. The following Sunday, his congregation learned that "the deYoungs' approach nearer than any other persons in history whether man or devil, to the monstrous model of consummate and unrelieved depravity." Then, for good measure, he added that the deYoungs were "hyenas of society…hybrid whelps of sin and depravity…moral lepers."[12]

Charles responded to that volley with a threat. In a reference to the transcript of Kalloch's trial for adultery in Boston, he promised in print that "if Kalloch doesn't step down and out before the election, I know good reasons why he should and he knows what they are."[13]

Now Kalloch really piled on the vitriol. "Charles deYoung," he told his audience, "is the wickedest man in the world. He may be without rival in hell. If he does not go to hell, then that institution should be abolished." And then Kalloch threw caution to the wind. "The deYoungs are the bastard progeny of a whore, conceived in infamy and nursed in the lap of prostitution."[14]

That did it. The subject of his mother's alleged one-time occupation was Charles' flashpoint. On the morning of August 23, 1879, Charles heard the report of Kalloch's diatribe. He went berserk. He took a revolver out of his desk and tucked it under his belt. He left the building and hailed a hack, ordering the driver to take him to Kalloch's mansion at 961 Mission. When he was informed that the minister was not at home but was at the Metropolitan Temple, he had the carriage take him there. At 10:00 A.M., Isaac Kalloch left the temple and was in the process of mounting his own carriage when he was informed by a messenger boy that a lady in the carriage ahead wished to give him her respects. It was the kind of invitation that Kalloch couldn't resist.

He approached the carriage confidently, removing his right glove in anticipation of shaking the hand of his admirer. As he reached for the carriage door, Charles deYoung whipped back the curtains and leveled his revolver at Kalloch. "Now I've got you," he screamed.[15] He fired point blank at the astonished minister, and this time deYoung was too close to his target to miss. The ball tore into the left side of Kalloch's chest.

Kalloch clasped his chest, where the wound was spouting blood and stumbled back toward the temple. DeYoung stepped halfway out of the carriage, steadied his foot on the fender, and fired again at the retreating Kalloch. This time he hit him in the thigh. "Oh, my God!" yelled Kalloch, as he staggered on toward the temple, a trail of blood marking his path.

Charles leaped back into his carriage and ordered the driver to return to the *Chronicle*. But the carriage was suddenly surrounded by members

De Young shoots Kalloch. *Frank Leslie's Illustrated Weekly*

De Young being rescued from the Workingman's Party mob.

of the Workingman's Party who happened to be having a political rally nearby and who had come running at the sound of the shots. They tried to pull Charles from his carriage, but he waved his gun at them and yelled, "I will shoot dead the first man who lays a hand on me!"[16] Obviously unfamiliar with Charles' reputation as an inferior marksman, they backed off.

Within minutes, however, the crowd regained its courage, set up a cry demanding that deYoung be hanged immediately, and dispatched a man to find a rope. However, before the lynching could progress, a squad of police, led by the valiant and ubiquitous Captain I. W. Lees, rescued deYoung and carted him off to jail. At nightfall, as Charles languished in his cell, thousands of angry men marched up and down the street outside, yelling, "Kill him! Kill him! Hemp! Hemp! Hemp!"[17]

In the meantime, Isaac Kalloch lay in his bed, hovering between life and death. The first bulletins were grim, and the city's newspapers all but declared him a dead man. The *Examiner* gave the story massive coverage:

> "Blood Spilled!—Dr. Kalloch Shot by DeYoung—Kalloch Mortally Wounded In Two Places—Threats To Inflict Summary Punishment On DeYoung—Kalloch Still Alive But Unconscious—City Hall Surrounded By An Excited Crowd!"[18]

Coverage in the *Chronicle*—as opposed to coverage in the *Call*—showing a marked difference in reportage.

The Morning Call was equally exuberant in its coverage of the event:

"ATROCIOUS! Dr. Kalloch Shot By Charles DeYoung!—Cowardly Attempt At Assassination!—A COLD BLOODED CRIME!!—Citizens Horrified And Aroused To Indignation!"[19]

And how did the *Chronicle* cover the event? Hardly at all. The next day, on page four, on an inner column and under a quiet heading called "The Shooting of Kalloch," the paper stated,

"We do not propose to comment in detail on the deplorable events of Saturday morning. The time has not yet come for a calm and candid discussion of the merits of the case. When men present themselves before the people as candidates for office, they become fair and proper subjects for criticism. Let them who have been so insulted (as our publisher) consider what they would have done, etc."[20]

The Workingman's Party subsequently felt compelled to issue an official proclamation on the subject of the *Chronicle*:

"Whereas that ulcerous running sore, the *Chronicle*, true to the antecedents of its infamous founder, has ever lived by blackmail and pandering to the debased low and lustful taste for obscene literature and scandalous depravity...."[21]

Doctors attending Kalloch predicted an early demise. His admirers formed a circle around Kalloch's blood that had splashed on the roadway, in order to prevent the street cleaner from washing it away. Firebrands in the party continued to make inflammatory speeches. One was Milton Kalloch, son of the wounded minister. "I yet believe my father will live to be Mayor of San Francisco and will tread on the grave of that brute deYoung. If deYoung does not hang, then help me kill him!"[22]

The infamous "slander pamphlet" that outraged Kalloch's son.

Better news began to emanate from the Kalloch residence. He had "the constitution of a grizzly bear." He had regained consciousness. He was fighting back gamely. Kalloch was surrounded by two surgeons and five attending physicians who were "working feverishly." Then it was reported that Kalloch had "a slim chance of living." Finally, after nine days, it was announced that "if anything, he is better. He is losing some flesh but looks well."[23]

On election eve, Kalloch rallied at last and his doctors announced that he would live. The next day, a relieved and grateful citizenry, sensing the intervention of divine Providence, elected Isaac Kalloch the eighteenth mayor of the City of San Francisco. His election to the city's highest office shocked many people. He had never been favored to win and his amazing victory was generally attributed to the shooting by deYoung. As Henry George later wrote, "The crack of deYoung's pistol from behind the curtain of a coupé fired Kalloch into the mayoralty."[24]

Charles deYoung, in the meantime, was out of jail on a $25,000 bond. After posting the bond, he quickly skedaddled down to Mexico to wait out the storm. After five months, he decided it would be safe to return to San Francisco. Subsequent events proved he would be wrong about that.

DeYoung quickly returned to work at the *Chronicle*, vowing to remain at the helm and promising to dispense wisdom and truth until the time of his trial. He also announced that he had dispatched one of his best reporters to the East to document all of the charges he had leveled at Kalloch during the campaign.

On the evening of Friday, April 23, 1880, Charles deYoung was working late in the offices of the *Chronicle*. He was consulting with E. B. Read, an employee, on the first floor when suddenly the front door flew open. There, standing in the doorway, his face an ashen white, was Milton Kalloch, son of the new mayor. Young Kalloch had a five-shot Wesley revolver in his hand. He fired at deYoung from a distance of only six feet. The shot went wild, smashing a glass door behind Charles. DeYoung quickly jumped behind Read, holding the employee like a shield. Milton Kalloch moved in closer, reached his gun over Read's shoulder and fired again. His second shot also missed and slammed into a window frame. DeYoung then ducked behind the counter, tugging at his tightly buttoned jacket in an effort to free his own revolver. Kalloch fired a third shot, this time grazing deYoung's skin, as the bullet tore through his jacket. DeYoung finally extracted his gun and was in the process of trying to aim it at Kalloch when Kalloch, now just two feet from his target, pulled the trigger once again.

This time he was too close to miss. The bullet smashed into the right side of deYoung's jaw, tore through his jugular vein and lodged in the back of his neck. Charles deYoung fell heavily to the floor. He was dead.

A number of Sandlotters, enemies of deYoung, so-called for their rabble-rousing speeches in the open, sandy area west of town, were celebrating in the nearby Irish-American Hall. When they heard the sound of gunfire from the *Chronicle* offices, they rushed over. Hearing of deYoung's assassination, they quickly relocated their party to the street outside the crime scene. Their singing and dancing went on for hours, pausing only to applaud as deYoung's corpse was loaded into the coroner's hearse.

Diagram of the room in which de Young was murdered.

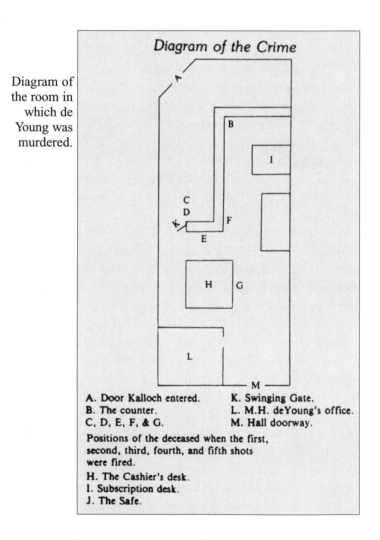

Diagram of the Crime

A. Door Kalloch entered.
B. The counter.
C, D, E, F, & G.
K. Swinging Gate.
L. M.H. deYoung's office.
M. Hall doorway.

Positions of the deceased when the first, second, third, fourth, and fifth shots were fired.

H. The Cashier's desk.
I. Subscription desk.
J. The Safe.

Funeral services were held for Charles two days later, conducted appropriately enough by the Odd Fellows. Charles remained as controversial in death as he had been in life, and as the funeral cortege of the thirty-nine-year-old publisher wound its way through the streets of San Francisco on its way to the cemetery, it was softly hissed and booed by some of the spectators.

The trial of Milton Kalloch for the murder of Charles deYoung was assumed by most observers to be perfunctory. There were a number of witnesses to the deed, all of whom testified that Kalloch emptied his revolver in the shooting. DeYoung's weapon had been recovered fully loaded and showed no signs of having been fired.

It was difficult to find jurors who did not already hold strong opinions on the principals involved. It took twenty-three days to select the jury, twenty-two days to hear testimony and four days for rebuttals. In all, 208 witnesses were examined, while nine shorthand recorders scribbled away, turning out thousands of pages of testimony.

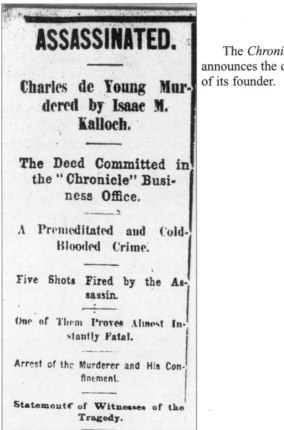

The *Chronicle* announces the demise of its founder.

As the trial droned on in the superior court in late January of 1881, everything seemed headed for a routine conviction. Then, near the end of the trial, the new mayor of San Francisco and father of the accused, took the stand. As Isaac Kalloch testified as to the outrages and perfidies that Charles deYoung had inflicted on his family, he continually jiggled two small objects in his hand, like an early-day Captain Quegg. As he talked on and continued to move the two objects about in his hand, the prosecuting attorney finally could stand the distraction no longer. He leaped from his chair and demanded, "Tell us, Mayor Kalloch, what is it you have in your hand?"[25] That was the moment Kalloch had been waiting for.

The mayor sprang from the witness box, proclaiming in a loud voice, "These are the two bullets from deYoung's murderous weapon which were extracted from my body."[26] Kalloch strode to the jury box and handed the two bullets to the astonished jurors. The shaken jurors then retired, deliberated, and returned to announce their verdict. They found Milton Kalloch not guilty of the crime of murdering Charles deYoung because of extenuating circumstances. The prosecuting attorney was so astonished that he swallowed his tobacco cud.

In an absurd miscarriage of justice, the *Chronicle* employee who had seen and testified that Milton Kalloch had fired five shots at Charles deYoung was convicted of perjury and sent to prison. Milton Kalloch quickly left town, only returning later when memories of the murder had dimmed. He practiced law in San Francisco until his death in 1930.

Isaac Kalloch spent two contentious years as mayor of San Francisco, dedicating most of his time to making eloquent speeches and fighting with the board of supervisors. He declined to stand for re-election and briefly returned to his post at the Metropolitan Temple, finally resigning in July of 1883. He moved to what was then the Washington Territory, where he tried his hand at farming. His peaceful life there came to an end just four years later in 1887.

Charles' brother, M. H. deYoung, took over the reins of the *San Francisco Morning Chronicle* and for the next half century shepherded the paper to new heights of circulation and glory. Today, some 120 years after Charles' death, the *Chronicle* is the dominant newspaper of Northern California. The words "Charles deYoung, Founding Editor" still appear on the masthead.

A crowd gathers outside the *Chronicle* building on news of de Young's death.

Chapter Five

The Phosphorescent Brides—1885

San Francisco, during the mid-1880s, was a city of growth, pride, and optimism. America had seen nothing like the explosive growth of the city and the area around its glorious Bay. San Francisco, to the country's astonishment, laid claim to being one of the ten largest cities in the United States. It was said that you could ask anywhere in the West for a railroad ticket to "the City," and you would be handled a ticket to San Francisco.

Of course, San Francisco still had its occasional economic crisis, bank failure, earthquake, and, yes, murder. By the 1880s, murder was perhaps not quite as commonplace as in previous decades, but it was still far from unusual. And, there were differences now in the way murder was adjudicated. Just a decade or so earlier, if the murder was unwitnessed, it simply went unpunished. But now "circumstantial evidence" was an accepted method of prosecution in most courts. Also, medical findings and the testimony of medical experts were becoming more acceptable in murder cases. Autopsies were held to determine the cause of death, if it were in doubt, and the opinions of medical experts were becoming highly regarded by California juries.

Nowhere in the history of this period is there a murder trial that better exemplifies these developments than what came to be called the case of the "Phosphorescent Bride"—or should it have been "Brides"? And, nowhere is there a better example of the growing complexity of the San Francisco court system and the uncertain course of criminal justice in California.

The Directory of San Francisco for the year 1885 listed more than five hundred men of medicine practicing and specializing in the treatment of a wide variety of ailments.[1] Among these was the name of Dr. J. Milton Bowers, a specialist in the treatment of women's ailments, who practiced out of his offices at 32½ Geary Street.[2] There seemed nothing remarkable about Dr. Bowers to those who knew him at the time. He was a man of average height; he was nice-looking but not really handsome, mustached and bearded like so many professional men of the day, and comfortable in his manner of living, but scarcely wealthy. Bowers was a man of limited social standing, but he often boasted of direct kinship with Robert E. Lee. It was said that he performed abortions.

In one regard, however, he was much different from most men in San Francisco: At the age of forty-two, he had already been married three times, and he had had singularly bad luck in his marriages. The first Mrs. Bowers was the former Fannie Hammond, whom he had married in his mid-twenties while living in Chicago. Unfortunately, she had died only a few years later, in 1874, of undetermined causes, and when Dr. Bowers' home burned

San Francisco in 1885, a south of Market view dominated by the original Palace Hotel.

down soon after her death, he almost immediately departed the scene of two such tragic losses and moved to New York. There he met his second wife, a beautiful young Jewish actress named Theresa Sherek. With the new Mrs. Bowers, he soon migrated to San Francisco and set himself up in medical practice. His credentials for doing so seemed quite splendid.

He first studied medicine in Germany, where he used his considerable inheritance from his father to travel and study in hospitals there. Later he joined the staff at Patterson Hospital in Washington, D.C., where he helped care for Civil War wounded, but he did not formally become a diploma-bearing doctor until he later graduated from the Electric Medical College of Chicago.

Dr. Bowers and his pretty wife had been in San Francisco only a few years when he once again became unexpectedly widowed. On January 28, 1881, the new Mrs. Bowers passed away after a brief and painful illness. Her obituary described her as both attractive and talented.[3] She had, it seems, somewhat out-distanced her husband in local fame during their brief time in the city, being an acclaimed writer and literary figure. Among her published works was a small and very successful book entitled *The Dance of Life*, which she had written in response to Ambrose Bierce's *The Dance of Death*, a satirical work proclaiming the evils of dancing the waltz. Bierce, the literary giant of San Francisco, paid dubious tribute to Theresa in his column in *The Argonaut* on September 28, 1877—and also ridiculed the custom of a wife using her husband's full name and title. Wrote Bierce, "I am proud to have been deemed worthy to receive a book entitled `The Dance of Life,' by Mrs. Dr. J. Milton Bowers—an engagingly vulgar title—that of the lady not the book."[4]

The death of the second Mrs. Bowers, stated by the doctor to have been caused by "abscess of the liver," seemed a heavy blow to Dr. Bowers, and he was seen weeping openly at the funeral. However, his grief was short-lived, and within less than a year, he took a third wife, Cecelia Benhayon. Cecelia was twenty-nine, a pleasant woman, short and somewhat plump, but known for her gaiety and high spirits. After just four years of marriage, the doctor's unlucky streak continued. The most recent Mrs. Bowers died on November 3, 1885, after a short and painful illness. However, while not much is known about the final days of the first two Mrs. Bowerses, the last illness of the third was chronicled in minute, painstaking, and somewhat disgusting detail. In fact, it became a major story in San Francisco newspapers for more than a decade.

Cecelia Bowers' death seemed almost more than the good doctor could handle. Overcome with grief, he had turned to the doctors attending her in her death throes and wailed, "Baby's going, doctor—is there nothing we can do for her?"[5] But nothing could be done, and, at the funeral and the graveside, J. Milton Bowers appeared a broken man, weeping with his head bowed. Perhaps it was because he knew he was in big trouble.

On learning of Mrs. Bowers' death, rumors immediately circulated in the city that perhaps Dr. Bowers' wives were victims of more than bad luck. The *Daily Alta*, one of the city's leading papers, did its best to put the rumors to rest:

> "Last evening startling rumors were circulated about town that Mrs. Bowers' death had been the result of foul play. Subsequent investigations, however, completely refute these groundless conjectures of thoughtless or vicious-minded persons. When the bereaved husband heard of the rumors, he immediately notified the Coroner and requested that official to hold an inquest that forenoon upon the deceased."[6]

Well, this was not exactly true. An anonymous letter had been sent to San Francisco coroner C. C. O'Donnell, alerting him to Mrs. Bowers' death, telling him that the body was still at the Bowers residence at 930 Market Street, and suggesting that an inquest should be held before the body was buried. The coroner hurried to the scene. There he found the bereaved husband, Mrs. Bowers' corpse, and a death certificate saying that Mrs. Bowers had died of "an abscess of the liver."[7] The coroner decided to take no chances, and he informed Bowers that he was ordering an inquest and that the body should not be disposed of. Dr. Bowers protested, but to no avail.

The inquest was held that day, with Dr. Bowers and a large number of witnesses in attendance, including two others doctors who had attended Mrs. Bowers during her illness. Both doctors declared that they agreed with the conclusion that "abscess of the liver" had been the cause of death, and that they had no reason to have any suspicions of foul play. Charlotte Zeissing, a nurse who had attended Mrs. Bowers in her final days, declared that Mrs. Bowers had told her that "her husband was her best friend," and that "she had always wanted her husband to give her her medicine," and that "her last request was that no autopsy be held."[8] She also spoke of Dr. Bowers' devotion to his sick wife, spending his nights sleeping on a cot near her bed and administering medicine to her personally.

This probably would have concluded the matter, except for the presence of two agents of insurance groups at the inquest. They represented fraternal organizations to which the deceased had belonged, and they informed the coroner that Dr. Bowers had recently obtained policies totaling $14,000 and that the doctor was the beneficiary of these policies. These agents demanded an autopsy. One reporter present recorded, "These suggestions were not kindly received and some sharp words were spoken by the parties."[9] The coroner subsequently ordered that the body should be placed in a receiving vault following the funeral, and that the body should then be returned the next day to an undertaker so that an autopsy could take place.

What happened next was described on the front page of the *Daily Alta* as "A Queer Proceeding."[10] Queer, indeed! At four o'clock the following day, Coroner O'Donnell received a phone call from Dr. Black, the city physician, that he was at the undertaker's to perform the autopsy at the scheduled time, but the body was not there. O'Donnell immediately drove to the cemetery, believing that someone there had simply forgotten to have the body delivered from the vault. But when he arrived, he discovered that the body was not there either. He demanded to know where it was. The cemetery superintendent informed him that Dr. Bowers had the body buried immediately following the funeral. Mrs. Bowers was now underground and out of sight.

The furious coroner ordered the body exhumed, but the cemetery officials refused, saying it could not be disinterred without a certificate from the board of health. The coroner refused to yield the point, cited additional law on the subject, and finally succeeded in having the corpse dug up and sent to the city morgue where the autopsy was rescheduled for the following morning.

The results of the autopsy were made public when the inquest was resumed on November 6. Dr. Black made such a detailed report on the state of each vital organ that Mrs. Sarah Benhayon, mother of the deceased, fainted dead away and had to be carried from the room. Black flatly stated that there were no abscesses in the liver. There was, however, an ulcer in the stomach, which he said was "of a suspicious nature."[11] As a result, Dr. Black ordered the stomach and intestine to be delivered to a chemist at Cooper Medical College for analysis.

When the inquest continued the following day, the doctors announced a shocking conclusion: Traces of phosphorous were found in the stomach. Mrs. Bowers had died as a result of being poisoned. Suddenly, the entire tenor of the proceeding took on another tone and direction. Mrs. Bowers' mother testified that her daughter had been frequently abused by her husband, that they often quarreled about Dr. Bowers' infidelities, and that he had prohibited her family members from visiting during Mrs. Bowers' illness. Her brother testified that he had heard Mrs. Bowers cry out several days before she died, "You are torturing me to death with medicine!"[12]

Dr. Bowers himself was questioned by the magistrate and professed absolute incredulity about the subject of poisoning. He was asked, "How do you account for the discovery of phosphorous in the stomach?" Bowers replied with seeming astonishment, "What's that, you say? Did you say that phosphorous was found in her stomach? I can hardly believe what you say, but if so, I did not give it to her. She must have taken it herself!"[13] Bowers was asked if it was true, as the autopsy also revealed, that a criminal operation, that is, an abortion had been performed on her. Bowers decided to stick with his previous ploy. "Yes...but I did not perform it. She did it herself."[14] That seemed enough for the inquest jury. Dr. Bowers was placed under arrest for the murder of his wife and sent packing to the county jail.

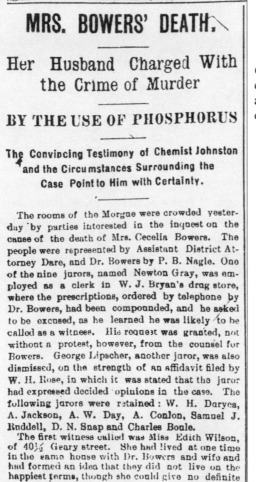

MRS. BOWERS' DEATH.

Her Husband Charged With the Crime of Murder

BY THE USE OF PHOSPHORUS

The Convincing Testimony of Chemist Johnston and the Circumstances Surrounding the Case Point to Him with Certainty.

The rooms of the Morgue were crowded yesterday by parties interested in the inquest on the cause of the death of Mrs. Cecelia Bowers. The people were represented by Assistant District Attorney Dare, and Dr. Bowers by P. B. Nagle. One of the nine jurors, named Newton Gray, was employed as a clerk in W. J. Bryan's drug store, where the prescriptions, ordered by telephone by Dr. Bowers, had been compounded, and he asked to be excused, as he learned he was likely to be called as a witness. His request was granted, not without a protest, however, from the counsel for Bowers. George Lipscher, another juror, was also dismissed, on the strength of an affidavit filed by W. H. Rose, in which it was stated that the juror had expressed decided opinions in the case. The following jurors were retained: W. H. Daryea, A. Jackson, A. W. Day, A. Conlon, Samuel J. Ruddell, D. N. Snap and Charles Boule.

The first witness called was Miss Edith Wilson, of 40½ Geary street. She had lived at one time in the same house with Dr. Bowers and wife and had formed an idea that they did not live on the happiest terms, though she could give no definite reasons for such impression.

The *San Francisco Chronicle* informs the city of Dr. Bowers' arrest for the murder of his wife.

Artist's drawing of Dr. Milton J. Bowers during the trial. *San Francisco Examiner*

Once in his new abode, Dr. Bowers seemed outwardly calm and controlled, and he was generous with his time, giving frequent interviews to reporters. Had he poisoned his wife? That was clearly preposterous. Had he wished to do so, he would certainly not have used phosphorous, but rather some other chemical more difficult to trace. Had he been married to two other women who died mysteriously? He would marry twenty times if he chose, and the previous deaths resulted from natural causes. The insurance money? Money was not important to him, only his reputation. Did he expect to be found guilty? He was confident that freedom was only a few days away. "I am not a bit nervous," he said, holding his hand out at full length. "My hand does not tremble the slightest." But one reporter wrote, "This was clearly a piece of bravado on the part of the harassed man...His palled countenance and restless eyes belied his effort."[15]

Bowers' trial got underway some four months later, on March 9, 1886, before Superior Court Judge D. J. Murphy. It lasted for six weeks, and from the outset San Francisco's newspapers fed the city's appetite for information on a daily basis, often in excruciating detail. The prosecution was handled by City Attorney Eugene Duprey, while the defense was headed by Colin Campbell, a veteran trial lawyer. The early weeks featured duel-

Sarah Benhayon, Mrs. Bowers' mother, who suspected her son-in-law from the beginning.

ing medical experts, clashing on the amount of phosphorous, if any, found in the body of the deceased, the effect of poisons on various organs of the body, and the likelihood of poison being administered without detection by the patient. The prosecution claimed that Bowers had an ample supply of phosphorous; the defense claimed none could be found in his office.

The second half of the trial was largely devoted to motive. The prosecution made much of the insurance money, claiming that the time the insurance was taken out and the amount involved pointed clearly to murder for money. The defense claimed that there was nothing unusual or suspicious about either—that both Dr. Bowers and Mrs. Bowers had jointly insured one another and that $14,000 was scarcely a fortune.

Much was made of Dr. Bowers' reputation as a faithless husband. Various witnesses, mostly relatives of Mrs. Bowers, claimed that the doctor had been an incorrigible womanizer. Descriptions of some of his activities were, according to the *San Francisco Chronicle*, "unfit for publication, even in technical terms."[16] Particularly damning was the testimony of Mrs. Bowers' brother, Henry Benhayon, who stated that the doctor once brought home "a European woman" and forced Mrs. Bowers to share a bed with the two of them. Benhayon also testified that he had removed two pills from Mrs. Bowers' deathbed and submitted them to chemical analysis and that one of them contained phosphorous. Benhayon added, for good measure, that Dr. Bowers had already been planning to marry his sister while still married to his second wife, and that he had even encouraged her to buy a trousseau while his wife at that time was on her deathbed!

Dr. Bowers was not without his champions. His nurse, Charlotte Zeissing, stated that Bowers had been attentive to his wife throughout her illness, that the banning of visitors from the sickroom had been at Mrs. Bowers' request, and that, as far as she knew, the Bowerses' marriage had been tranquil and happy. A Miss Farrell, who had once been a maid in the Bowers household, testified that Mrs. Bowers was an extremely jealous woman, and that Dr. Bowers was a model of patience and understanding.

Bowers himself took the stand for a full day to deny all of the accusations, to say that he loved his wife dearly, and to repeat that under no circumstances would he have done anything to endanger her health. He then re-stated the strange thought that if he had killed his wife, he would certainly have used a poison more difficult to detect than phosphorus.

Still, most of the testimony seemed to portray Bowers as a man who had abused his wife frequently, who had over-insured her with himself as the beneficiary, and as a doctor who had every opportunity to administer lethal drugs to his wife. Hanging constantly over the trial was the specter of his two earlier wives who had both died of undesignated causes at very early ages, and, according to one observer, might still be "glowing in their graves."

By the time the trial was concluded in late April of 1886, it had become the longest murder trail in the history in San Francisco. The trial had lasted almost six weeks, 130 witnesses had paraded to the stand, and the clerk's shorthand notes filled seventeen large volumes. The prosecutor concluded his closing statement with a florid literary conceit:

> "If an angel," he said, "had dipped his pencil in a ray of light streaming from heaven and pictured on a canvas brutality and mercenary heartlessness in all their hideousness, we would know that the defendant alone had sat for the portrait."[17]

The jury pondered for a mere thirty-five minutes. Its verdict: guilty of murder in the first degree. The demeanor of the defendant astonished most of the onlookers. Some said he seemed the calmest man in the room as the verdict was read. As he left the courtroom, he saw someone he knew, slapped him on the back, and said matter-of-factly, "Well, it's murder in the first degree." Later, he spoke of the crime to a reporter "as if he were passing an opinion on the case of someone else."[18]

On June 3, Bowers was brought back into court before Judge Murphy. Asked if he had anything to say, Bowers made a short, self-serving speech during which he again claimed his innocence. The judge listened carefully and then sentenced him to death by hanging. Bowers seemed to take the news calmly and was returned to his cell to await execution.

And, that should have been the end of the story. But it wasn't. In some ways, it was only the beginning.

On Tuesday, October 18, 1887, some eighteen months after the close of the trial, a young man rang the doorbell of a rooming house at 22 Geary Street, immediately next to the house where Dr. Bowers had kept his offices. The door was answered by Mrs. Higgins, the manager of the building, and when the young man expressed interest in renting a room, she showed him several that were vacant. He was not interested in these rooms, but asked specifically about room 21. Mrs. Higgins stated that room was occupied but would be free as of the following Saturday. The man left.

The next day, a second man appeared at 22 Geary, told Mrs. Higgins that he heard room 21 would be available as of Saturday, made a five-dollar deposit and, in return, was given a key.

The following Sunday, the Chinese houseboy who had the job of keeping all the rooms clean, entered room 21 to prepare it for its new occupant. He was scarcely prepared for the sight that greeted him. On the floor was the body of a man. He was fully clothed, lying on his back, with his arms straight out at his sides. He was quite dead.

The servant ran shrieking from the room and his cries summoned Mrs. Higgins. She stared in disbelief at the corpse on the floor, and her shock was not relieved by the fact that it was neither the man who rented the room nor the man who originally inquired about it. She had, in fact, never seen this man before. She hastily summoned the police, and it seemed only a matter of minutes before detectives were in the room undertaking their examination. There was no luggage or other clothing to indicate that the man had moved into the room. There were, however, a number of other unusual objects on and near the body: a partly consumed bottle of whiskey, a bottle of chloroform, and more disturbingly, a bottle of cyanide of potassium. And there were three letters on the bedside table, along with ink and a pen.

The personal items on the body of the corpse indicated that he was Mr. Henry Benhayon, the brother of Mrs. Bowers and the man who had been so vigorous in his testimony against his brother-in-law, Dr. J. Milton Bowers, during the trial of the previous year. All three letters left in the room were signed "H. Benhayon."

The first letter was addressed to a local newspaper and contained an advertisement, directed to be run the following day. It stated: "Lost, October 20, near City Hall, a memorandum-book with a letter! A liberal reward will be paid if left at this office."[19]

The second letter was addressed to Dr. J. Milton Bowers. It said,

"Doctor: I only ask that you do not molest my mother, as Tilly is not responsible for my acts. I made all the reparation in my power. I likewise caution you against some of your friends who knew Cecilia...Among them C. W. McClennan, C. Eisenchiminel, H. Stern, J. W. Harborn, F. H. Ackerman, J. Horn and others. I cannot think of them now, but you will find some more of your friends when the memorandum-book is found. I think you will find many of your diamonds changed for Parisian paste. Cecilia lost the money in stocks. Farewell."[20]

The third letter was addressed to the San Francisco coroner. It said:

"The history of the tragedy commenced after my sister married Dr. Bowers. I had reasons to believe that he would leave her soon, as they always quarreled and on one occasion she told me she would poison him before she would permit him to leave her. I said in jest, "Have him insured." She said, "All right." But Bowers objected for a long time, but finally said, "If it will keep you out of mischief, go ahead." They both joined several lodges and I got the stuff ready to dispose of him, but my sister would not listen to the proposition and threatened to expose me. After my sister got sick I felt an irresistible urge to use the stuff on her and finish him afterward. I would then become the administrator for my little niece, Tilly, and would have the benefit of the insurance. I think it was Friday, November 24, 1885, that I took one capsule out of her pillbox and filled it with two kinds of poison. I didn't think Bowers would get into any kind of trouble, as the person who gave me the poison told me it would leave no trace in the stomach. This person committed suicide before the trial, and as it might implicate others if I mention his name I will close the tragedy."[21]

The news of the event hit the city like an earthquake. Did this mean that Dr. Bowers was completely innocent? Had the trial that lasted three months been a sham? Had the jury made a dreadful mistake?

Reporters were quick to interview Dr. Bowers in his jail cell and tell him of the letters. Bowers was jubilant. "I was surprised," he told them, "at the confession of Benhayon.... I always looked upon him as a pleasant and agreeable young man. Yet, those letters put a new complexion on his character.... Strange, that with all my watchfulness and despite the fact that I was continually at her bedside that he should be able to get in and poison her in such a mysterious manner."

Opinions on the incident were divided. Many San Franciscans thought the letters vindicated Dr. Bowers. But others were highly suspicious. One newspaper quoted a young man identified as "A. Reuf, an attorney" on the subject. Decades later, Reuf would achieve notoriety as the chief culprit in the celebrated San Francisco graft trials, but in this instance he was on the side of the angels. Said Reuf, "The circumstances of his death are such as to lead me to believe that the young man [Benhayon] was the victim of foul play at the hands of a conspiracy to free J. Milton Bowers."

Reuf was not alone in his suspicions. Two principal inspectors had been involved in the Bowers case: Captain of Detectives I. W. Lees and his assistant, Robert Hogan. During the original investigation of Mrs.

Henry Benhayon, whose curious death seemed to exonerate Bowers. *San Francisco Chronicle*

*Henry Benhayon, from a photo taken before
June 1, 1879.*

85

Bowers' death, the two had arrived at opposing opinions. Lees became convinced of Dr. Bowers' innocence; Hogan had become convinced of his guilt. But now they both agreed that the latest development didn't add up. The position of the corpse seemed unnatural and contrived. The bottle containing the poison was tightly capped. The pen lying on the end table had never been used. The "confession" letter was too artfully composed. The landlady's tale of the earlier visitors to the room was very strange.

The detective quickly theorized that Benhayon had been murdered by someone anxious to free Dr. Bowers from jail, that he had been killed somewhere else and his body brought to the rented flat, that the poison was placed on the table to make it look like suicide, that the so-called "confession letters" were forgeries designed to place the blame for Mrs. Bowers' murder on her hapless brother.

And yet, if the entire affair was a setup, who would do such a thing? Ands how could Dr. Bowers be involved? After all, he had been under tight security in a jail cell at all times since the trial.

Their suspicions aroused, the detectives first analyzed the records of visitors to Bowers' cell during his confinement. A number of people had come to see him, but none more frequently than Charlotte Zeissing and Theresa Farrell, the two women who had been his most vigorous defenders at the trial. They had been almost daily visitors. Further inves-

The famous city detective Captain Lees, who first thought Bowers innocent, but later changed his mind. *Bill Secrest collection*

tigation led the detectives to a third party they thought might be involved— John Dimmig, the husband of Theresa Farrell. Dimmig had also been a frequent visitor to Bowers' cell. He was a man of dubious character who had been involved in several scrapes with the law. The detectives placed Dimmig under arrest on suspicion of complicity and brought him before Mrs. Higgins, the housekeeper. She immediately identified him as the second man who had come to 22 Geary and the man who had given her a five-dollar deposit for room 21.

John Dimmig quickly demonstrated a quixotic personality. He was thirty-three years old, blond and husky, a one-time drugstore clerk, cab-driver, and door-to-door salesman. When he was taken to police head-quarters, he was dressed elegantly and even sported a tall silk hat. His plain-featured face was highlighted by an extravagant mustache waxed at either end in a dramatic curl. When he was officially photographed at the station, he seemed to lose interest in why he had been arrested, and instead he became obsessed with how his photograph had turned out.

John Dimmig, whose two trials for the murder of Benhayan, gave Bowers a chance to claim innocence.

When asked at his inquest why he had rented the room at 22 Geary, he replied in a somewhat braggadocio tone that, even though he was a happily married man, he needed a place for his sexual liaisons, in this case with a certain Mrs. Timkins from San Jose. To bolster his argument, he claimed to also have another trysting spot on Market Street. When pressed for more details on the Market Street lady, he could only come with the name "Dimples."

When neither Miss Timkins nor "Dimples" could be located, Dimmig's argument fell apart, and he quickly made a complete reversal of his position. Now he claimed to be a devoted family man, a doting father, and a loving son to his parents. His only concern, he said, was clearing his good name so that no shame would fall upon his family. The inquest jury decided to give him that chance and charged him with murder.

Dimmigs' trial began on December 14, 1887, and lasted almost three months. The evidence against the defendant was circumstantial, but it was also considerable. Yet Dimmig seemed to have an answer, however unlikely, for every aspect. Did he know the deceased?—only casually. Why did he make a number of visits to Dr. Bowers in his cell?—to keep his wife company. Why had he purchased cyanide poison from his druggist?—to treat a skin ailment. Why had he hired Benhayon to do some copying for him?—certainly not to obtain samples of his handwriting. How had Benhayon found his way into the room Dimmig rented on Geary Street? He must have stolen the key from him.

Then there was the question of the authenticity of the handwriting. Dueling experts testified that it certainly was and certainly was not Benhayon's penmanship. On the witness stand, Dimmig once again changed the reason why he had rented the room. Now, he claimed it was for the purpose of storing art books that he planned to sell door-to-door in the neighborhood. Curiously enough, and for no apparent reason, Dimmig then produced on the witness stand a fourth "Benhayon letter," this one addressed to Dimmig himself. It purported to invite Dimmig to visit Benhayon at 22 Geary Street, which seemed to complicate Dimmig's story that he did not know how or when Benhayon got into the room in the first place.

To say the least, the testimony was so bewildering and paradoxical that even the city's reporters had trouble keeping it straight. Apparently, it had the same effect on the jury, for when they retired to consider the evidence, they argued for sixteen hours and reported themselves to be hopelessly deadlocked. The frustrated judge called the jurors back to his courtroom and dismissed them. The jurors later revealed that five had been for conviction and seven for acquittal. The judge sent Dimmig back to his jail cell and announced that he would set a date for a new trial.

But now another trial was afoot. Dr. Bowers had earlier appealed for a new trial for himself, but it had been rejected in June of 1888 by the state supreme court. Now Bowers made yet another appeal, based largely on the authenticity of the Benhayon confession letter. This time the supreme court granted the re-trial. Bowers was exultant, stating, "What I look for is exoneration, no jury will be found to convict me."[23]

Just six months later, the second Dimmig trial commenced. This time the testimony was even more confusing, if possible, than during the first trial. Dimmig had new excuses and rationales for almost everything. The prosecution, now woefully short of witnesses due to the passage of time, put on a somewhat more feeble case. Again the jury deadlocked, but the frustrated judge announced that this time he would keep them locked up until they reached a decision. Eventually, the exhausted jury announced to a weary judge that they could only find the defendant not guilty. A jubilant Dimmig left the court a free man. Mrs. Zeissing and Theresa Dimmig wept with joy.

And just where did this leave Dr. Bowers' case? The prosecutors pondered that question for eight months as Bowers endured his fourth year in jail. Finally, District Attorney Page announced his decision: All charges against Dr. Bowers were being dismissed as the Benhayon confession letter made further prosecution extremely difficult. Once again, Mrs. Zeissing and Mrs. Dimmig wept copiously.

Newspapers protested that the idea of Bowers going free constituted a civic outrage and an historic miscarriage of justice. Others simply breathed a sigh of relief. Said the *Morning Call*, "Altogether, his arrest, trial, conviction and sentence of death, intertwined with the mysterious Benhayon tragedy, and sudden discharge form probably one of the most remarkable chapters in the criminal history of the world."[24]

Dr. Bowers walked out of Cell 33, down the jail corridor, and out into the sunlight. Knowing there was no possibility of a new trial, he was sufficiently emboldened to express regret. "I would rather have a new trial," he said, "as I would show evidence to clear me beyond a doubt." However, with apparent reluctance, he settled for his freedom.

Bowers, after a brief vacation in Southern California, once again set up practice, first in San Francisco, then in Oakland. But apparently there was not a sufficient number of patients in the Bay Area willing to submit to the medical ministrations of the infamous Dr. Bowers.

A few years later, Bowers moved his practice to San Jose, where he was less well-known. He spent the remainder of his life there in relative obscurity. Astonishingly, he married once more, this time to a Miss Mary Bird, a schoolteacher who had been one of his patients. Not long after, on March 7, 1904, Dr. J. Milton Bowers died of a paralytic stroke. One of the San Francisco newspapers concluded its obituary of Dr. Bowers by mentioning his fourth wife, and by remarking that she "fortunately survives him."[26]

The death of Dr. Bowers in 1904 did not stop speculation that he had murdered three wives and a brother-in-law. *San Francisco Call*

DR. J. MILTON BOWERS IS CALLED TO RENDER ACCOUNT TO MAKER

Man Deemed Murderer of Three Wives and Brother-in-Law and Who Was Sentenced to Death, but Was Saved by Supreme Court, Dies in San Jose

PRINCIPAL IN SENSATIONAL MURDER CASE WHO DIED YESTERDAY.

Chapter Six

The Revenge of the Tongs—1887

The first Chinese immigrant of record came to California in 1847. The next year, three more immigrants, two men and one woman, came to the state. By 1862, Chinese were coming to California and, more specifically, to San Francisco by the thousands. In April of that year, The Annals of San Francisco *reported that "by this month, it was supposed that upwards of ten thousand of that people had arrived in San Francisco, while as many more were estimated to be on the way. Considerable public discussion exists on the desirableness of such a vast migration of that race."[1]*

Almost all of the immigrating Chinese were brought in under work contracts by what were called the Six Companies or, less formally, the Chinese "Tongs." These were tightly organized, hierarchical groups which controlled the lives and the labor of their members, and which established their own laws, customs, and standards of behavior. Originally, they had been labor agencies operating in the six districts of Canton, China, but in 1850 they all moved their headquarters to San Francisco, where they established a virtual monopoly on which Chinese would be permitted entry and on every aspect of how they would lead their lives once they were in the city.

The Tongs quickly assumed complete control over all gambling, opium, thievery, and prostitution operations. And, they meted out their own form of justice to those who violated their codes, in the form of limiting employment opportunities, ostracism, and, not infrequently, death.

It was not long before the Chinese and the Tongs were widely re-sented, hated, and even feared by the white population of the city. The argument was made that no good could come from allowing an "inferior race," willing to work long hours for low wages, to compete in the labor market. Even worse was the specter of a foreign element that "lived in squalor and filth, ate strange food, suffered from strange diseases, wor-shiped strange gods, and lived by its own laws."[2] The cry of "The Chi-nese Must Go!" became a slogan of more than one politician looking for votes amongst the white populace of San Francisco.

It was against this background that a remarkable man called "Little Pete" came to prominence in the city. In Chinatown itself, he would be

The only known photograph of Little Pete, as an inmate at Alcatraz. *Celebrated Criminal Cases of America*

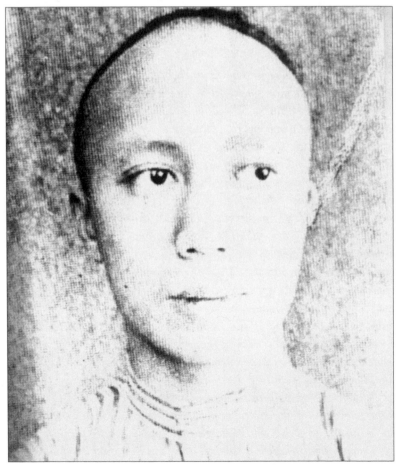

known as a successful businessman, a clever and fearless politician, and a rich and powerful leader. In the rest of the city he would be known simply as "The Evil King of Chinatown." His life—and his death—would have a profound effect on both parts of the San Francisco cultural climate.

Born in the mid 1860s in the district of Kow Gong in the province of Canton[3], he was given the conventional Chinese name of Fong Ching, but that was not the name under which he would make his mark in history.

When he was just five years old, Fong Ching came to San Francisco with his father, who immigrated under the auspices of the Sam Yup Company. Ching was educated at the Methodist Chinese Mission, where he quickly became proficient in the English language. His father was a merchant, and young Fong Ching was soon schooled in the art of buying and selling, but Fong knew early on that he did not want to be just a merchant, for he had already discovered the excitement and the mystery of what was called "underground Chinatown."

Initiation ceremony of a Chinese Tong. *Bancroft Library*

Chinatown, home of the Highbinders, at the time of Little Pete. *Arnold Genthe Collection*

This was the strange and exotic world that existed outside the sight of the white man's law—the world of slave girls, opium dens, fan tan clubs, prostitution, and gang warfare. This was where the Tongs exerted their jurisdiction over vice and corruption, and where they exacted tribute from both honest businessmen and their own members.

Outside of Chinatown itself, in the white community surrounding the Chinese enclaves, it was rumored that there actually was an "underground Chinatown," where, over the years, the Tongs had burrowed down beneath the city like animals fleeing from the light. It was said that they had carved out a warren of rooms and labyrinths that extended as deep as five stories beneath the street level. Here, the dark business of drugs and gambling and slave girls could hide from the white man's law. No such underground actually existed, but the idea that it did underscores the gulf between the two worlds of San Francisco.

By the time he was a teenager, Fong Ching had already been initiated into both aspects of the city. During the day, he helped his father, selling goods and produce, learning the ways of legitimate business as well as the culture and language of America. But at night, he did the work of the Tongs, running numbers, acting as lookout for the gamblers, and finding customers for the slave girls. As he grew to manhood, he became the most Westernized citizen in Chinatown. Handsome and intelligent, he moved easily in the San Francisco business world. Shrewd and manipulative and outfitted in the finest Oriental wardrobe, he could match wits with the cleverest Tong leaders. He spoke both English and Chinese with no discernible accent, combining Western friendliness and informality with Oriental sagacity and cunning. He parted his hair in the front like an American, but in the back he wore a carefully braided queue, the pigtail that signified his allegiance to the land of his birth.

It was not long before Fong Ching became the official interpreter for the Sam Yup Company, and, as such, he came to know the intricate secrets of the Tong organization. He was especially fascinated by the Tong's "hatchet men," the enforcers of the Tong rule. These were the ruthless Chinese gangsters, easily identified by the their black costumes, loose flowing robes, black, circle-brimmed hats, and pistols, not too artfully concealed in their sleeves. The terms of the contract under which the hatchet men, also referred to as "highbinders," operated were strict and clear.

The Sam Yup Company rules were especially detailed:

> "All who undertake the service of this Tong must obey orders, and without orders they must not dare to act. If any of our brethren are suddenly molested it will be necessary to act with

resolute will. When orders are given, you will advance valiantly to your task. Never shrink or turn back. If, in the discharge of your duty, you are slain, we will undertake to pay $500 sympathy money to your friends. If you are wounded, a doctor will be engaged to heal your wounds, and if you are maimed for life, $250 shall be paid to you and a subscription taken up to defray the costs of your journey home. Furthermore, whenever you exert your strength to kill or wound the enemies of the Tong, and in doing so are arrested and imprisoned, $100 will be paid for every year you are in jail."[4]

Another of their rules was more benign and evidenced the traditional Chinese veneration of age: "A young man must let an old man strike him three times before he strikes back."[5]

As interpreter for the Tong, Fong Ching began to move in important political circles, both in Chinatown and in San Francisco City Hall. He was an eager student and had a keen memory. His most outstanding characteristic, however, was obvious to all who watched him: He was ambitious.

The turn-of-the century hatchet man. *Bancroft Library*

At the age of twenty-one, he borrowed a large sum of money and started a shoe factory, perhaps the one honest thing Fong did in all his adult life. The factory was an immediate success, but the demand for his product was limited because the larger white community was reluctant to buy Chinese products. So he changed the name of his company to F. C. Peters, adding an American name to his own initials.[6] The company prospered, and before long Fong Ching became known by a new nickname: Little Pete.

With the riches from his shoe enterprise, Little Pete soon set himself up in the truly rewarding businesses of Chinatown: gambling, opium, and the slave trade. He became a major importer of girls from mainland China and with his new wealth he bought into the fan-tan parlors and the gambling houses. Little Pete also began blackmailing a number of important people, a lucrative but dangerous enterprise. By the time Little Pete was twenty-five, he became the undisputed leader of the Sun Yap Company.[7] He also did something that shocked Chinatown: In addition to ruling the hatchet men of the company, he established his own personal fighting Tong, the Gae Sin Seer, devoted entirely to protecting him and instilling fear in his enemies.

Little Pete had moved too far too fast for some of the other companies, and the Bo Sin Seer Tong ordered that Little Pete be disposed of. Little Pete responded by adding the deadliest of all the hatchet men, Lee Chuck, to his team of personal bodyguards. For several months, a cat and mouse game between Lee Chuck and Yen Yuen, the principal killer of the Bo Sin Seer Tong, dominated the activities of Chinatown life. Then,

San Francisco's Chinatown Squad, the detectives charged with seeing that the white man's law was obeyed. *Society of California Pioneers*

in the autumn of 1886, Lee Chuck and Yen Yuen finally met each other face to face in a back alley. It was no contest. Lee Chuck fired five bullets into the body of the Bo Sin Seer executioner while he was still struggling to get the pistol out of his sleeve.[8]

Lee Chuck was pursued and captured by a policeman who happened to be in the area, and he was subsequently placed on trial for murder. Little Pete then made one of the few mistakes of his life: He tried to bribe two policemen to give favorable testimony to his protector at the trial. To his astonishment, the policemen refused the bribes and Little Pete was indicted by a grand jury. At his trial, Little Pete gave the following astonishing testimony:

> "Yes, gentlemen, I paid those two officers a bribe, but it was honestly done, as I asked them to take the money and testify only to the truth.... They came back for more money, and when I refused their demands they not only convicted my friend but arrested me."[9]

This remarkable testimony, plus additional bribes to the jurors, resulted in a hung jury. A second trial also failed to result in a verdict, but a third trial, despite additional perjury and massive bribery charges, resulted in a conviction. In all, Little Pete had spent more than $75,000 to corrupt justice and buy favors, a record of chicanery unmatched in a city notorious for corruption.[10] In fact, Little Pete's efforts to buy San Francisco officials was so massive that it won the begrudging respect of the city's editorial writers. It also made him a folk hero in Chinatown.

Little Pete served several years in the Folsom prison, but he was scarcely idle. Through intermediaries, he continued to run his dark businesses in Chinatown, and when he was released he immediately plunged back into the business of crime. He stepped up his extortion and protection rackets until almost every Chinese business was paying tribute. He began importing crib girls from China at an unheard-of rate. When the authorities tried to clamp down on him, Little Pete simply outfoxed them. During San Francisco's Midwinter Fair of 1894, a boatload of 103 Chinese women was imported as "hosts" for the Chinese pavilion. The girls' chaperone turned out to be none other than Little Pete's cousin. Several months after their arrival, only thirty-seven of the girls could be accounted for at the fair. The papers estimated that Little Pete netted more than $50,000 on the deal, plus continuing income from the girls as they worked in the cribs.[11]

Next, horse racing caught Little Pete's attention. Although he knew little about the sport, he made more than $100,000 at the Bay District track in just two weeks by the simple expedient of bribing the jockeys. In one race, Little Pete put $6,000 on a lightly regarded horse named Rosebud. He cleaned up when Rosebud nipped the favorite Wheel of Fortune at the wire. Witnesses reported that Wheel of Fortune's mouth was actually bloody from being reined in. For years, Little Pete continued to clean up at the track, even though he was banned from personally appearing at the tracks. He simply used confederates to bribe the jockeys and place his bets.

Over the ensuing years, Little Pete's power and wealth continued to increase, until his activities reached such a crescendo that he became a threat to both the legal and illegitimate businesses of Chinatown. The leadership of the Tongs finally met in solemn conclave to determine what should be done to remedy the situation.

The result was a hastily drawn four-count indictment against Little Pete that condemned him for recent actions:

> "One. False information he had given to immigration officers had barred Chinese merchants from bringing their wives and daughters to America.
> Two. He had deliberately given highbinders a thousand dollars in gold to strike down one of his countryman.
> Three. He had ordered two of his men to kill Yee Foo in Ross Alley—Yee Foo who, at the time, was peacefully cursing his own cats.
> Four. He had, through his efforts, forced the peace plans of the Tongs to collapse."[12]

The sentence was death. Since homicide was in violation of the white man's law, it was concluded that Tong chiefs should devise the means of disposal, with an understanding that, should one Tong member get into trouble over the disposal, the other Tongs would come to his aid.

Len Jok Lep of the Suey Sing Tong was appointed to supervise the mission. A methodical man, he went about his task with great care, sending out his most trusted men to chart Little Pete's movements and to seek out the best assassins to handle the task.

Little Pete was immediately alerted to his precarious position, and he began to take extraordinary precautions. He spent most of his time barricaded in his quarters on the third floor of his building at 819½ Washington Street.[13] He slept in a windowless room behind a bolted door. Whenever he ventured outside, he walked with a bodyguard of three men, one in front, one in back, and one at his side. As Little Pete was knowledgeable as to the ways of city law and Chinatown custom, one of his bodyguards was a white man, C. H. Hunter. Little Pete knew that his enemies would hesitate to fire on a white guard because it would involve the full force of the white man's law. He also kept two fierce attack dogs in his apartment, and he frequently had them at his side as he moved about the city. Additionally, Little Pete wore a sheet of steel mesh about his upper body and inside his hat he wore a thin sheet of steel curved to fit his head.

The Tongs promised a $1,000 reward to any hatchet man who would assassinate Little Pete. Days passed, and there were no takers. The prize was raised to $2,000, and still no one cared to take the risk. In desperation, the Tongs increased the bounty to $3,000, an unheard-of amount for the taking of a single life. Word of the prize swept the West Coast, and one day two hatchet men from Oregon, Lee Jung and Chew Chin God, were seen for the first time on the streets of San Francisco's Chinatown.

Over the next few weeks, the two highbinders followed Little Pete's every turn. They plotted the diagram of his apartment building and determined that Little Pete and his family lived on the third floor, over a second-floor shoe warehouse and a first-floor barbershop. They determined that their best chance to assassinate him was through the window of the bath-

Righteous punishment for a Chinatown violator. *The Illustrated Wasp*

room where he shaved and combed his hair. But by the time they gained access to the next-door apartment where Little Pete would be accessible, the wary Chinaman had shuttered the window and was no longer visible.

Next the two hatchet men learned that Little Pete had his hair shampooed every Saturday afternoon in the barbershop on the first floor, gaining access to the shop by means of interior stairs in the rear of the building. Yet, even there, Little Pete was always carefully guarded by his men and dogs. Still, they noted that he was personally defenseless once the barber's towel was over his head. They hoped that perhaps one Saturday he would be unguarded and vulnerable in the shop.

Time would prove them correct. On January 23, 1887, just several days before the Chinese New Year, Little Pete left his apartment for the barbershop. He decided at the last minute to leave his dogs behind and descended the stairs with only bodyguard Hunter at his side. He entered the barbershop, noting that there was only one other customer present.

The barber placed a warm towel over Little Pete's face and untied his pigtail in preparation for the ritual of cutting and washing his hair. Little Pete, suddenly realizing that he had two horses racing that afternoon at the track, dispatched Hunter to go to the Western Hotel down the street to pick up the afternoon paper. For the first time in weeks, he was completely defenseless. As soon as Hunter was out of sight, Lee Jung entered the barbershop and indicated to the barber that he would wait for service. The barber offered him a cup of tea, which Jung accepted and sipped quietly. Then Chew Chin God also entered the shop. The two men nodded to one another, and Jung put down his tea and walked over to Little Pete, pulling a revolver from his waistband. When he reached Little Pete, he leaned over and spoke into his ear, saying, "It's time for you to celebrate the New Year."[14] Jung jammed his gun into the space between Little Pete's neck and his bullet-proof vest. The shot was heard for blocks around. Before Little Pete could even slump in the chair, Chew Chin God stepped forward and fired two more bullets into his head. Little Pete slipped from the chair and sprawled out on the floor, a pool of blood circling his head. The barber fainted dead away.

The two hatchet men fled, running across the street and through the door of an apartment building on Waverly Place. Within minutes, the police arrived, briefly studied the corpse, and then began asking questions. The other customer in the barbershop claimed that he had a towel over his head and saw nothing. The revived barber pleaded ignorance, saying that he had suffered what was translated as "mist before the eyes."[15]

Newspaper drawing of the assassination of Little Pete. *San Francisco Chronicle*

The two assassins were now hiding in the basement across the street. They hoped to use a pre-planned escape route which involved climbing to the top of the building and then walking across a pre-set plank to the adjoining building. But when they reached the roof, they discovered that someone had removed the plank. They hastily retreated down the back stairs into the dark of the basement. When the police entered the building, they found two well-known hatchet men, Wing Sing and Chin Poy, playing cards on the second floor. Happy with their discovery and unwilling to look further, they promptly arrested the two men for the murder of Little Pete.

News of the murder electrified the city. Entire front pages of the leading newspapers were devoted to the event, with banner headlines that proclaimed, "Little Pete Murdered by his Enemies," "The Great Jury-Briber Shot Down by See Yup Assassins," and "Chinese Highbinders Assassinate the Most Famous of Local Mongolians." Artist sketches of the shooting,

FONG CHING, Alias Little Pete, the Famous Chinaman Who Was Assassinated Last Night.

A portrait of Fong Ching (alias Little Pete) following his death. *San Francisco Call*

WONG SING and CHIN FOY, the Two Men Under Suspicion of Having Murdered Little Pete.
(Sketched from life in the City Prison last night by a "Call" artist.)

Drawing of the two alleged assassins. *San Francisco Call*

diagrams of the barbershop and portraits of Little Pete himself, some with his entire family, were featured. The language describing the event was florid: "The ephemeral sensation of an ordinary Chinese murder has no place on the list with the feverish anxiety, bitter vindictiveness and cuss-dog deviltry that have been engendered through the cold-blooded assassination of Little Pete on Saturday night in Chinatown."[17]

Newspaper descriptions of subsequent activities in Chinatown revealed the suspicions and fears of the white community. "Chinatown is afire with passion and venom. The wealthy Sam Yups, with little regard for social customs and the right of individuals to live their allotted lease of life, are sending out fighting men to annihilate the highbinders of the See Yups. Placards on street corners in flaming red are read by the dirty scum of Chinatown who gather about with bloodshot eyes and twitching fingers."[18]

There now remained the task of giving Little Pete a proper burial. There was a feeling in Chinatown that a man so powerful in life might also be powerful in death. The body was laid out in the fashion of Chinese royalty. Little Pete was dressed in spectacular burial raiment. His head was crowned with a formal consular cap that featured a golden tassel usually worn only by Chinese nobility. Almost everyone in Chinatown who had ever known, loved, hated, feared, or despised the deceased passed by in solemn procession as the body lay in state.

The funeral that followed was a cross between a royal procession and a hilarious carnival. Little Pete's body was transported by an elaborate hearse pulled by six black stallions. There were dozens of marching bands, Oriental dance groups, and singing ensembles, interspersed among several miles of mourners who trooped all the way from Chinatown to the San Yup cemetery in the Richmond district. A hundred-foot dragon, ordinarily used for only the most festive holidays, snaked its way through the assemblage. Official mourners were carried in 112 carriages.

At the cemetery, there was an attempt at decorous ceremony, with mandarin priests burning incense and chanting ancient dirges, but the crowd got out of control. Whole pigs and sheep had been roasted as sacrifices for the event, and when they were brought out, a frenzy ensued and the frenzy quickly turned into a riot. The altar was plundered by souvenir hunters and even the corpse was threatened. Suddenly, the family announced that Little Pete would not be buried there after all, but would be returned to China. So the King of Chinatown made a return trip, this time without nearly as much ceremony, to the undertaker.[19.]

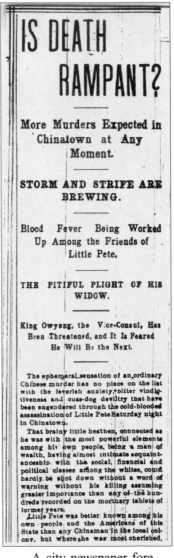

IS DEATH RAMPANT?

More Murders Expected in Chinatown at Any Moment.

STORM AND STRIFE ARE BREWING.

Blood Fever Being Worked Up Among the Friends of Little Pete.

THE PITIFUL PLIGHT OF HIS WIDOW.

King Owyang, the Vice-Consul, Has Been Threatened, and It Is Feared He Will Be the Next.

The ephemeral sensation of an ordinary Chinese murder has no place on the list with the feverish anxiety, bitter vindictiveness and cuss-dog deviltry that have been engendered through the cold-blooded assassination of Little Pete Saturday night in Chinatown.

That brainy little heathen, connected as he was with the most powerful elements among his own people, being a man of wealth, having almost intimate acquaintanceship with the social, financial and political classes among the whites, could hardly be shot down without a word of warning without his killing assuming greater importance than any of the hundreds recorded on the mortuary tablets of former years.

Little Pete was better known among his own people and the Americans of this State than any Chinaman in the local colony, but where he was most cherished.

A city newspaper foresees the start of a Tong War.
San Francisco Call

In the meantime, the white man's law was progressing slowly. Despite the best efforts of police and detectives to pin the crime on Wing Sing and Chin Poy, it soon came obvious that they were not involved. Their innocence was further confirmed when Little Pete's wife, uniformly and ingloriously referred to in the city newspapers as "Mrs. Little Pete," posted reward notices throughout Chinatown for the real killers.

The actual perpetrators, Len Jung and Chew Chin God, had been quickly smuggled out of town by the Tongs and sent back to the Chinese settlement in Portland. Reports filtered back to San Francisco that they were feted by their fellow countrymen as heroes.[20]

In Little Pete's case, fame was fleeting and time became the enemy of historical fact. The murderers were never officially identified. No one ever determined the extent of Little Pete's holdings and control. No one was ever certain how far the tentacles of his organization reached into the legal and illegal businesses of San Francisco. Through he was apparently in his early thirties at the time of his death, no one ever knew the exact date of his birth. And, there is no record of his ever having made the long journey back to Canton.

A Chinatown opium den, as imagined by an artist at the turn of the century.

Chapter Seven

The Belle in the Belfry—1895

As the twentieth century approached, San Franciscans felt they had a great deal to brag about. In the previous two decades, the city's population had doubled to almost 300,000. It had survived fire, earthquake and lawlessness to become the jeweled metropolis of the West. In 1894, San Francisco decided to show itself off to the rest of the world with The Midwinter Exposition, an extravaganza held in Golden Gate Park, for which more than one hundred buildings were constructed, and which featured educational exhibits, carnival games and musical entertainments. More than 2,500,000 people travelled to San Francisco for the exposition. There they saw a city that had become a financial capital, a manufacturing heartland, and a cultural center. It was also an extremely religious city, with the number of churches and synagogues actually rivaling the number of bars and saloons. But even as visitors marveled at its progress, San Francisco was about to witness a startling event that would once again transform the city's image in the eyes of the world, and not for the better. San Francisco was about to endure what many came to call "The Crime of the Century."

There was never any doubt as to whom Blanche Lamont was with when she disappeared. No doubt at all. In fact, it is unlikely that any other final journey of a murder victim was ever as well documented as was hers. At 8:00 A.M. on April 3, 1895, her aunt bid her farewell at her home at 209

Twenty-first Street, as Blanche began her brief journey to Boy's High School where she was taking a course.[1] She was dressed for a day in the city, in a flowing black skirt and a fashionable jacket with feathers and ribbons. She was an attractive young lady of twenty-one, and a number of people on the street remembered seeing her pass by. At 8:15 A.M., she was seen meeting a young man named Theo Durrant at Twenty-first and Mission. Those who witnessed the meeting remembered that it seemed to have been pre-arranged.[2] Together they boarded an electric street car, and the conductor later recalled that Theo placed his hand gently on Blanche's shoulder and spoke to her softly throughout the trip.[3] Along with several other passengers, he also remembered the two of them departing the car at Polk Street, where they were then seen walking a short distance, then separating as Blanche continued on her way alone to the Boy's High School.

The only known photograph of Blanche Lamont at the age of seventeen. *From* Sympathy For The Devil, *Praeger publishers*

Blanche attended her class, along with a number of other students, and was then seen walking to the Normal School on Powell Street between Clay and Sacramento, where she took a cooking class between two and three o'clock. No one noticed anything unusual about her behavior. Immediately following class, three other students saw her meet Theo Durrant in front of the school. They also reported that she hurried to him, apparently eager to see him. A Mrs. Vogel, who lived across the street, stated that Theo had, in fact, been waiting outside the school for almost an hour, and when Blanche exited the school, he moved quickly to a passing cable car.[4] He boarded the cable car, tipped his hat to the conductor and then assisted Blanche into the car. A Mrs. Crosset later saw the two get off the cable car at Twenty-second and Valencia, and she remembered that the wind blew fiercely and that Blanche held onto her hat.[5] An attorney, Martin Quintin, saw them cross Twenty-second Street and head toward the Emmanuel Baptist Church. Mrs. Caroline Leak, looking out her window from across the street, saw Theo and Blanche enter the church through a side gate. She recalled that Theo entered first and that Blanche followed him.[6]

The city's first look at Blanche, an artist's sketch for the *Call*.

The *San Francisco Call* announces the disappearance of Blanche Lamont on April 10, 1895.

THE MYSTERY OF A GIRL.

Blanche Lamont Not Seen or Heard of Since Last Wednesday.

THE POLICE UTTERLY BAFFLED.

She Was Here From Montana Taking Lessons to Fit Her as a Teacher.

Blanche Lamont, a beautiful girl, 21 years of age, has disappeared as mysteriously as if the earth had swallowed her. Detective Anthony has been working on the case for nearly a week and he has been completely baffled to find any trace of the young woman.

She came here from Montana, where her mother, a widow, lives, in September last to her uncle, Charles G. Noble, 209 Twenty-first street. Her object was to attend the Lowell High School on Sutter street, be-

Then, Blanche Lamont simply disappeared. When she reappeared nine days later, the entire incident was immediately dubbed "The Crime of the Century," not only by newspapers in California and America, but by journals throughout Europe. And, to this day, there is great conjecture as to exactly what happened.

Who were these two young people whose lives would forever be intertwined in mystery and legend?

Blanche Lamont had come to San Francisco from her hometown of Dillon, Montana, just a year earlier. She had made the journey with her sister in the hope of improving her health and obtaining a better education. Somewhat frail when she arrived at the home of her aunt and uncle, Typhina and Charles Noble, at 209 Twenty-first Street, she quickly blossomed into a robust and spirited young lady. She was popular with her schoolmates, devoted to her studies, and active in the affairs of the nearby Emmanuel Baptist Church, where she was a member of the Christian Endeavor. She quickly became admired by her friends and teachers for her charming disposition and her attractive and carefully groomed appearance.[6] Everyone agreed that she would have no trouble realizing her ambition to become a school teacher.

The Emmanuel Baptist Church at the time of the murders.

Theodore Durrant was born in Toronto, Canada, in 1871, and came to San Francisco with his parents while still a youngster. He attended private schools, had an uneventful childhood, and graduated from Cogswell's Polytechnic School at the age of nineteen. Intelligent and well-liked, he was promptly accepted as a student at Cooper Medical School, where he was pursuing an intensive course of study in preparation to become a physician. Deeply religious, he had been a member of the Emmanuel Baptist Church for a number of years, and he had become one of its most active members. His fellow parishioners elected him secretary of its social society. He was also a superintendent of the church's Sunday school and was honored with possession of his own keys to the church.

No one was surprised that these two young people had been attracted to one another, and none of the witnesses to Blanche's final journey was surprised to see them together. When Blanche did not return at the usual hour, her aunt became concerned. When evening arrived and Blanche had still not returned, Mrs. Noble went to the church, thinking that perhaps Blanche had simply visited another friend's home and would be at that evening's prayer meeting. At the prayer meeting, however, she was unable to locate Blanche. During the service, she was startled to be tapped on the shoulder by someone in the pew behind her. It was Theo Durrant. "Is Blanche here tonight?"

Mrs. Noble replied, "No, she did not come."

Durrant then said, "Well, I regret that she is not with us tonight, and I have a book called *The Newcombs* for her, but I will send it to the house."

Several days passed before Blanche's distraught aunt reported her niece's disappearance to the police. Theo Durrant immediately called on Mrs. Noble and offered his services in determining Blanche's whereabouts. He also related to her a disquieting rumor that Blanche was believed to have departed from a life of morality and had entered a house of ill-repute. He further stated that if this were true, he would endeavor to find Blanche and return her to a life of righteousness. The dumbfounded aunt expressed her thanks and gratitude.

Several more days passed with no news of Blanche. A janitor at the church reported that he had come across Theo Durrant at the Oakland ferry and Durrant had told him that he was busy pursuing a clue that had come his way regarding Blanche Lamont's whereabouts.

More days passed, and finally her disappearance became a matter of city-wide concern. On April 10, the *San Francisco Call-Bulletin* ran a sketch of Blanche along with the headline, "Mystery Of A Girl. Blanche Lamont not seen since last Wednesday. The police are utterly baffled"[7] Then on the eighth day, a remarkable event occurred. When Blanche disappeared, she had been wearing three rings, all of which were well known to Mrs. Noble. That morning, Mrs. Noble opened her copy of the *San Francisco Examiner*, wrapped in the usual fashion for delivery. When she unwrapped it, Blanche's three rings fell out of the paper onto the floor. The astonished Mrs. Noble immediately notified the paper, which quickly publicized the extraordinary event. Within hours, an Adolph Oppenheimer, the owner of a pawn shop on Dupont Street, identified a man who had earlier tried to pawn one of the rings. It was Theodore Durrant.[8]

But by now, Durrant was involved in another activity, which would soon break the mystery of Blanche Lamont wide open. He was about to keep a date with another young lady, named Minnie Williams.

Minnie was, like Theo Durrant, a Canadian by birth. She had come with her parents to San Francisco as a young girl, and, when the rest of her family returned to Canada, she decided to stay in the Bay Area as a domestic and as a live-in companion. Minnie was now twenty years old and attractive, with dark, curly hair and clear, even features.[9] She had first been employed by a family in Piedmont but then transferred her loyalties to another employer, a casket manufacturer named Clark H. Morgan. Minnie was especially pleased with this change of venue because she was now close to the church she had belonged to since a youth: the Emmanuel Baptist Church on Twenty-first Street. When the Mor-

A newspaper artist's portrait of Minnie Williams. *San Francisco Chronicle*

gans later announced to Minnie that they would be moving to Tacoma, Washington, she was able to secure a job as housemaid to Mrs. A.D. Voy on Market Street which would permit her to remain close to the church.

Minnie and Theo had had an earlier encounter and she confessed to a friend that he had once taken her to a lonely spot in Fruitvale and proposed that they should have intimate relations. She refused and insisted on being taken home. But now they had another date. They would meet at a Dr. Vogel's home in San Francisco where the church's Christian Endeavor meeting would take place. And once again, the record of witnesses is astonishing.

On Friday, April 12, Minnie left the Morgans' home to go to Mrs. A. D. Voy's home in San Francisco where she would begin her job as housemaid and companion. Mr. Morgan remembered that she sent her trunk off in the morning. Minnie next appeared at her hairdresser's in Alameda at 3:30 in the afternoon. Before she left, she told the hairdresser she intended to catch the 4:00 P.M. ferryboat back to San Francisco.[10] Earlier, at 3:00 P.M.., three medical students recalled seeing Theo waiting at the ferry depot. At 4:00 P.M., Frank Sandeman, a janitor at the Emmanuel Baptist Church, also saw him in the ferry terminal.[11] At 5:00 P.M., Adolphe Hobe, an Oakland commuter, saw Theo conversing with Minnie in that same building.[12] Between six and seven o'clock, Minnie appeared at the Voys' house, without Theo, to report that she was on her way to Dr. Vogel's house for the Christian Endeavor meeting. She never arrived there.

At 8:00 P.M., a laundress named Ann McKay remembered seeing Theo and Minnie arguing in front of the Emmanuel Baptist Church.[13] A little after 8:00 P.M. a young boy, C. Y. Hilly, passed by the church and saw Theo and Minnie enter through the back door.[14]

And then Minnie Williams, like Blanche Lamont, simply disappeared. But not for long.

At 9:30 P.M., Theo Durant joined the Christian Endeavor group at Dr. Vogel's house. He seemed pleasant and amiable and joined calmly into the events of the evening. At the conclusion of the evening, he went home with friends, none of whom noted anything unusual in his behavior.

On Saturday morning, April 13, a group of ladies proceeded to the church with flowers to decorate the altar for Easter services the following morning. On arriving at the church, they first went to the library to arrange the flowers. They were scarcely prepared for the sight that greeted them: the horribly mutilated body of Minnie Williams.

The corpse was partly stuffed into an open closet door. Her clothing was mostly torn from her body and she had been repeatedly stabbed. Parts of her own clothing had been stuffed down her throat. A broken knife was stuck in her breast, and there was blood everywhere.[16]

The police were immediately summoned to the horrible scene. Captain Lees of the detective force was placed in charge of the case, along with a number of the city's top investigators. They quickly ascertained that Minnie had last been seen in the company of Theo Durrant. The detectives went to Theo's room, where they found Minnie Williams' purse. A warrant for his arrest was issued immediately. Theo was eventually located in Walnut Creek where he had traveled on Sunday to join the signal corps of the state militia, a group with which he had previously affiliated. He was placed under arrest, although he protested violently that he was completely innocent and had no connection whatsoever with any criminal activity. On April 23, he was officially charged in court with murder, while continuing to adamantly protest his innocence.[16]

But where was Blanche Lamont all this time? The mystery was soon solved when detectives finally made a thorough and painstaking search of the Emmanuel Baptist Church. Eventually, one detective climbed the stairs to the church belfry. There in the half-light of the belfry, he beheld a startling sight. At first, it looked like a marble carving of a completely nude girl lying on the floor. She was on her back, her body

The belfry where Blanche Lmont's body was discovered. *Police photo*

straight and dignified like a statute. Her hands were folded over her breast, her hair carefully arranged behind her head. But it wasn't a marble statute. It was Blanche Lamont.

When the detectives carried her body from the coolness of the belfry to the heated rooms below, it turned almost immediately from white to black. A further search of the room uncovered Blanche's clothing and her school books were found stuffed into the studding behind the plaster of a wall.[17]

An autopsy on the two bodies revealed that both women had died in similar fashion. Both girls had been the victims of violent sexual frenzy. Both had struggled valiantly but ineffectually. Both had been strangled and violated before and possibly after death. Minnie's screams had obviously been so loud that the murderer, in a panic, had stuffed clothing down her throat to silence her. So great was his frenzy on the occasion of Minnie's murder that he had taken a knife from a table in the room and slashed her wrists, forehead, and chest. He then made a half-hearted and unsuccessful attempt to hide her body in a closet.

Blanche died of strangulation during the assault on her, which also took place in the church library. The attacker stripped her of her clothing and dragged her body, probably by the hair, up two flights of stairs into the belfry. Then, for some unknown reason, he arranged her body in a precise and formal position on the floor, placing a block of wood under her head and folding her arms over her breast in the manner in which cadavers were frequently positioned at medical school.

Once Durrant was cited as the likely perpetrator, stories and rumors about his past behavior quickly surfaced. As one detective later recalled, "As soon as the finger of suspicion pointed at Durrant, information poured into Captain Lees, proving that the prisoner was a degenerate of the most depraved class. For obvious reasons, names cannot be given of young ladies to whom he made the most disgusting propositions, and the wonder of it is that he was not killed, or at least exposed before."[18] But, in most instances, the nature of his insults was such that the offended ladies feared to inform their relatives, lest they would take the law into their own hands.

The crime seemed to electrify newspapers through California, America and Europe. This was a crime that had everything—sex, murder, mayhem, mystery, discovery, denial, and, yes, even religion. In short, it instantly put San Francisco in the front rank of celebrated crime cities—New York, New Orleans, Paris, and even London.

San Francisco seemed obsessed with the murders. The city's papers were filled with reportage and speculation on Durrant's motives and actions, on Blanche's and Minnie's earlier lives, and on details of the official investigation. There were rumors of other debaucheries at the church, that the pastor himself was somehow involved, and that others were proffering confessions to the crime.

So intense was public interest in the events that a play dramatizing the murders, entitled "The Crime of the Century," was mounted successfully at the Auditorium Theatre at Eddy and Jones streets.[19] A short novel entitled *Letter F*, or *Startling Revelation in the Durrant Case* was quickly published in both San Francisco and New York.[20]

The international interest in the crime and its outcome was recorded by British writer Guy Logan:

"I well remember the interest which the protracted trial aroused in England, and the feeling of satisfaction, amounting almost to relief, when the news came that the perpetrator of these deeds would not be allowed to escape the extreme penalty."[21]

Throughout the formal court proceedings that followed, Theo Durrant claimed that he was totally innocent, that he had not even seen Blanche following her arrival at the high school, that he did not see Minnie at all on the day of her death. The trial that followed required the screening of over

William Durrant, seated between his parents at the trial. *San Francisco Examiner*

115

a thousand potential jurors before twelve impartial citizens could be found.[22] The trial itself began on April 22, 1895, and lasted almost a month. The prosecution paraded more than fifty witnesses to the stand. They all placed Durrant at the scene of the crimes, despite his protestations. One girl testified that Durrant had earlier tried to entice her into the library for purposes of a "physical examination." Another revealed that she had been in the library with Durrant when he suddenly disappeared, only to reappear completely naked.[23] The girl stated that she fled in terror. The jury deliberated for a full five minutes and returned with its verdict: Guilty of murder in the first degree with the death penalty attached.[24]

In jail, Durrant continued to protest that he was completely innocent. The verdict was appealed to a higher court and denied. Two years of additional legal maneuvering ensued and finally the date of June 11, 1897, was set for the execution. Durrant's lawyers appealed to Governor James Budd for clemency. The governor made an extensive examination of the case, determined that Durrant was guilty, and refused to interfere.

On April 10, Durrant was taken to San Quentin to await execution. Still more appeals were made to higher courts and all were denied.

Durrant as San Quentin prisoner number 17260. *California State Archives*

116

During the months that Durrant languished in prison at San Quentin, his behavior ranged from the predictable to the bizarre. He became obsessively religious, calling on God to reveal the real perpetrator of the crime. He claimed to have prophetic dreams concerning a scroll on which were strange ciphers that only he could interpret and which pronounced his innocence. He gave interviews to reporters in return for money. He began work on an autobiographical manuscript, now happily lost to history. He came to see himself as a martyr: "I am not afraid to die. Such a death as mine may be the means of abolishing capital punishment in this state."[21]

His time came on the morning of January 7, 1898. After a hearty breakfast of steak and eggs, William Henry Theodore Durrant was led from his cell to a specially prepared scaffold, where hangman Amos Lunt and an audience of California sheriffs awaited him. To make certain that Durrant died only in the prescribed manner, the sheriffs had all been relieved of their firearms.[26]

As the noose was placed around his neck, Durrant began to make what was obviously a carefully practiced speech:

> "I would like to say this: I have no animosity against anyone, not even those who have persecuted me and have hounded me to the grave innocent as I am. I forgive them all. They will receive their justice from the holy God above, to whom I now go to receive my justice, which will be the justice given to an innocent boy who has not stained his hands with crimes that have been put upon him."

Durrant making his "farewell address." *San Francisco Examiner*

Eleven Minutes After the Drop Durrant Was Dead.

It was 10:38:02 when the drop was sprung. Eleven minutes later Drs. W. P. Lawlor, the prison physician; P. F. Casey, R. E. Williams, W. J. Whitman and M. F. Jones pronounced Durrant dead. The body remained motionless after it fell and there was not a single respiration. The neck was broken and the head bent far over under the rope. The hands which the doctors grasped to catch the speeding pulse first grew pale and then blue and ashen. A little patch of the neck showed between the cap and the collar and it ran from an ashen to a purple in color. The record of the pulse by half minutes was as follows: 67-60-54-50-50-40-50-55-56-70-40-45-36-60-40-42-22-20-30. When the physicians raised their hands announcing the death of the gibbet's victim Father Lagan ceased his prayers and left the scaffold and the crowd filed out of the death chamber.

Durrant at the end of his rope, proclaimed dead by the prison physician. *San Francisco Chronicle.*

The witnesses assembled for the hanging began to grow restless but Durrant droned on:

"The fair name of California will be forever blackened with the crime of taking this innocent blood. I am innocent of the crimes charged to me, before God who knows my heart and can read my mind. I am inno…."[27]

But hangman Lunt had heard enough. Theo Durrant's final word was cut short by the loud slap of the trap door.

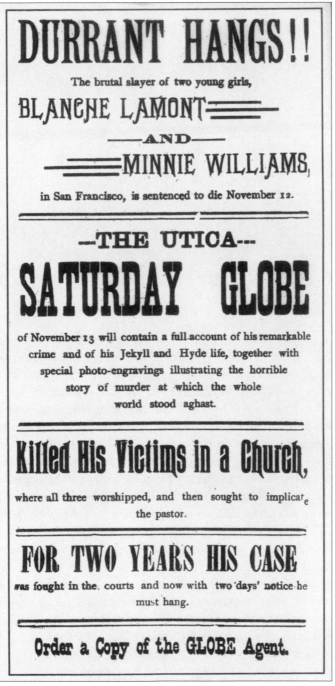

Death notice of the murderer in an Eastern newspaper.
Utica, N.Y., Globe

Chapter Eight

The Stockton Trunk Stuffer—1906

*In the early days of California, death was the customary penalty
for a wide variety of crimes—murder, of course, but also rape, treason,
claim-jumping, and horse-thievery. The sentence was often carried out
without the benefit of a formal trial, for, in fact, a true jury system was
not in effect in the state until the mid 1840s. At that time, jails did not
even exist in most parts of California. Therefore, according to one historian, "immediate execution was the most effectual and lasting process of
elimination and it was often employed."[1] A typical example of this rough
justice occurred in 1849 in Placerville, then known as Dry Diggins, when
four Mexicans were accused of robbery. According to the official history
of El Dorado County, "They were tried by a crowd of half-intoxicated
miners. They tried to defend themselves in Spanish, but no interpreter
was found, and they were immediately hanged from the branches of a
tree in the center of the camp."[2]*

*The death penalty was legitimized by the California state legisla-
ture when, in 1851, it passed a bill "permitting a jury to impose the
death penalty for serious offenses including robbery and grand larceny."[3]
Over the next half-century, juries eagerly availed themselves of the opportunity to dispatch evildoers by means of the "ultimate sentence." Death
by hanging was, in fact, the principal tool employed by both of San
Francisco's vigilance committees.*

*There is no official record of the number of hangings that took
place over the next half-century in California, but there can be little*

doubt that they numbered in the hundreds. As far as can be determined, however, all of those so dispatched were males. Almost all law on the subject referred to "men charged with a capital crime" or to "lawless men." The idea that women would commit crimes deserving death seemed unthinkable. As one moralist of the time proclaimed, "The very thought that a woman should be hanged is morally repulsive and beyond the realm of serious contemplation." Several women, including the infamous Laura Fair, received death sentences, but all had subsequently escaped the gallows. Yet, there always remained the possibility that, at some time and at some place, some woman would perpetrate a criminal offense sufficiently heinous and repulsive that the death penalty could be employed. Such a crime did occur shortly after the turn of the century—in a town not far from San Francisco.

The city of Stockton sits at the crossroads of the San Joaquin Valley, about equidistant from San Francisco and the foothills of the Sierra Nevada mountains. At the start of the twentieth century, it served as the region's business center, thanks to its deep-water port at the head of the Bay tributary called the San Joaquin River and because of its railroad freight yards which served the rich farmlands to the west.

In the spring of 1906, Stockton had something of a dual personality. During the week, it was a quiet and respectable town of some 20,000 hard-working citizens. But on the weekends, its hotels and rooming houses welcomed an influx of fun-seeking visitors from San Francisco, from the farming communities to the south, and from the gold and silver towns to the north. The visitors crowded its streets, filled its restaurants and dance halls, and poured money into its stores. The citizens of Stockton tended to ignore the weekend transients and to heave a sigh of relief when the weekends were over and the visitors returned home. Sometimes, however, the visitors stayed on—and sometimes they did things that were impossible to forget.

On Saturday, March 24, 1906, the afternoon train pulled into the Stockton depot of the Southern Pacific Railway at about 5:00 P.M. Baggage man N. J. Vizelich began the task of putting bags and trunks on the freight car for the journey to Sacramento. His job completed, he turned to walk back into the station. Then he heard a heavy thump behind him and turned to find that one of the trunks he had loaded had been thrown off the train. "Can't take it," the man on the train yelled at him, "It's got no tag!"[4] Vizelich hurriedly examined the large trunk and was surprised to see that it had no identification of any kind. Reluctantly, he loaded it

The Union Pacific Train Station in Stockton in 1905, scene of the grisly discovery. *Courtesy of the Haggin Museum, Stockton, CA*

back onto his transit truck and wheeled it to the door of the baggage room. He left it there temporarily as a reminder of the carelessness of some of his customers.

Before leaving for dinner that evening, Vizelich finally took the trunk inside and weighed it in at 225 pounds. Then he locked up the freight room and went home.[5]

Several hours later, the baggage man was back on the job, accompanied by his boss, John Thompson, the baggage master, and an express man named McGuire. The room was warm and stuffy, and the three men began to complain to each other about an unpleasant aroma. At first they attributed it to the long, hard day they had all put in, but as the minutes dragged on, they became increasingly concerned with the growing unpleasantness. Then Vizelich, who, over the years, had handled a number of corpses that came through the freight room in their coffins, announced that he recognized the odor. It was, he said, the smell of a decaying body. The other two men dismissed the idea, but eventually the stench reached such a level that they began searching for the source. They walked around

The trunk that contained the bloodied body of Albert N. McVicar.
The Haggin Museum, Stockton, CA

sniffing the room until they found themselves standing in front of the large trunk with no label.

At first they considered opening the trunk, but then they decided that this was a matter for the police. Just before 10:00 P.M., Police Captain John Walker entered the baggage room with an order from the district attorney's office to open the trunk. With the help of the baggage men, he removed the rope that bound the trunk, and then he cracked open the trunk itself. When he raised the lid, a pair of shoeless feet popped out into full view. Inside was the bloodied body of a man lying on its back with its legs doubled up so that the feet were on either side of the head. The body was fully dressed except for shoes. The face was covered with blood, which still ran freely from the nose and mouth, and the interior of the trunk was smeared with gore. It was the body of a tall, spare man with brown hair and what was then known as a "waterfall" mustache. The body was surrounded by a variety of male clothing, including shoes, ties, trousers, and a pair of bib overalls. Captain Walker immediately summoned other members of the

123

police department, and the trunk was impounded as evidence. The body was surrendered to the coroner for an autopsy.

Walker quizzed the baggage men about the trunk and learned that it belonged to a lady who had arrived at the depot at about 2:00 P.M. that afternoon to check on her trunk's arrival. When she learned that the trunk was not yet there, she became extremely agitated and attempted to call the California House to see if it had been picked up. She was so nervous that she was unable to complete the call and asked for assistance. But just then the trunk arrived, along with a medium-sized straw suitcase. The woman was about thirty years old, rather pretty, and well dressed. She indicated the trunk should be put on the train to Sacramento, and she departed. Later in the day, she returned and took the straw suitcase and boarded a train for San Francisco, leaving the trunk behind.

The morning following the gruesome discovery, Policeman Frank Briare was detailed to find the express man who had hauled the trunk. There were only six men in Stockton in that business and Briare had little trouble locating Charles Berry, who informed the patrolman that he had hauled a large, heavy trunk from the California House to the depot on Saturday afternoon. Berry was then taken to the morgue, where he identified the trunk. He had hauled the trunk from room 97. The landlady at California House showed police the hotel register for the previous Friday night. Room 97 had been registered to "A. N. McVicar and wife, Jamestown, California."[6]

The heavily hatted Emma Le Doux and the luxuriantly moustached Albert N. McVicar, in portraits prior to their marriage. *The Stockton Evening Mail*

The landlady, Mrs. Englehardt, said that she remembered Mr. and Mrs. McVicar. They had rented a room from her several weeks earlier and then again on Friday night. She described Mrs. McVicar as an attractive lady, much shorter than her husband. Mr. McVicar, she said, had a large, dark brown, drooping moustache. The landlady then led the police up to the third floor to room 97. The room was clean and sunny, with no apparent evidence that it was a crime scene. In one corner, police found a dark-green valise. It contained a numbers of photographs. One was of a rather pretty woman with a head of dark hair piled high on her head. Another was a strip of "stamp pictures," showing images of a man with sharp features and a luxuriant moustache. "That's Mrs. Vicar and that's Mr. McVicar," said the landlord, pointing to the photographs.[7]

Charles Berry, the express man who delivered the trunk from room 97 to the depot, told police that he had also, earlier in the day, delivered that same trunk to room 97 from Rosenbaum's General Store on Main Street. The investigators hurried to Rosenbaum's, where the sales clerk remembered selling the trunk to a woman for ten dollars in gold. He then referred the lady to express man Berry for delivery of the trunk to her rooming house. He also remembered telling her she should go to Shaw's Store to purchase rope to bind up the trunk. At Shaw's Store, salesman Bee Clark recalled the lady clearly. He had sold her a length of the best Manila hemp and, as the lady was leaving, he jokingly admonished her, "Look out, now, and don't hang yourself!"[8]

The happy couple in their wedding photograph, Jamestown, CA. *The Haggin Museum, Stockton, CA*

Still another store owner then came forth with information on the now notorious Mr. and Mrs. A. N. McVicar. A sales clerk at Breuner's Furniture Emporium recalled that a couple, identifying themselves as the McVicars, had purchased a quantity of furniture to be shipped to an address in Jamestown. The clerk was surprised when they gave their names as Mr. and Mrs. McVicar, because that same lady had been in the store two weeks earlier and had given a different name. He looked up the sales slip and confirmed his suspicion. Earlier, she had called herself "Mrs. Emma Le Doux."

The Stockton police were now confident that they knew who was responsible for the body in the trunk. They telegraphed the authorities in San Francisco and at all intermediate train stops to be on the lookout for a woman approximately thirty years old, well dressed, short in stature, with brown hair worn in high-fashion style, and identifying herself as either Mrs. A. N. McVicar or Emma Le Doux.

In the meantime, the coroners had completed their work on the murder victim. The autopsy disclosed "congestion of the inner lining of the skull and several contusions, sufficient to cause death. No fracture. No sign of poison discovered, and urine clear, showing conclusively that no carbolic acid was employed."[9] Their shocking conclusion: The victim was still alive when he was put in the trunk!

The crime was instantly celebrated in San Francisco, as well as in every town and village in between San Francisco and Stockton. Shrieked the *San Francisco Examiner:* "Trunk Murderess Headed Here."[10] It wasn't long before the alleged murderess was in tow. The police in Antioch, a town a few miles east of San Francisco, had the privilege of arresting the suspect on Monday morning. They were alerted that a woman calling herself Mrs. Jones, but answering the description of Mrs. Le Doux/McVicar, had checked into the Arlington Hotel. Marshal Thomas B. Sharon took her into custody. On being arrested, the woman said that her real name was Emma Le Doux and that she knew all about the crime. Sheriff C. C. Case was dispatched to bring her back to Stockton, and he arrived accompanied by a number of reporters from both Stockton's *The Evening Mail* and *The Daily Evening Record.*

Marshal Sharon had already examined Mrs. Le Doux's straw suitcase, and the list of contents was intriguing, to say the least. It included, in addition to Emma's own clothing, men's shaving equipment, neckties, shirts, collars, a man's watch, small sacks of Durham tobacco, a bottle of cyanide of potassium, a bottle of morphine pills, a bottle of carbolic acid, a bottle of tablets of carbolic acid, a knife, a meat cleaver, a small saw, and a buggy lamp covered with mud.[11]

On the train back to Stockton, Emma Le Doux was far from reluctant to talk. In fact, the sheriff and the accompanying reporters could hardly shut her up. She not only answered every question put to her in excruciating detail, but also rambled on without any encouragement. Was she married to Mr. McVicar? No, but she had been. They were divorced last year and now she was married to Eugene Le Doux, who lived in Jackson in Amador County. Had she murdered Mr. McVicar? Certainly not. He was murdered by a man she had met but did not know well. How had he murdered McVicar? This man had forced McVicar to drink carbolic acid while the three of them were in the room at California House. Then he had forced her to help him put McVicar's body in the trunk. Why had she helped him? She was frightened that the man would kill her if she didn't help. What was the man's name? Well, it was...Joe Miller. Did she really think anyone would believe the man's name was Joe Miller? Well, it wasn't Joe Miller, actually. It was Joe Healy and he was a plumber in San Francisco. Where was Joe Healy now? He had returned to San Francisco with her and disappeared. Did she buy the trunk herself? Yes, but Joe Healy made her do it. After buying the trunk, she had stayed in town and bought a new hat, which cost eight dollars. She reported it was the hat she was wearing now, and didn't they like it? The reporters agreed with Sheriff Case when he said that he had a very unusual prisoner on his hands.

News of the bizarre murder and the apprehension of the alleged perpetrator of the crime swept through Stockton like a prairie fire. Nothing this weird and horrible had ever happened before in the city, and it had galvanized the citizenry. When the train arrived at the Santa Fe station, more than fifteen hundred people were waiting, hoping to catch a glance of the already infamous Emma Le Doux. Another thousand, less well informed, waited at the Southern Pacific depot and missed her completely. At the Stockton jail, hundreds lined both sides of the entrance to jeer and applaud. Even more ghoulishly, hundreds of other Stocktonites, including women and children, crowded into the morgue to gaze upon the lifeless body of A. N. McVicar as it lay on a marble slab following the autopsy.[12]

Emma Le Doux was locked up for the night in a cell with a window where she "passed a quiet night, seemingly cool and unmoved, after which she ate breakfast with apparent relish."[13] Joe Miller/Healy was, from the outset, referred to in the Stockton press as "the mythical accomplice." It turned out, however, that there really was a Joe Healy, who lived in San Francisco on Florida Street, and who did, in fact, know Emma Le Doux. It was quickly established by the authorities that he had been in that city the entire weekend and had nothing to do with the crime.

The enterprising reporters of Stockton were quick to ferret out other facts concerning the principals in the case. Mr. McVicar was Albert N. McVicar, a timber man who had come to California from Kansas in 1904. He was employed by a Captain Neville at the Rawhide mine in Jamestown. He was thirty-six years old, more than six feet in height, and apparently quite well-off. His employer described him as "one of the best workmen and the handiest man I ever had in my employ." He further stated that "McVicar quit his job last Thursday and was coerced away by (Emma Le Doux), whose reputation up here is not good."[14]

The facts about Emma herself were somewhat more elusive. It was determined that she had been married a number of times. She took her first husband, a man named Barrett, when she was sixteen, but the marriage did not last. Several years later, while working as a domestic in Jackson, she married again, this time to a Cornish miner named Williams. The couple soon moved to Bisbee, Arizona, where Williams developed "miner's consumption." He died shortly thereafter and Emma took the insurance money and returned to Jackson, where she eventually married Eugene Le Doux. Investigators could find no record that she had ever married McVicar, despite Emma's protestations that she had both married and divorced him. It was clear that Emma Le Doux was a woman of shifting loyalties and principles, who frequently acted on impulse without really weighing the consequences. As Stockton District Attorney Norton later stated, "The woman is beyond me. I never saw an accused person more cool or unconcerned. She seems to take everything as a matter of course...as though she were on a pleasure trip or sightseeing. She seems to give no thought to the terrible crime with which she is charged."[15]

Relatives of both Mrs. Le Doux and Mr. McVicar suddenly materialized, professing their disbelief and outrage and eagerly giving interviews to reporters. McVicar had two brothers, both of whom quickly projected themselves onto the scene. One brother, who owned a laundry in Cripple Creek, Colorado, grandly announced that he was in Stockton to claim his brother's body. The second brother, however, demanded that the body be sent to Wichita, Kansas. Still another McVicar relative, announcing that the murder victim had been named after him, declared that he was on his way to Stockton out of a sense of family duty to protect his nephew's interests.

Emma Le Doux was also soon to be gifted by a visiting family member—her mother. The mother, referred to in the press simply as "Mrs. Head," reportedly took the news calmly when informed in Jackson that her daughter was accused of murder. However, she soon rallied, announcing grandly that she would never desert her daughter, and that she would "mortgage her ranch and exhaust every means to secure her release."[16] She also promised that she was on her way to Stockton to comfort and assist her daughter. It would prove a long and unforgettable visit.

A bogus relative also emerged. On Wednesday, March 28, a woman presented herself at the jail and announced that she was Emma Le Doux's sister and had come to visit with the accused. The jailer was just leading the visitor into the jail cell when he suddenly remembered his instructions to allow no one to see the prisoner without a court order. So, he took the lady to the sheriff's office where she admitted that she was not Mrs. Le Doux's sister but was instead a reporter from the *San Francisco Bulletin* seeking an exclusive interview.

The citizenry learns of the shocking murder in full and florid detail. *The Stockton Record*

The efforts of the San Francisco newspapers were, however, more successful on another front. A reporter from the *San Francisco Examiner* decided to see if Mrs. Le Doux's cyanide of potassium had been procured in San Francisco. He made a tour of the city's pharmacies with a photograph of Emma Le Doux, and at the Baldwin Pharmacy at 119 Ellis Street he hit pay dirt. The pharmacist immediately recognized Emma's photograph, searched his files, and determined that she had purchased a large quantity of the poison on March 14, ten days before the murder. When asked why he had sold the cyanide without a prescription, the pharmacist said that Mrs. Le Doux told him it was for photographic purposes and she had a calm, reassuring demeanor.[17] This revelation inspired Dr. John F. Dillon, also of San Francisco, to come forth with the information that Mrs. Le Doux had purchased twelve grains of morphine from him, presumably for stomach pains.

That was all the Stockton newspapers needed to condemn the alleged murderess. The headline in *The Evening Mail* informed readers that "The Facts are Conclusive!"[18] *The Daily Evening Record* was only slightly more reticent, announcing in bold type that "Le Doux Woman Faces Damaging Circumstances."[19] The authorities, of course, still had their work to do.

The murder room, number 97 at California House, as sketched by an artist for the *Stockton Record. The Haggin Museum, Stockton, CA*

On Friday, March 30, the coroner announced his autopsy findings, and a grand jury, receiving the evidence, proclaimed its official verdict: "We believe that the deceased came to his death from the combined effects of having been drugged with morphine and chloral, and in a dazed condition having been forced into a closed trunk, where there was not sufficient oxygen to sustain what life there was present. We also believe that one Mrs. Emma Le Doux was responsible for the death of Albert N. McVicar and, as far as we have been able to determine from the evidence submitted, that she was unaided."[20] Judge Nutter, of the Stockton city court, set a date of May 22 for the trial of Emma Le Doux for the murder of Albert N. McVicar.

The intervening weeks were filled with a variety of events, all covered in copious detail by the Stockton newspapers. Emma's mother, Mrs. Head, breezed into town, accompanied by defense attorney Charles Crocker. Mrs. Head quickly became a fixture in the city, granting interviews to one and all, and issuing bulletins proclaiming her daughter's

Sheriff Sibley whose method of jury selection resulted in a new trial for the convicted murderer. *The Haggin Museum, Stockton, CA*

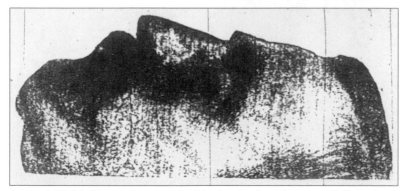

A.N. McVicar, photographed in death after his removal from the trunk. *The Stockton Record*

innocence. The McVicar brothers came to Stockton, expressed their outrage at the events surrounding the murder, and then took the murdered man's body back to Jackson with them.

Then, on April 16, an event occurred that finally knocked what had become known as "the trunk murder" off the front page. It was the San Francisco earthquake. The great quake destroyed most of the city of San Francisco, ruined Stanford University, and even shook up the city of Stockton. The headline writer at *The Evening Mail*, possibly exhausted from the demands of the McVicar murder, tried his best to rise to this new challenge. He almost, but not quite made it. Screamed the front page headline—"AWFUL CATACLASM!" The next day, he fared no better. His headline read—"IS ABSOLUTELY NO HOPE!"

On April 18, 1906, the case of Emma La Doux was put on hold by the great San Francisco earthquake and fire.

Eventually, of course, things got back to normal, and Emma Le Doux was restored to her rightful place on the front page. At her arraignment, she was described as "becomingly gowned, dignified and composed,"[21] As she languished in her cell, Emma continued to grant interviews to reporters, all of them self-serving. On one noteworthy occasion, she accused District Attorney George McNoble of bullying her. She declared that McNoble, after interrogating her, snapped his fingers and said, "I wouldn't give *that* for your neck, you contemptible hussy!"[22]

More important, prosecutors in the case finally revealed what they believed to be the motive for the crime: one too many husbands. It seems that Emma had married Eugene Le Doux without bothering with the nicety of obtaining a divorce from Albert McVicar. When McVicar journeyed down from Jamestown to be with his beloved, Emma realized she had a major problem. Her simple solution was to eliminate Mr. McVicar. The assignment of a motive to this previously baffling crime seemed to remove the last element of doubt from the minds of the citizens of Stockton.

The trial finally got underway on Tuesday, June 5, with a massive turnout of both spectators and press. Reporters' interest in the empaneling of the jury was surpassed only by their interest in how Mrs. Le Doux and her mother were attired. Mrs. Le Doux, it was reported, was "dressed entirely in black, with hat and veil of the same somber hue…Her breast heaving with deep breaths," and "Mrs. Head was dressed entirely in black, except for a white ribbon at her throat." One paper also reported that the two could pass as sisters, then adding somewhat cattily that Mrs. Head "is probably much older than she looks."[23]

There was equal interest paid to the interactions between the two women. When Mrs. Head approached her daughter from behind at the defense table, squeezed her shoulder, and then patted her breast, Emma made no response. Later, when one prospective juror was asked if he had any moral compunction against hanging a woman, Emma remained passive, showing no visible emotion. Her mother, however, fainted dead away.

By Friday, June 8, twelve jurors took their seats in the jury box to hear prosecuting attorney Norton make his opening remarks, concluding with his demand for the death penalty. The trial droned on for five days, without anyone learning anything really new concerning the case. The facts of the case, as well as the rumors and conjectures surrounding it, had been so extensively publicized by the papers and so eagerly ingested by the people of Stockton that there was little for anyone to learn. That did not keep the prosecution and the defense from exploring every aspect of the case in excruciating detail.The prosecution did everything imaginable to blacken the already soiled reputation of the defendant. A parade of witnesses who had known Emma over the years portrayed her as a naughty girl, a troubled teenager, an unreliable employee, a faithless wife, and a conniving widow. The result was a portrait of a woman who led a careless life, moving from one thing to another with little thought of what she was doing or what the consequences would be. She seemed to marry and re-marry almost on impulse, without always going through the inconvenience of divorce.

District Attorney Norton, who came close to poisoning himself during the trial. *Artist's sketch for The Stockton Record*

Endless testimony was presented concerning the contents of Mr. McVicar's intestine, bowels and blood, as competing experts dueled with conflicting facts and theories. The most compelling testimony was delivered by Professor Roy R. Rogers of Cooper Medical College, who had examined the organs of the deceased. Rogers informed the jury that they contained knockout drops and morphine in a quantity sufficient to kill a man several times over. The professor also dazzled the court by testifying that McVicar could have lived up to forty-five minutes in the trunk, because he, Rogers, had actually spent that length of time in the trunk as an experiment and obviously had no trouble surviving!

The defense threw out a number of arguments, some of them highly creative. One was that McVicar had committed suicide, intentionally or not, and Emma was simply trying to get rid of a dead body. Even more astounding was the contention that McVicar was still alive when the trunk was opened and that he had been killed by the effects of the autopsy!

The trial itself came close to causing a second tragic death. While prosecuting attorney Norton made his final arguments, he paused several times to take a drink of water. Just as he was concluding, he reached behind himself once again to obtain the water glass, but instead he grabbed a glass filled with water and carbolic acid which had been used as an exhibit by the defense. As he was lifting it to his lips, another attorney leapt forward and took the glass from his hand. The headline that evening in the *The Evening Mail* proclaimed, "District Attorney Norton Nearly Poisons Himself!"

Emma kept her composure throughout the trial, showing what one newspaper referred to as "indifference." Another reported that, "The trial seemed to greatly interest everyone in the courtroom except Mrs. Le Doux."[24] Her mother, on the other hand, seemed passionately involved in everything that occurred, and even managed to faint several more times.

The jury retired at 2:30 P.M., following the completion of concluding arguments, to contemplate all that they had seen and heard. It did not take them long to come to a conclusion. On the first ballot, the jury was unanimous in finding Mrs. Le Doux guilty. When it came to deciding between life imprisonment and the death penalty, there were four holdouts. After six hours and sixteen ballots, however, there was finally a unanimous vote for the death penalty. Mrs. Le Doux was ordered to appear in court the following day for her sentencing.

Because of the seriousness of the occasion—and with her life hanging in the balance—Emma wanted to be appropriately garbed for the event. She concluded that she needed new shoes. The *Mail* gave its readers the important details: "Yesterday Mrs. Le Doux made known to jailer Benjamin that she desired a new pair of shoes…. A local dealer sent over part of his stock in order that she might make a selection. The woman said that she wanted the very latest in French heel shoes and declared she wore a 'four-three A' shoe. Arthur K. Thorpe, the shoe clerk, doubted the truth of Mrs. Le Doux's statement. Accordingly he took out two pairs of shoes…the 'four-three A' proved too small, whereupon he tried on the other which was a 'five-single A.' Mrs. Le Doux inquired, 'What size is that?' 'That's a four-four A,' responded Mr. Thorpe, professionally prevaricating in order to spare the feelings of his customer…. Mrs. Le Doux seemed satisfied and she made the purchase. She still believes her foot is smaller than it is."[25]

When the sentence was read, there was a look of puzzlement on Emma's face. She was asked if she had anything to say. She replied slowly, looking down at her new shoes, "I don't know what I can say to you. I haven't anything to say. I can't say anything."[26]

Judge Nutter intoned the sentence as Emma stood quietly before the bench: "It is the judgement of the Court that you shall be hanged by the neck until you are dead. The Court now issues the death warrant and fixes the time for the execution upon Friday, October 19, 1906, between the hours of six o'clock in the morning and noon at the State Prison at San Quentin."[27]

Had Emma actually become the first woman to be hanged in the state, it would have brought the story of this feckless woman to a tidy conclusion. But that was not to be. She did not hang, and the reasons for that are truly historic.

WOMAN DOOMED TO DEATH ON GALLOWS

Emma LeDoux Found Guilty of the Murder of A. N. McVicar

Jury Arrived at the Verdict Quickly, Then After Some Argument, Agreed to Verdict Carrying Penalty of Death on the Scaffold

Justice is done, according to the *Stockton Evening Mail*. *The Haggin Museum, Stockton, CA*

No sooner was Emma Le Doux settled in her new windowless cell in the Stockton jail than her lawyer began petitioning for a new trial. The grounds for the appeal were numerous and elusive, but the courts took them seriously, and the matter wound its way slowly up the court hierarchy until it finally settled in the lap of the California Supreme Court. Its decision, reached three years after the original trial, outraged the people of Stockton as well as much of the population of California. The court

Mrs. La Doux was permitted to wear her latest hat for her official mug shot at San Quentin prison. *The State of California Archives*

found that the jury in the trial had been improperly empanelled because the sheriff who had arrested Emma and had been so outspoken about her obvious guilt was also the person who selected the pool of citizens from which the jury was drawn. This was not an uncommon practice in California, but the supreme court now decided it was improper, and granted Emma Le Doux a new trial. A cry of anguish went up from the press. "No one," wrote one paper, "is anxious to have the wretched woman hanged, but no one who does not want to see anarchy ultimately prevail in our country can look with composure on the breakdown of criminal justice in this State."[28]

By the time a new trial date was set, Emma had spent three years in the Stockton jail. She had served her jail time in the same way she endured her trial—quietly, stoically, and without giving things much thought. While in jail, for instance, she entered a mail-in contest sponsored by a piano company. She was one of the winners and received as a prize a certificate good for $92 on the purchase of a piano—hardly a contest that a jailed inmate would reasonably have entered in the first place.

On January 10, 1910, Emma Le Doux stood before Judge Nutter once again, but this time her plea was different. Said Emma, "Owing to the condition of my health which has been shattered by years of confinement, I do not feel able to stand the strain of another trial. I therefore have decided to plead guilty, and I want you to do what you can to dispose of the matter quickly."[29]

Whether or not there was prior collusion with the prosecutors and the court is not known, but the judge promptly withdrew Emma's sentence of death and instead sentenced her to life imprisonment. Emma received the news with characteristic calm, and a short while later she was driven under guard through San Francisco and then to San Quentin, where she would presumably spend the rest of her life. At the prison, she listed her occupation as "dressmaker," though there is no record of her ever having made a dress, and she was given the prison number 24077.

There was a strong suspicion in Stockton that a "life sentence" meant no such thing in the case of an attractive young woman, despite the grievous nature of her crime. And this suspicion proved correct. Emma first applied for parole after just seven years. She applied again just a year after that, and then again after still another year. In the meantime, Emma led the life of an ideal inmate in her usual quiet and unobtrusive way—with one notable exception. In 1919, Emma Le Doux saved the life of a jail matron who was being beaten by other inmates. Again, without thinking of the consequences, she impulsively threw herself into the fray and protected the matron against her assailants. This act of impromptu heroism apparently exerted a powerful influence on the parole board. On July 30, 1920, Emma walked out of San Quentin into the protective custody of her sister in Lodi. She had served just ten years for the infamous trunk murder of Albert McVicar.

Freedom did not alter the character of Emma Le Doux any more than imprisonment had. She continued to lead the same random, careless life she had always led. She spent the next year doing her best to violate her parole—drinking and carousing, driving her car dangerously, seducing young men, and generally being a pest to her guardian and the community. After the violations to her conditions of parole became too numerous to ignore, she was welcomed back to San Quentin prison after just eleven months of freedom.

Again, she was a model prisoner, and a generous parole board decided after little more than three years that she deserved still another chance at freedom. This time Emma took advantage of her time on the outside to search out still another husband, a hapless gentleman named Mr. Crackbon, who lived in Napa Valley. As her other husbands seemed so often to do, the unfortunate Mr. Crackbon died within a short time and Emma was once again a widow. The insurance must not have been adequate, for Mrs. Crackbon was picked up within months on both an immoral loitering charge and a bad check charge. By this time the authorities seem to have become exasperated with Emma, for they quickly slapped her back into prison and more or less told her to stay there.

She was now in her fifties, running out of luck and health, but she was still determined to return to her wayward life outside. She continued to petition the board for parole, periodically claiming that life in San Quentin was much too hard for a woman of her delicate nature. In 1933, Emma was transferred to the new women's prison in Tehachapi, where she was once again a model prisoner. She continued, year after year, to file her carefully argued petitions for release, in an increasingly shaky hand. But the parole board had wearied of her continual transgressions on the outside, and ruled that both she and society were better off with Emma in confinement.

In July of 1941, Mrs. Barrett-Williams-McVicar-Le Doux-Crackbon died in the prison hospital at Tehachapi. The woman whom many assumed would be the first female legally executed in California had outlived all of her husbands and most of those involved in her original prosecution. And she left behind a legal legacy that impacts the actions of the California courts to this day.

Chapter Nine

The Movie Star
and the Party Girl—1921

From the beginning, San Francisco was an entertainment-loving, theatre-adoring town. Its first theater, Washington Hall, was built in 1849, almost coincidental with the creation of the city, and by the turn of the century more than thirty theaters of all kinds welcomed the greatest actors of the time—Lola Montez, David Belasco, Lillie Langtrey, Edwin Booth, and Lotta Crabtree, all of whom thrilled San Francisco audiences and went away singing the city's praises. Even the fire and earthquake of 1906, which destroyed almost all of the city's theaters, could not dim San Franciscans' appetite for entertainment. Within months, new theaters were under construction—the Colonial, the Orpheum, the Van Ness, the Valencia.

However, only a few years later, a dramatic change began to take place in the nature of San Francisco theatrical entertainment. Motion pictures came on the scene. At first, they were added to the beginning and the end of theatrical shows as novelties, but it wasn't long before they took over the main entertainment venues. The first theater to devote itself exclusively to the showing of films was Grauman's Imperial, in 1912. This was the start of an avalanche. Two years later, there were thirty-five motion picture theaters in the city. By 1917, there were more than a hundred movie houses operating within the city limits of San Francisco.

As the 1920s got underway, the movie industry was still in its in-

fancy. And even though films were in black and white and had no sound, they already had a profound effect on the citizens of San Francisco and of America. In darkened theaters across the land, people sat before flickering screens as they laughed and cried, cheered and marveled, at the new heroes of the land: movie stars!

Not everyone, however, was happy with the new entertainment. The Women's Vigilance Committee and other guardians of the public morality worried that movies might be corrupting the morals of the nation's youth. Even more unsettling were rumors of loose living by the movie people of Hollywood. It was inevitable, perhaps, that there would be some incident that would bring all these suspicions and fears to a head. As it happened—well, it happened in San Francisco.

Whether or not you believed it was murder depended on whether you were the prosecuting attorney or a member of the grand jury—and on whether you were a reader of *The Hollywood Reporter* or the Hearst newspapers. It also depended on which of three juries you served on. But two things were clear: Someone died—and someone was responsible.

The person most people believed was responsible was Roscoe "Fatty" Arbuckle. Arbuckle was second only to Charlie Chaplin as the most popular movie star of the day—and he was also one of the best known and best loved personalities in the world. How he came to his unhappy predicament is a story filled with contradictions and clouded by conjecture.

Arbuckle was born in 1887 in South Center, Kansas, but his family moved to Santa Clara the next year. Roscoe was a huge baby and grew into an even larger youngster. By the time he was twelve, Arbuckle was sixty-seven inches tall and weighed two hundred pounds. Roscoe was also on his own. His parents had separated, and his family put him on a train to San Jose, where his father was to meet him. But his father failed to meet the train, and the young boy found himself abandoned in a strange city. Eventually, he found a job with a local vaudeville group and began his theatrical career even before he became a teenager.[1]

By the time he was seventeen, Arbuckle was already a seasoned performer, traveling throughout Northern California as a singer and a physical comedian. Despite his weight, which now approached two hundred and fifty-five pounds, he was unusually gracefully and acrobatic. His travels regularly took him to San Francisco, where he performed in virtually every vaudeville house in the city.

During one of his San Francisco appearances, Roscoe fell in love with a fellow performer, Minta Durfee. Within months, they were mar-

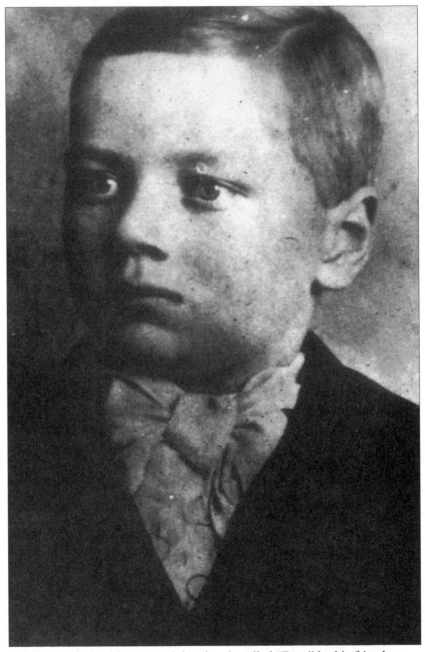

Roscoe Arbuckle at age eight, already called "Fatty" by his friends.

ried, and they went on the road as a team. Arbuckle, however, was not content being just a vaudevillian, and he soon branched out as a legitimate stage performer, appearing in Gilbert and Sullivan roles and traveling with touring companies presenting *Ruggles of Red Gap* and *The Count of Monte Cristo*.[2] But physical comedy was still his forte. His eye-catching bulk, his ability to move, even to fall, with a kind of elegant grace, and his keen sense of timing, guaranteed a laughing, even howling audience wherever he performed. It wasn't long before the producers of a brand new medium, two-reel motion picture comedies, sought him out.

Mack Sennet had already made his reputation as the master of movie comedy. His Keystone Kops were a national hit in movie theaters across the nation. Their madcap antics made little sense, but movie audiences didn't seem to care. In Sennet's films, custard pies flew without provocation, cars rocketed through traffic lights without incident, buildings exploded for no apparent reason, and the Kops ran and scrambled and collapsed without any clear purpose.[3] This was Roscoe Arbuckle's kind of comedy.

In 1913, Arbuckle filmed his first comedies with Sennet—five shorts, with established co-star Mabel Normand. The films were wildly popular and Arbuckle was film-named "Fatty" by Sennett himself. In these first films, Arbuckle also made motion picture history by being the recipient of the first custard pie ever hurled into a comedian's face.[4]

Mack Sennet's celebrated "Keystone Cops.

Over the next half dozen years, his movie career continued to soar. Hit followed hit, and "Fatty" Arbuckle was on the road to fame and fortune, through films such as *Fickle Fatty's Fall*, *The Feud*, *The Moonshiners* and *The Traveling Salesman*. Over a three-year period, "Fatty" made 105 one- and two-reel films, after which he starred in a dozen films with Charlie Chaplin. With a "derby hat on his big round skull, the vacant stare of a country bumpkin, and oversized trousers hanging loosely from the vast and billowy expanses of his waist,"[5] Arbuckle won the hearts of movie fans not just in America but throughout the world.

With millions flocking to movie theaters across the land, the nation's moralists expressed concern that films were having a corrosive effect on young people. But Arbuckle, safely ensconced in comedies rather than serious films, felt emboldened to separate himself from such concerns. Said "Fatty,"

> "I shall produce nothing that will offend the proprieties of either children or grown-ups. My pictures are turned out with clean hands and therefore with a clean conscience. Nothing would give me more grief than to have mothers say, 'Let's not go there today. Arbuckle is playing and he isn't fit for children to see.'"[6]

By 1921, Arbuckle had achieved world fame and some of the rewards of success, including a large Los Angeles home. But Sennet was notoriously tight-fisted and Roscoe felt his income was not commensurate with his position as a major movie star. Then in 1917, Paramount Pictures offered him an astonishing contract that included a salary of $1,000 a day, complete control over his pictures, and the possibility of making one million dollars after three years, if his pictures were successful. "Fatty" became the highest paid actor in films. He celebrated by buying a Tudor mansion on West Adams Boulevard for $250,000 and a custom-made Pierce Arrow for $25,000.[7]

Arbuckle as a young film star, earning $150 a week.

While Arbuckle's movie career flourished, his private life was deteriorating. Never a good drinker, he began drinking heavily and experimented with cocaine. His marriage to Minta, who had played opposite him in a number of films, fell apart and the couple separated. "Fatty" became involved in a number of unsavory incidents, none of which reached the press, and he was known frequently to seek out the company of ambitious starlets.

Still, his movies continued to grow in popularity. When America became involved in World War I in 1918, Arbuckle spent the better part of a year entertaining American soldiers and making charity appearances, which carried his popularity to a new high. He was lionized wherever he went. On a publicity trip to France, he was mobbed by more than 4,000 fans and had to flee for his life.

In 1920, Arbuckle starred in *Brewster's Millions*, a film that was a huge critical and financial success. The next year, he made three more features, *Crazy to Marry*, *Freight Prepaid*, and *Leap Year*. By August of 1921, he could look back on the greatest successes of his career.

Labor Day was approaching and "Fatty" was in a mood to celebrate. His friend and frequent co-star, Buster Keaton, invited him to join a yacht trip to Catalina Island. Arbuckle was tempted, but he finally told Keaton that he had already promised two friends that they would drive up to San Francisco for a few days of fun.

It was a trip that would destroy "Fatty" Arbuckle, shock the nation and shake the movie industry.

On the afternoon of Saturday, September 3, 1921, Arbuckle and two friends, Lowell Sherman, a fellow actor, and Fred Fischbach, a Sennet movie director, pulled up in front of the Saint Francis Hotel on Union Square in Arbuckle's Pierce Arrow. They checked into rooms 1219, 1220, and 1221 and settled in for some serious partying.[8]

"Fatty" as a child monster in *Brewster's Millions*.

Despite the fact that the Volsted Act was in force, the revelers had little trouble finding fuel for their party. Within hours after their arrival, a case of gin and a case of whiskey arrived at the Arbuckle suite. Next came a record player and a stack of records. Three showgirls, whose names were never revealed, were the next arrivals. They spent the remainder of the day, as the party moved into full force. Word was out that Arbuckle was celebrating, and friends and well-wishers dropped in and out of the suite. Arbuckle received them wearing only his pajama bottoms, drink in hand.

On Monday morning, September 4, there were three new arrivals. They were Al Semnacher, an actor's agent, Maude Delmont, a fashion model, and Virginia Rappe, a sometime actress. All three were friends of Arbuckle from the Hollywood studios.

Virginia Rappe had appeared in several films, usually in minor roles, and a year earlier she had been named the "Best Dressed Girl in Pictures." She had also achieved some minor celebrity as the face pictured on the sheet music of the hit song "Let Me Call You Sweetheart."[9]

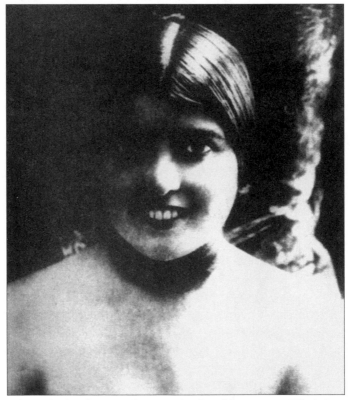

The last known photograph of aspiring actress Virginia Rappe.

This new trio of celebrants arrived at the Arbuckle suite at 10:20 A.M. and immediately joined in the festivities. An hour or so later, they were joined by two additional ladies, named Zey Prevon and Alice Blake.[10] Both were "models" on the fringe of show business. Now the party got into full swing. The record player blared loudly, the liquor flowed freely, and there was constant dancing and noisemaking, much to the distress of those in adjoining guest rooms. As the triumphant host, "Fatty" Arbuckle sat by the record machine, supervising the dancing and telling jokes, encouraging the merry-makers to drink up and party on.

By mid-afternoon, as the party veered toward its woozy climax, Virginia Rappe suddenly announced that she was feeling ill. She stumbled into the bathroom of room 1221 and disappeared. Exactly what took place over the next hour has been studied and debated ever since. No one can be certain exactly what happened. There are several reasons for this uncertainty and confusion. First, no single person present in the Arbuckle suite was a witness to all the different incidents that took place. Second, so much alcohol had been consumed by those in attendance (Maude Delmont later admitted to having consumed at least ten whiskeys by herself) that their observations were confused and their memories blurred. And third, judgments were clouded both by loyalties to Arbuckle, by some, and friendship with Miss Rappe, by others.

The most sanitized version of what followed came from Arbuckle's later testimony:

"Shortly after Miss Rappe had taken a few drinks, she became hysterical and complained that she could not breathe and then started to tear off her clothes. ...

I had been sitting nearby on a chair, but I had been kidding around, dancing, eating, drinking, playing the phonograph. I remember distinctly it was three o'clock when I went into room 1219 to dress. I closed the door and locked it. I went into the bathroom. I found Miss Rappe lying on the floor, doubled up, moaning.... That was the first time I knew she was in the room.

The door struck her on the head as I opened it, and I had to squeeze through the aperture to get in. She was holding her stomach. I took a towel and wiped her face, then handed her a glass of water. She drank it. She said she would like to lie down. I put her on the small bed with her head to the foot of the bed. Then I went to the bathroom and closed the door. Returning from the bathroom, I found her lying on the floor between the beds, holding her stomach and rolling around. I couldn't pick her up very well. I got her into the big bed and went out and told someone—believe it was Miss Prevon—that Miss Rappe was sick....

She came into room 1219 with me. Miss Delmont came a few seconds later. Miss Rappe was sitting up tearing at her clothes. She was frothing at the mouth. I saw her tear her waist. She had one sleeve almost off. I tore it off completely and went out."[11]

At the other end of the spectrum is this lurid description of the same event from a retrospective article in *Newsweek* magazine. "During the revelry, Arbuckle seized Rappe and escorted her to another room from which the guests later heard hysterical screams and Rappe crying, 'I'm dying. He's killing me!' Then Arbuckle walked out giggling, wearing Rappe's hat. 'She's acting it up,' he said. 'She's always been a lousy actress.' He also threatened to throw her out of the 12th story window unless she stopped moaning. But Rappe wasn't acting. Arbuckle had told others that he had jabbed a large, jagged piece of ice into her vagina."[12]

There would be still other versions of that fateful hour in rooms 1219 and 1221 as the days and months wore on, but the conclusion of each version was the same: Virginia Rappe was dying.

Maude Delmont, for instance, said that when she went to Arbuckle's bedroom, she had to kick at the door several times before he opened it. When Arbuckle opened the door, according to her account, he was standing alongside Rappe in his pajamas. Virginia was semi-conscience, yelling, "He did it! I know he did it! I'm dying."[13]

In the hope of alleviating Virginia's pain. Maude rubbed ice over her abdomen. When Roscoe attempted to re-enter the bedroom, Maude angrily ordered him out. Fred Fischbach came in and suggested that immersion in cold water might alleviate her pain and help her hangover. The two of them ran a tub of cold water and immersed her. It seemed only to aggravate her discomfort and she continued screaming. They wrapped Virginia in Arbuckle's robe and put her back in bed. If anything, she seemed worse. Maude got on the phone and called H. J. Boyle, the assistant manager of the hotel, who hurried to the room but was unable to be of much help.

At this point, Arbuckle came back into the room, and he and Boyle carried the screaming Virginia Rappe to a vacant room at the end of the hall. Still uncertain as to the gravity of her condition, they left her there. Maude's whiskeys had caught up with her and she retreated to a room provided her by Boyle. But one thing was now clear: The party was over.

The guests at the party gathered their wits and their belongings and quietly left. The bottles of gin and whiskey were packed up and sent out of the room. Chairs and tables were restored to their original positions. The phonograph and records were given to bellhops to return to storage. It seemed to Roscoe and his companions that with things tidied up, sanity had returned. They put on their traveling clothes, packed their bags, checked out of the hotel, and headed back to Los Angeles. Maude Delmont could deal with Virginia Rappe in the morning if, in fact, she was really ill and needed any further help. It was now Tuesday afternoon. The celebration in San Francisco was history. The talk turned once again to work, upcoming films, and plans for the rest of the week.

On Wednesday morning, a sober but suffering Maude Delmont awoke in her room at the Saint Francis. She washed, dressed, and then made her way down the hall to see how Virginia was. She was horrified to find that Virginia was even worse, moaning and clutching her abdomen. Hurriedly, she called for the hotel doctor. The physician, M. E. Rumwell, rushed over to the hotel and examined Virginia. He failed to find any obvious source for her pain and prescribed a sedative, promising to return if needed. Maude spent the remainder of the day nursing her hangover, catching catnaps, and checking periodically on the pathetic figure lying doubled-up on the bed and writhing in agony. Virginia was still in Arbuckle's bathrobe, her torn clothing piled in a heap on a nearby chair. The day went by, and that night Maude slept quietly as Virginia lapsed in and out of consciousness.

On Thursday morning, Maude and Dr. Rumwell decided Virginia needed to be in a hospital. But no real hospital was nearby, and they both felt it was important to make as little fuss over the situation as possible. Instead, they took her to a small office-sanatorium at 1065 Bush Street, just a few blocks away.[14] It was run by a doctor, W. Francis B. Wakefield, whose practice was reputed to include the termination of unwanted pregnancies. There, Virginia Rappe was diagnosed as suffering from "systemic upset from alcohol poisoning."[15]

The diagnosis was incorrect. The next day, Friday, September 9, Virginia died. An autopsy, conducted by Dr. Shelby Strange later that day, found that the immediate cause of death was "peritonitis, the result of a rupture caused by an extreme amount of external force."[16]

Before the day was out, Roscoe "Fatty" Arbuckle was charged by the San Francisco district attorney's office with murder. The penalty for murder in California at the time was the gas chamber.

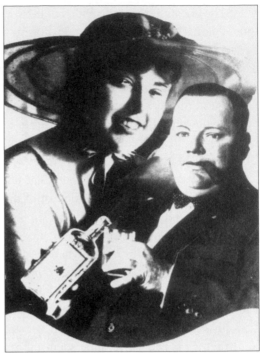

A Hearst mock-up of Rappe and Roscoe, seeming to share a bottle of whiskey. *San Francisco Examiner*

The assistant district attorney, Milton U. Ren, stated to the press that "the evidence of the various witnesses clearly indicated that a felony was committed and was the super-inducing cause of the injury that ended in the girl's death."[17]

The witnesses and their testimony were scarcely consistent, but taken as a whole, they were certainly inflammatory.

One of the revelers reported that Roscoe was heard to say, "I've been trying to get you for five years," that he then disappeared into the bathroom where Virginia was and slammed the door, and that fifteen minutes of silence ensued.[18]

Zey Prevon, another guest in the suite, stated, "When I walked into the room, Virginia was writhing on the floor, and in pain, and she said to me, 'He killed me. Arbuckle did it.'"[19]

The nurse who cared for Virginia at the Wakefield Sanatorium, Mrs. Jean Jamison, stated that her last words were, "Get Roscoe. Follow this up to the end."[20]

A second autopsy reported "bruises on the body, thighs and shins and fingermarks on Virginia's upper right arm."[21]

A bewildered Roscoe Arbuckle returned to San Francisco with his attorney, Frank Dominguez. He was greeted with bold-faced head-

GIRL WHO DIED AFTER BOOZE PARTY

Miss Virginia Rappe, beautiful movie actress of Los Angeles, who died Friday at a hospital here, af g taken ill in apartments of Roscoe "Fatty" Arbuckle, at the St. Francis. The center picture is a portr e girl; the other pictures show her in characters she played in film comedies.

A romantized pictorial of "Miss Rappe, beautiful movie actress of Los Angeles." *San Francisco Examiner*

lines that screamed "Arbuckle is Charged with Murder of Girl" and "Arbuckle Booze Party Kills Actress." The press, both in San Francisco and the nation generally, was having a field day. The Hearst papers, leading the way, would eventually come out with up to eight editions a day to keep an eager public satisfied.

Nattily dressed in dark-green golf pants and tan shoes, Arbuckle reported to city hall and surrendered. On the advice of counsel, he refused to make a statement. He was placed under arrest and put in the city jail.

The sympathy of the city and the nation seemed to be entirely with the dead woman, while Arbuckle was roundly condemned as the villainous lecher responsible for her death. Virginia Rappe was the "beautiful film actress, a leading woman in films who was noted in the film colony for the richness of her taste in clothes." She was "the best dressed woman in movies" and "a woman of financial means because of investments in Texas oil."[22]

Henry Lehman, a sometime movie director, surfaced at a press conference in New York claiming to be Virginia Rappe's fiancee. He announced that if Arbuckle was acquitted he, Lehman, would kill Arbuckle. "Arbuckle is the result of too much ignorance and too much money. There are some people who are a disgrace to the film industry...people who resort to cocaine and opium and indulge in orgies of the lowest character. You know what the death of Virginia meant to me. Her last words were to punish Arbuckle, that he outraged her. She died game, like a real woman."[23] Six months later, Lehman would assuage his grief by marrying Follies beauty Jocelyn Leigh.

Reporting on Virginia Rappe's funeral, the Hearst papers were almost poetic on the subject of the departed. "Little Virginia Rappe...whose up-to-the minute clothes have been the admiration and the envy of thousands, wears today the oldest known garment in the world. It is a shroud....The remains of the girl whose death has shocked the nation...wrapped in a winding sheet of white silk, a sheaf of dead white roses on her breast, her lips parted showing her pearly teeth...this dead girl, whose every impulse was said to have been wholesome and kindly...etc."[24]

It is likely, however, that Miss Rappe was not the vestal virgin the Hearst newspapers would have had its readers believe. One co-worker who knew her said later that "Virginia Rappe was one of those poor girls who came to Hollywood looking for a career and wound up being used more in the dressing room or in some executive's office than in front of the camera. At Sennet's place she spread syphilis all over the studio."[25]

It was widely rumored in Hollywood that Rappe had undergone a number of abortions. An even gamier rumor was that on the Sennet set she had infected so many of her co-workers with lice that Sennet closed down the studio and had it fumigated.

However, if the early reporting on the Rappe case was misleading, it should also be said that the rush to judgment on Arbuckle was also unfair. "Fatty" was almost uniformly portrayed in the media as a hard-drinking, lust-filled rapist whose perversions had driven him to murder. The Hearst papers reached all the way back to ancient Rome for a comparable example of outrageous behavior:

"Will anyone remember another dead Virginia who lay in state in the Forum of Rome? The Virginia slain by the hand of her own father to save her from the rapacious embrace of the licentious Claudius? Will any pause and recall that the death of Virginia was the means of ending the corrupt saturnalia of Rome, which is said to have no parallel until the present day?"[26]

A *San Francisco Examiner* drawing portrayed Arbuckle at the center of a spider web, holding two bottles of liquor, with the web ensnaring the seven women who had been guests in the suite. It was captioned, "They Walked into his Parlor."[27] Even the staid *New York Times* bannered one story with the headline, "Arbuckle Dragged Rappe Girl to Room."[28]

The effect on "Fatty" Arbuckle's status as a movie star was immediate and corrosive. Overnight, he became a pariah. "Arbuckle Film Withdrawn at Two Theatres"[29] was the heading of an article in the *San Francisco Examiner* just one day after Virginia Rappe died, as the New Fillmore and the New Mission theaters both announced a policy of never showing Arbuckle's films. This was just the beginning. Before the week was out, theaters all across America were pulling Arbuckle's films. The *New York Times* reported that, in the theaters still showing "Fatty's" pictures, audiences were hissing when he appeared on screen. Kansas state censorship officials urged that Arbuckle films be banned throughout the state. The Proctor chain announced the permanent banning of all Arbuckle films from its theaters.

The most bizarre incident of anti-Arbuckle sentiment came from Thermopolis, Wyoming, where a theater manager claimed that 150 townspeople had stormed his movie house, shot up the screen when Arbuckle's picture appeared, seized the reel of film, taken it to the street, and burned it. The incident was later denied, but the story became headline news across the country. Adolph Zukar, the head of Paramount, announced that whatever pictures Arbuckle was scheduled to make would be tailored to the talents of other actors. The movie career of "Fatty" Arbuckle was in shambles.

The district attorney of San Francisco was an ambitious lawyer named Matthew Brady. Brady was out of town when the scandal broke, but when he realized the magnitude of the event, he rushed back to the city and took over the case personally, granting interviews, making pronouncements, and outlining the strategy of the prosecution. It was Brady who announced that an indictment of murder would be sought.

A grand jury called to determine the charges was convened on Monday, September 12, and although testimony was secret, it was clear that some witnesses had changed their testimony and that others had simply disappeared. An outraged Brady threatened to bring perjury charges and went public with his accusations. Two days later, the grand jury returned a preliminary indictment of manslaughter rather than murder. Brady was apoplectic. Brady had, however, succeeded in obtaining a murder charge against Arbuckle in the San Francisco courts, and he urged

A fanciful portrayal of Arbuckle as a spider catching women in his web. *San Francisco Examiner*

the members of the grand jury to "return to the jury room and reach another decision tonight. Do not make a farce of this investigation."[30] Brady's persistence seemed to be carrying the day, and later in the week, on September 17, the *Examiner* carried a banner headline on its front page reading, "Arbuckle will be Tried For Murder."[31]

The final decision on the conflict between the San Francisco court and the grand jury was settled by Judge Sylvian Lazarus. She ruled that the charge would be manslaughter and she set the trial date for November 7.

The assault on Arbuckle's reputation and career continued, as theater owners and theater goers vented their outrage. In Chicago, two firms operating motion picture houses canceled all Arbuckle films and announced that "said pictures of the comedian will be laid on the shelf."[32] The mayor of Bedford, Massachusetts, ordered all movie houses to cease showing Arbuckle films. Sid Grauman, owner of the largest theater in Southern California, ceased an Arbuckle film in mid-screening. At the Arbuckle home in Los Angeles, there were daily deliveries of hate mail and numerous threatening phone calls. Tourists, instead of stopping to admire and photograph the home of the great Keystone star, now pelted the house with rocks and yelled obscenities.

The decision to try Arbuckle for manslaughter disturbed not only the district attorney's office, but also much of the citizenry. The Women's Vigilance Committee was especially upset. A San Francisco institution devoted to preserving the public morality, the Women's Vigilance Committee appointed an eighteen-member task force to monitor the Arbuckle trial and see that justice was done. During the trials, members would stand on the courthouse steps and yell, "Do your duty!" as the jurors arrived.[33]

After one postponement, the trial finally got underway in mid-November. Reporters from all over the world massed in San Francisco. Everyone involved in the trial was an automatic celebrity. Anyone acquainted with the principals seemed good for an interview or a pronouncement. In a total breech of protocol, the empanelled jury, consisting of eight men and four women, sat for a formal portrait which appeared in the *Examiner*, with each juror carefully identified by name, street address, and occupation.[34]

The trial itself was filled with all the lurid details the press and the public had hoped for. Numerous witnesses recounted the event of the fateful Sunday, often with conflicting recollections. The coroner reported his conclusion that Virginia Rappe's death was due to "application of external force." As the days dragged on, the testimony heated up. Nurse Jean Jamison testified that Virginia had whispered to her that she did indeed have syphilis and that it had been the gift of a certain unnamed

Hollywood director. Doctors then testified that this was a disease that could cause a bladder to burst. A chart of Virginia's inner workings was introduced into evidence and physicians conjectured on their significance.

The highlight of the trial, quite naturally, was Roscoe Arbuckle's own testimony. With his estranged, but still loyal, wife at his side, Arbuckle had sat impassively through the early phases of the trial. But now emotion in the court reached its peak as Arbuckle took the stand. Calmly and deliberately, he told how he had found Virginia Rappe in pain in the bathroom, how he assisted her into the adjoining bedroom and got her in bed, how he returned moments later to find her on the floor, how he had gone into the next room and sought aid, and how he had tried to ease her pain. The interchange that followed, between Leo Friedman, the prosecuting attorney, and Arbuckle, is revealing:

Friedman: Mr. Arbuckle, the fairy tale you just told the court. Had you told anyone else that story before this morning?

Arbuckle: Yes sir. Mr. Dominguez and Mr. McNab, my two attorneys.

Friedman: Weren't there several other stories you told friends and others as to what happened in that bedroom?

Arbuckle: No sir.

Friedman: Would it surprise you to know I have seven versions of the story you just related to the court, told to different people by you?

Arbuckle: There was just one true story of what happened. I just told you that...

Friedman: Virginia Rappe had a few drinks and you lusted after her. You pulled her into the bedroom, locked the door, threw her on the bed despite her protestations, tore some of her clothes off and raped her and Lord knows what other perversions you practiced on a helpless girl who was at your mercy. When you tore her insides out and she screamed for mercy you callously said you'd throw her out the window if she didn't shut up. That's the true story, isn't it, Mr. Arbuckle?

Arbuckle: No sir, is isn't.

Friedman: Then what is the true story? What did you mean when you told several friends that you shoved ice into Virginia Rappe's vagina?

Arbuckle: I never said that.[35]

Arbuckle on
the witness stand,
proclaiming his
innocence.

A parade of witnesses followed, but the central question was already before the jury: Which version would they believe? The trial droned on until early December, and it finally went to the jury after prosecutor Friedman in his summation portrayed Arbuckle as an inhuman monster preying on an innocent, young girl.

After two days of deliberation, the jury announced that it was hopelessly deadlocked. The vote was ten to two for acquittal. District Attorney Brady immediately announced that he would seek a new trial.

"Fatty" returned to Southern California, a depressed and beaten man. He had expected to be cleared of the charges, and even though the majority of jurors had voted for acquittal, he felt defeated. With the exception of Charlie Chaplin and Buster Keaton, he had been abandoned by his friends and his career had all but evaporated. The press continued to flay him and he dreaded the prospect of another trial.

It was a subdued Arbuckle who re-entered the San Francisco courtroom in January of 1922. The second trial was essentially a replay of the events of November, with a few notable exceptions. Several of the witnesses for the prosecution gave altered versions of their earlier testimony, now more favorable to Arbuckle. Gavin McNab, the Arbuckle attorney, seemed oddly distracted during the trial, and he even took time off during the proceeding in order to travel to Nevada to assist movie star Mary Pickford in some divorce proceedings. McNab also made a cardinal error in not putting Arbuckle on the witness stand—in the belief that, because his earlier testimony had already been read into the record, it would be redundant. Even more disastrously, he failed to make a summation to the jury, believing that the prosecution's case had been so weak that a defense summation was unnecessary.

The jury completely misunderstood both Arbuckle's failure to testify and McNab's failure to make a closing argument. McNab thought these decisions would be taken as expressions of confidence on the part of the defense. The jury assumed them to be expressions of guilt. However, after six hours of deliberation, they announced that they could not arrive at a clear verdict, although the vote had now been ten to two for conviction.[36] Brady, encouraged by this turn-around in the jury vote, announced that he would seek a third trial.

Arbuckle was devastated. He knew the additional damage to his reputation would be immense, and he was right. By now, the cancellation of "Fatty" films was epidemic. Arbuckle was banned from all screens in New York, Michigan, Chicago, Philadelphia, Portland, Pittsburgh, Buffalo, Massachusetts, Missouri, and Kansas—all in response to the growing public perception that Arbuckle was guilty.

The third trial began on March 13, 1922. This time, Arbuckle's defense team took nothing for granted. It put Roscoe on the stand for four hours. It savagely attacked all the prosecution witnesses with telling effect. It pulled out all the stops in soiling the reputation of Virginia Rappe, detailing her sex life, her abortions, her medical history, and her reputation for tearing off her clothes at the slightest provocation. It even brought before the jury Miss Rappe's bladder, encased in a jar of preservative. A succession of doctors described the organ as diseased, distended, inflamed, and cystitic, as well as prone to self-rupture. Attorney McNab's final oration to the jury was eloquent and persuasive.

After just five minutes of deliberation, the verdict was unanimous. Roscoe Arbuckle was found not guilty. The jury was, in fact, so persuaded of his innocence that it presented the judge with the following statement:

> "Acquittal is not enough for Roscoe Arbuckle. We feel that a great injustice has been done him. We also feel that it is our duty to give him his exoneration, under the evidence, for there was not the slightest proof adduced to connect him in any way with the commission of crime. We wish him success, and hope that the American people will take the judgement that Roscoe Arbuckle is entirely innocent and free from all blame."[37]

Arbuckle poses with the jury that acquited him

Arbuckle returned to Los Angeles, assuming that he would be able to pick up the threads of his life and to resume his career in motion pictures. However, a transformation had occurred in Hollywood during the Arbuckle trials. Fearful of the public's reaction to the morals of movie people and to the life portrayed in some Hollywood films, the industry had established a board to regulate the standards of all movies and the morals of the studios and their stars. Will Hays, who had been the post-master general in President Harding's administration, was hired at an annual salary of $100,000 to police the industry. All performers' contracts were now to include a morals clause. It was forbidden for an actor and an actress in films to appear in bed together, even if they were man and wife. Women could not show any part of the leg above the knee. Kisses could not last more than seven feet of film. Only villains and seductresses could smoke.

In keeping with the new high standards of motion picture morality, Will Hays, on April 18, 1922, banned Roscoe Arbuckle from acting in motion pictures.[38]

"Fatty" in a studio shot with child star Jackie Coogan.

The seeming injustice of this dictum was generally recognized in Hollywood, but the decision was hailed in many quarters of the country, as ministers and ladies' groups in particular gave it wide support. The *New York Times* was one of many newspapers that saluted Arbuckle's banishment, applauding the fact that "fellows of the baser sort will not have the opportunity to disease themselves and the rest of us by applauding the man the jury pronounced 'not guilty.' "[39]

The years that followed saw Roscoe Arbuckle undertake a variety of jobs, all capitalizing on his now-soiled celebrity, and all designed to rehabilitate his reputation. He made a number of tours in his old role of vaudevillian, usually to appreciative audiences. He directed some comedy films under an assumed name. He opened a nightclub and acted both as host and entertainer. But the industry and the public were slow to forgive.

Arbuckle's legal fees as a result of the three trials exceeded $700,000, a sum so enormous that that was no real prospect of his ever paying it off. When he died in his sleep at the age of forty-six, the first "million-dollar movie star" left an estate of less than $2,000.[40]

The tragedy of Roscoe "Fatty" Arbuckle's life is that he is remembered in the public mind, not as the world's first great film comedian, but as the villain who, through an act of sexual perversion, caused the death of a beautiful young movie actress.

Was it really manslaughter—or even murder? For many that question still lingers. Years later, Arbuckle's wife, Minta, in an interview with author Stuart Oderman, recalled a statement by her husband that sheds additional light on the subject—and could even be interpreted as a confession.

"I'd have been diseased if I had sex with her, right? I'd have gotten what some other guys at Sennet got. How would that have looked to the jury in San Francisco if I'd come down with syphilis or gonorrhea? I would have been guilty. I did put ice on her, but the evidence *melted*. That's why there was no basis for a trial. The evidence *melted*." [41]

Chapter Ten

Mr. Schwartz, Mr. Warren and Mr. Barbe—1925

Criminologists and students of homicide have long been fasci-nated by the idea of the "perfect" crime—a murder in which there is no chance that the perpetrator will ever be caught. There is little doubt that many such crimes have taken place in San Francisco's Bay Area. If, for instance, the estimate of some 1,200 murders in the city during its first two decades is accurate—and history shows there was only one success-ful prosecution for murder over that period—it might be assumed that there were a great many perfect crimes in the city's early history.

But the preferred definition of the "perfect crime" is one that suc-ceeds through the cleverness of the murderer and not through the incom-petence of the authorities. To be sure, we know only of the "perfect crimes" that failed—such as the celebrated Leopold and Loeb case in Chicago or the case of Dr. Kel in Lodi, California, who in 1925 killed and incin-erated a tramp, disguised the body as his own, and then saw that it was given an elaborate funeral. The deception failed when Dr. Kel inexplica-bly neglected to flee the area and was promptly recognized by his friends.

Just a year later, there was another noteworthy attempt at a "per-fect crime." It is historic for a number of reasons—the elaborateness of its planning, the nearness of its success, and the early use of scientific methods to solve it. It is also an early example of how police depart-

*ments of different cities—in this case, Walnut Creek, Berkeley and Oak-
land—can work together to prevent such a crime from succeeding.*

There are three names—Schwartz, Warren and Barbe—that will
forever be associated with one of the most bizarre and bewildering crimes
in the history of the Bay Area. From the time it first came to public
attention on August 7, 1925, until its dramatic conclusion nine days later,
the police, the press, and the public abounded in theories and wallowed
in confusion. Even to this day, there is uncertainty and debate as to many
of the details of the case. One thing was certain: The extraordinary personalities involved were what made it so memorable.

Charles Henri Schwartz was a respected chemical engineer and the
founder and principal owner of the Pacific Cellulose Company, a business
pioneering in the manufacture of artificial silk. His investors included a
number of prominent and monied citizens in Northern California. Schwartz
resided in the university city of Berkeley, directly across the Bay from San
Francisco, where he lived with his attractive wife, Alice, and their three
young sons. The offices and factory of Pacific Cellulose were located in
the town of Walnut Creek, just a short drive from the Schwartz residence,
and Schwartz himself had recently announced to his associates that his
work on the formula for artificial silk was nearing completion and that
production would soon begin. Schwartz was thirty-six years old, short,
somewhat stocky, and carried himself with what was described as a "military air." He had a full head of brown hair tinged with gray and a carefully
trimmed moustache. He was generally regarded as "handsome."[1]

Harold Warren first appeared in Berkeley in 1923. A clean-shaven
bachelor in his mid-thirties, he was known to his friends and acquaintances
as a successful construction engineer. Warren was something of a man of
mystery and seldom talked about his past or his place of origin. He was
known to be a great "admirer of the ladies," although his behavior was believed to be entirely circumspect toward the wives of his friends. One of his
closest friends was Charles W. Heywood, owner of the Nottingham Apartments on 41st Street, not far from the Santa Fe station in northern Oakland.
Harold Warren had, in fact, recently arranged to lease one of the Nottingham
units so that he could live closer to Mr. and Mrs. Heywood, whose company
he enjoyed. Warren was known to the Heywoods and their friends as a great
wit and storyteller, and they eagerly anticipated his arrival.[2]

Gilbert W. Barbe was a deeply religious man who was devoting his
mature years to spreading Christ's word and the conversion of souls to
Christianity. Now fifty years old, Barbe had come to his religious fervor

Charles Henry Schwartz, chemical engineer, entrepreneur and the inventor of "artificial silk." *Oakland Tribune*

due to his experiences in the first World War, where he saw death and suffering first hand. Some, in fact, described him as "a shell-shocked war veteran."[3] Although Barbe had been raised and educated in the East, he had spent his recent years in California, wandering about the state as an itinerant preacher. In the summer of 1925, he was living in Los Gatos, an hour's drive south of San Francisco, searching for work in the orchards and farmlands of the area and trying to spread the Gospel to all who would listen. In mid-July, he was on his way to Walnut Creek in search of promised employment and more souls to save.

On July 30, 1925, the paths of these three singular personalities converged in a way that would transfix and confound the Bay Area. The *Oakland Tribune* described this event in florid detail under the headline, "Chemist Dies in Explosion of Invention":

"Within a few hours after he had completed a process for the manufacture of artificial silk, Charles Henri Schwartz, prominent Oakland chemist and general manager of the Pacific Cellulose Company, by a queer twist of fate was killed when the formula he had apparently perfected exploded in his laboratory at the company's plant at Walnut Creek.

After a 12-hour investigation of the explosion, during which they questioned numerous persons and eliminated theories of possible suicide and murder, Contra County officials reached the conclusion that the chemist's death last night was accidental.

Schwartz was killed by his own invention, and his secret formula which he predicted would revolutionize the artificial silk industry will probably never be known as the blast left no trace in the laboratory.

The blast, which wrecked a portion of the company's plant and burned the chemist's body almost beyond recognition, came five minutes after he telephoned his wife. The explosion occurred at about 10 o'clock last night. The body will be shipped to Oakland where it will be cremated. Services will be held tomorrow at 2 o'clock."[4]

On the night of the explosion, the plant watchman was on his way to the plant from one of the outbuildings when the blast occurred. It lit up the night sky, blowing the main door out into the yard. The watchman grabbed a fire extinguisher and plunged into the blazing inferno. He called out for Schwartz but received no reply. The fire became so intense that he then fled, rushed to a nearby telephone and called the fire department. Within ten minutes, the fireman arrived and put out the flames.

The fire had done considerable damage to the building. Although the windows remained intact, the paint on the walls had been scorched and much of the furniture was charred. Still smoldering beneath two benches was a charred bundle of fabrics that contained the body, almost completely burned except for the top of its head and its feet. The face looked like a blackened skull, with the skin shrunken back to reveal white teeth forming a hideous grin.

The coroner was soon on hand, and he noted the details of the position of the corpse: knees drawn up tightly to the body, one arm pointing up awkwardly into the air. Under the body were the remnants of a blanket. Some of Schwartz's cards and keys had survived the heat. His pocket watch and chain lay across one shoulder.

Mrs. Schwartz was the next to arrive. She was shown the charred corpse, illuminated only by a fireman's flashlight. "That's him," she screamed. "That's him!"[5]

This apparently eased the last doubts of the coroner, who then proclaimed it to be the body of Charles Schwartz. He ordered the corpse removed and taken to the morgue. Mrs. Schwartz quickly regained her

The Schwartz family. Was Alice his wife or widow? Or, as the *Oakland Post-Enquirer* asked, were they "the bereaved family or the plotter's kin?"

Bereaved, or Plotter's Kin?

The wife, or widow, of Charles Henry Schwartz, with his children. Left to right, Clifford, 4, Ralph, 2, and Gordon, 3.

composure and calmly requested that the body be cremated at the earliest opportunity, so that she would not have to suffer continuing thoughts about her husband's unfortunate condition. She was informed the cremation would probably take place on Thursday after the necessary formalities had taken place. Mrs. Schwartz was driven back to her home and her children at 2:00 A.M. Friday morning.

Two hours later, at 4:00 A.M., Harold Warren, the construction engineer, arrived at the Nottingham Apartments and awakened his friend, Mr. Heywood, the owner. He apologized for his untimely arrival, explaining that he had been in an automobile accident and that, rather than setting out for his residence which was some distance away, he decided to claim the apartment for which he had previously arranged. Heywood was very understanding, especially when he noted that Warren was limping as a result of the accident. Warren then explained that he had not notified the police, because he had liquor in his car, and because prohibition was in force, he feared that he would be liable for prosecution. The two men

A reporter examines the crime room. The position of the body, here outlined in white, was one of the things that aroused suspicion. *Oakland Post-Enquirer.*

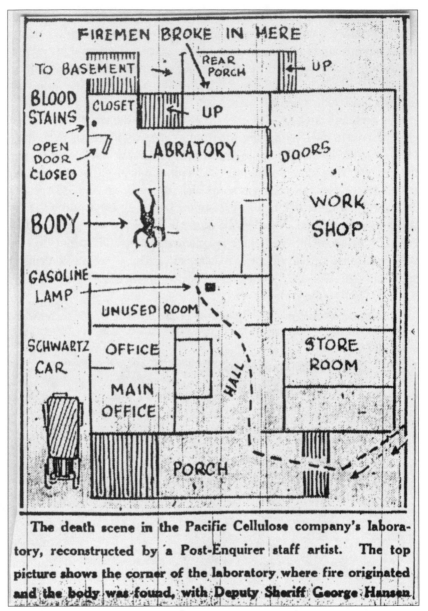

The death scene in the Pacific Cellulose company's laboratory, reconstructed by a Post-Enquirer staff artist. The top picture shows the corner of the laboratory where fire originated and the body was found, with Deputy Sheriff George Hansen

The death scene in the laboratory of the Pacific Cellulose plant, as sketched by the *Oakland Post-Enquirer*..

shared a laugh about the follies of prohibition, and Heywood showed Warren to his suite. Warren explained that he would send for his clothes and effects the next day. Heywood wished his friend good night and retired for what remained of the night.

The following morning, the Schwartz family physician, Dr. Alfred H. Reudy, and a close friend of Schwartz, Mr. Edward Domballe, viewed the charred remains. Both proclaimed it to be "without a doubt the remains of Charles Schwartz."[6] As if that were not sufficient confirmation, Schwartz's attorney, A. S. Bell, announced in a separate statement that "the corpse now lying in the little white morgue at Walnut Creek is Charles Henri Schwartz."[7]

However, it wasn't long before doubts began to set in. One of the first skeptics was Guy Spencer, the deputy state fire warden. When Spencer entered the basement of the fire-damaged building the next day, he was surprised to find blood stains on part of the ceiling above. Further examination showed them to be coming from a closet opening off the laboratory, some distance from where the body had been found. There on the floor was an unexplained pool of relatively fresh blood. He searched in vain for an explanation.

Another doubter was Deputy District Attorney James F. Hoey. The moment Hoey walked into the burned-out laboratory, he felt something was wrong. It made no sense to him that the body had been so seriously burned while the rest of the room was only lightly charred. He returned to his office and immediately contacted a man he knew who could give him a proper picture of what had happened in the laboratory; this was Professor Edward O. Heinrich, a consulting expert in legal chemistry and a famed Berkeley criminologist.

Heinrich was an experienced hand at analyzing crime scenes and arson sites. He knew how to "read" fires and how to reconstruct how they had started and how they had burned. Within hours, Heinrich was prowling the laboratory, searching for answers. They came quickly and surely.

Outside the door to the laboratory, Heinrich found a scorch mark that clearly showed that the fire had started at that location. This was corroborated by a fan-shaped burn on the floor just inside the door. He then found a small puddle of unburned benzine in a depression in the metal door sill. Clearly, this fire had been intentionally started from *outside* the laboratory. Next, he studied the intensity of the damage inside the room. He noted that the portion of the floor where the body had been found was the most severely burned, while a cabinet just a few feet away was virtually untouched. His study of the contents of the laboratory revealed no chemicals sufficiently inflammable to have caused the severe damage to the site where the body was found.

Heinrich analyzed the blood in the closet and determined it to have been discolored by the fumes of the explosion. This meant the blood was there before the blast. On the floor near a workbench, Heinrich found marks showing that a chair had been positioned there at the time of the blast. He also detected specks of blood on some nearby shelves.

Professor Heinrich drew these conclusions: The deceased had been earlier attacked as he sat in a chair, probably with a blow or blows to the head. The body had been stored for a while in the closet, then dragged out, saturated with benzine, and burned prior to the explosion. The explosion itself had been created by a fire from the outside. This was clearly a crime scene, with both murder and arson involved.[8]

At the Nottingham Apartments, Harold Warren read the story of the explosion and the subsequent events with great interest. He seemed to enjoy discussing it with his host and friend, Charles Heywood. Together with Heywood's attractive wife, Elizabeth, Warren speculated on the true nature of the event, agreeing that a crime was certainly involved.

Warren's leg was still bothering him and so he seldom left the house, preferring to remain sedentary while his leg healed. To pass the time, Warren and Heywood played cribbage. Warren exhibited remarkable skill and usually wound up the winner. During this time, he professed an eagerness to regain his health and get on with his life. In the meantime, he continued to amuse the Heywoods with his repertoire of stories and anecdotes. Eventually, the Heywoods convinced Warren that he should join them the next night at a surprise party that had been arranged for their daughter, Marjorie. Warren agreed and quickly became the life of the party, offering toasts to the young lady and leading a "Grand March" about the premises.[9]

In the meantime, Mrs. Schwartz was doing her best to have her husband's body cremated. Her demand for the release of the corpse, however, was frustrated by the coroner's decision to conduct a full autopsy. The Schwartzes' attorney then made the bizarre request that only the head of the body he preserved. The district attorney decided otherwise, stating, "The whole body will be placed in cold storage."[10]

The autopsy that followed was something of a shocker. Among the findings: Death was the result of two severe blows to the head. The other findings were no less startling. The corpse was that of a man between fifty and sixty years of age. The man had been dead between two to twenty-four hours before the explosion. The fingerprints had been blurred by acid burns. The eyeballs had been punctured in an attempt to conceal the color of the iris. Two teeth of the corpse had been knocked out after

Famed criminologist Dr. E. O. Heinrich renders his verdict after examining the evidence: It is not Schwartz's body. *Oakland Post-Enquirer*

death to correspond with teeth known to have been missing on Schwartz. There were no contents in the stomach conforming to the dinner Schwartz was known to have consumed the evening of the blast.

The final conclusion was clear: This was not the corpse of Charles Henri Schwartz, but that of a person unknown.

Mrs. Schwartz and the family doctor, Reudy, were having none of it. This was a murder, they agreed, but they were adamant that the murdered man was Schwartz.

Said Mrs. Schwartz, "Of course, it is my husband! I must see justice done. They say he isn't my husband. That makes me so mad!"[11]

The doctor was equally sure. "There are certain peculiarities of his physical contour of which I have knowledge. There is no doubt in the world in my mind but that it is Schwartz."[12]

At this point, family attorney Ray came up with a novel solution to determine whether or not the corpse was Schwartz. Schwartz was known to have unusually small hands and feet, so Ray suggested making a plaster cast of the feet of the corpse to see if Schwartz's shoes fit. The coroner doomed the suggestion with silence.

But now, the public image of Charles Schwartz as a chemical genius on the brink of a great discovery and as a loving husband and family man was beginning to tarnish, as investigators and reporters eagerly searched his background. In fact, they soon determined that Schwartz was not at all

A comparison of Schwartz's profile with that of the burned corpse showed some marked differences. *Oakland Post-Enquirer*

Mrs. Schwartz was the first person to identify the body as her husband's—and the last to admit that it wasn't.
Oakland Tribune

what he seemed to be. His original name was Leon Henry Schwartzhof, and he was born of Alsatian parents in Colmar, France, in 1887. His early life is unchronicled, but he claimed to have been brilliantly educated, acquiring degrees from a number of universities in both France and Germany, including a doctorate in chemistry from the University of Heidelberg. When inquiries were made at these universities, authorities were unable to find his name in their records. Schwartzhof also reportedly served as an officer in the French army and put in two years with the Red Cross in Morocco. It was during this time that he changed his name to Charles Henri Schwartz. His personal effects, examined by the Walnut Creek authorities, included a chemical degree from the French College of Chemistry. Inquiry revealed that no such institution existed.

While still in his early thirties, Schwartz had secured a job with a textile firm in England, and there he married a war widow named Alice Warden. During his stay in England, Schwartz developed a severe case of asthma and decided to move to California for his health. In 1920, he arrived with his wife and their two sons in Berkeley, directly across the Bay from San Francisco. He secured employment as chief chemist with the California Fibre Company, an organization devoted to manufacturing automobile tires made of Chinese grass. Quite naturally, the company failed, and Schwartz was subsequently accused of looting the company of some of its machinery and scrap iron. He responded by threatening the life of one of the other managers and was forced by police to surrender a revolver that he carried. It was at about this time that Schwartz began talking about people being "after" him—summoning up the specter of "evil enemies" who were trying to steal his valuable chemical formulas.[13]

Undaunted by early failures, in late 1925, Schwartz founded the Pacific Cellulose Company. His new company, he announced grandly, would manufacture inexpensive artificial silk made from wood fibre. He was, he reported, close to perfecting the formula that would make this possible—a formula to which he had devoted most of his life. This was an era of rapid, sometimes startling, manufacturing development as well as a time of ready money. Schwartz's new company seemed to have little trouble finding investors. Among them was his wife, who put all of her remaining inheritance into company stock. In return, Schwartz put her on the board of directors and made her treasurer of the company.

Schwartz purchased a frame building in Walnut Creek from a failed glove manufacturer, proclaimed it his laboratory and plant, and began purchasing equipment. For the next several years, he spent his time hiring and firing a small number of employees, drawing a generous salary, and "perfecting his formula."[14]

Eventually, Schwartz's shareholders grew restive, and Schwartz responded by announcing that his formula was on the brink of completion and that the company would soon be in production. The laboratory itself, which had always been off-grounds to visitors, was now partially opened so that he could be seen energetically stirring a large cauldron filled with a mysterious liquid. In early July, he purchased a roll of very expensive silk. When challenged as to the reason for this purchase, he replied that he needed it to compare his own future product with the best silk available.

Schwartz's love life was almost as perplexing as his business life. He was often seen in the company of attractive young women who called him by various names not his own. Frequently, when they discovered he was married and had a family, they would contact Mrs. Schwartz, who, in turn, would extract expressions of regret and pledges of future fidelity from her husband. The most flagrant of these infidelities had gone public just weeks before the explosion at the plant.

In mid-April, Schwartz was introduced by mutual friends to a Miss Elizabeth Adam, an attractive lady some fifteen years his junior. An apparently torrid love affair ensued that included money and gifts to Miss Adam, as well as journeys to San Jose for trysts. Schwartz was known to this young lady as Mr. Stein, and on one occasion he presented her with an engagement ring, saying they would marry at the earliest opportunity. When she finally realized that her Mr. Stein was, in fact, a married man named Schwartz, she took action. She filed a $75,000 breach of promise suit in the Oakland county court. Just one week before the laboratory explosion, Schwartz was in court, denying everything and claiming that Miss Adam had stolen money from him.[15]

This was not the only unsettling activity Schwartz was involved in during the weeks prior to the explosion. He also began taking out insurance policies on his own life. The policies eventually totaled $190,000 and they named Pacific Cellulose and his wife as beneficiaries. A number of the policies had a clause for double indemnity in case of accidental death.

Schwartz also performed several other curious acts in that final week. It was revealed by his dentist that Schwartz had called to see if any molds or casts of his teeth or his dental bridge still existed. Schwartz seemed relieved to learn that there were none. He also wrote lengthy letters to his wife and to his attorney, which were to be opened only in the event of his death. In these, he stated that he felt constantly in danger from his "enemies," who wanted to steal his secret formula, and he expressed concern for his safety because of the necessity of his working with dangerous and potentially explosive chemicals.[16] With the unsavory facts of Schwartz's

Miss Elizabeth Adam, Schwartz's "fiancée," who sued him for $75,000 for breach of promise. *Oakland Post-Enquirer*

personal life now exposed and with the damning conclusion of the autopsy on the burned body released—it was now clear to all involved that Charles Schwartz was a murderer of a person yet unknown. This was clear to everyone except Mrs. Schwartz, that is, who clung desperately to her belief that the body was that of her husband. "The poor man," she insisted. "He lies murdered."[17]

Detectives went to the Schwartz home at 6101 Rock Ridge Boulevard seeking further clues. They were surprised to find it cleansed of any sign that Schwartz had lived there. All of his belongings, his photographs, and even his clothing were gone. Said Sheriff Veale, "Schwartz cleaned out the house. Anything that might be likely to aid in tracing him or learning his plans is gone."[18]

A statewide hunt was now underway for Schwartz. His photograph and vital statistics were published in newspapers throughout California. Reports came in to the authorities placing Schwartz almost everywhere— in a car traveling south, at the local airport, dining at a Los Angeles restaurant, and hitchhiking on a highway heading north. One report that could not be ignored, however, stated that he had been spotted boarding the freighter *Nordic*, en route to Astoria. A wireless to that ship ordered the captain to account for all passengers. He did…and no suspicious person was reported to be on board.

While all involved were wondering where Schwartz was, they were also wondering who it was that he had murdered. The body was charred beyond any hope of recognition, and no one had come forward reporting a possible missing person. The *Post-Inquirer* tried to be helpful by publishing a list of seven men reported missing in Bay Area communities over the past two weeks.[19] None of these seemed to fill the bill. However, the press finally settled on Joseph Rodriguez, a local laborer who had not been seen since the day of the explosion. He fitted the general description issued by the coroner, and his friends set up a clamor that he either be found or proclaimed to be the deceased. One newspaper was so certain it was Rodriguez that it identified the "closed automobile in which his body had been transported to the death scene."[20]

Back at the Nottingham Apartments, Harold Warren read the newspaper accounts about the case avidly, and he expressed his opinion that Mrs. Schwartz was probably the last sane person involved in the case. He was also certain, he said, that it was either Schwartz's body in the morgue or that he had been killed in some nefarious plot. Mrs. Heywood, his hostess, told him she had read that Schwartz had $1,000 on him when he was supposedly killed, and that the funds had not been found. Warren speculated that it had probably been stolen by the police. At cribbage that evening, he won once again from Mr. Heywood. At an informal dinner gathering later that night, Warren was the life of the party, entertaining both the Heywoods and their guests, Mr. and Mrs. N. B. Edmunds, Jr. The Edmundses became so fond of Warren that they invited him to join them at their home the following evening. Warren was most appreciative, but declined as his leg was still giving him some pain.

In Walnut Creek on August 4, the friends of Joe Rodriguez were preparing an elaborate wake for their friend. Their plans were put on permanent hold however, when Rodriguez casually walked in and announced that he had been in Oakland with his brother-in-law, enjoying a long weekend of drinking and movie-going. The search for the identity of the charred corpse went back to scratch.

Once again, it was master sleuth Heinrich who came up with the important clues. In his examination of the crime scene, he had found the burned remnants of a backpack of the kind typically used by hobos. On a bench near the body, he discovered some partially burned religious pamphlets. Studying them later, he found certain passages had been underlined. They included, "The twelve Jesus sent forth, and commanded them…go to the lost sheep of the house of Israel. And as ye go preach, saying the Kingdom of Heaven is at hand. Provide neither gold nor silver nor scrip for your journey"—and "Behold, I send you forth as sheep in the midst of wolves."[21] The more Heinrich reflected on these clues, the more certain he was as to what kind of person had been murdered: an itinerant preacher.

Once Heinrich's conclusion was made public, reports flooded in of missing preachers. The most promising came from an undertaker in Placerville, who said that his friend Gilbert W. Barbe was a traveling preacher who had been visiting ten days earlier and told him that he was on his way to Walnut Creek where he had secured a job in a plant. This was followed by a report from another man who said he had picked up a hitchhiker south of Sacramento who answered Barbe's description. The hitchhiker had told him that he was on his way to answer an ad seeking a plant assistant "with small hands and feet."[22] It was then learned that Barbe had a somewhat deformed right arm, which investigators thought might explain the unusual position of the right arm of the corpse when it was first discovered. Handwriting found on a short note at the murder scene was compared to Barbe's handwriting from a letter he had written to a family member. The handwriting matched. On August 9, the authorities announced their conclusion: The murdered man was Gilbert W. Barbe. and the murderer was Charles Henri Schwartz.

Everyone knew where Barbe was: He was in the morgue. But where was Schwartz? None of the tips from around the state had panned out. At one point, police surrounded a house in Berkeley where Schwartz had supposedly been spotted, but it turned out to be a false lead. Then, in a case that had more than its share of bizarre twists, there was still another baffling turn of events. A bank teller reported that a woman he recognized as Mrs. Schwartz had claimed a safety deposit box in the name Alice E. Orchard. When police investigated the incident, they found that the box had been opened originally by a Mr. H. Orchard and a Mrs. A. E. Orchard.[23] Handwriting on the application was clearly that of Mr. and Mrs. Charles Schwartz. To this day, no one knows what was in the box.

Handwriting on the letter found near the victim and on a letter written by an intinerant preacher reveals the body to be that of Gilbert W. Barbe. *San Francisco Examiner*

BLAST VICTIM IS IDENTIFIED

On the evening of Saturday, August 8, the Heywoods were enjoying a dinner party at the Edwards home when the discussion turned inevitably to the Schwartz murder case. It probably resembled the conversations that were taking place in thousands of other homes that evening throughout the Bay Area—until Mrs. Edwards brought out that evening's *Oakland Tribune*. On the front page was a full-face photograph of Charles Schwartz. Heywood stared at it in disbelief. He knew that face. Yet, somehow it looked different. The man in the photograph had a mustache. Slowly, he reached out with his hand and covered the lower part of the face. Staring back at him were the eyes of his friend and tenant, Harold Warren. He said nothing to his dinner companions.

Back at the Nottingham Apartments that night, Heywood began to have doubts. He knew several officers at the Berkeley police station, so he called and asked for a more complete description of the wanted man. What he heard confirmed his suspicions. Height: five feet, four inches; weight: 140 pounds; eyes: dark brown; hair: brown with gray streaks; carriage: military bearing. Heywood hung up the phone and pondered what to do. He went to bed, but sleep did not come. Finally, at about 2:00 A.M., Heywood called the Berkeley station and told them that Charles Schwartz was in residence at the Nottingham Apartments.

Within the hour, police were knocking at the Warren/Schwartz apartment demanding entry. They heard sounds of someone walking inside, but there was no other response. They tried to force the door, but it was too sturdy. They rushed around to a rear entrance and again demanded entry. Their efforts were interrupted by the sound of a gunshot. The police battered down the door and rushed in. They found Schwartz lying on a bed, a .32 revolver in his hand. He had fired one shot into his right eye. The bullet had passed through his brain and lodged in the wall behind. There were still signs of life, so police called an ambulance. However, on the way to the hospital, Charles Henri Schwartz was officially pronounced dead.[24]

In his bedroom, Schwartz had left a letter addressed to his wife. "I made a dirty job of it," he wrote. But other than that candid confession, the rest of the letter was entirely self-serving. In it, Schwartz claimed that he had no intention of committing such a crime until the affair with Elizabeth Adam came to a head. This is entirely unlikely, since the murder required long and elaborate planning. Schwartz also wrote that he killed Barbe "in self defense," and that only after Barbe's death did it occur to him to try to conceal the real series of events.[25] This claim is ridiculous. There is nothing in Barbe's history to indicate that he would ever attack anyone. Barbe was killed by two blows to the rear of his skull, hardly the way an attacker would be killed. And, certainly, there is no way that the extensive details of the cover-up could be executed in a brief period of time. In fact, it was determined that Schwartz had established his other persona as "Warren" as much as two years earlier.

Two other significant items were discovered in Schwartz's effects. One was a train ticket on the Santa Fe line from Oakland to Barstow, California, for 11:00 P.M. on the night of the murder.[26] This would indicate that Schwartz's first option had been to flee the area after the crime, but that something had made him miss his train, and staying at the Nottingham Apartments was his backup plan. Further inquiry by the authorities revealed that there had been a car accident on Tunnel Road,

A *Post-Enquirer* graphic of the climactic scene in the case, the Heywood apartment building where Schwartz killed himself.

between Walnut Creek and Oakland, the night of the murder. The driver of the car was never found. If the driver was Schwartz, it would explain his missing the train, his injured leg, and his early morning arrival at the Nottingham Apartments.

Two other items of interest found in his effects in the apartment were more ominous: the passport and the naturalization papers of his friend and landlord, Charles Heywood. When informed by police that these items had been stolen from him by Schwartz, Heywood remembered that during his stay Schwartz had suggested that the two of them should consider taking a driving vacation somewhere.[27] It is entirely possible that Schwartz was considering, as the next part of his escape plan, the murder of Heywood. This would have permitted Schwartz to adopt the persona of Charles Heywood and further confuse his pursuers.

A formal inquest into the entire affair was held on Thursday, August 13. A coroner's jury formally found that Charles Schwartz was guilty of the murder of Gilbert Barbe by means of a blow or blows to the head with a blunt instrument. It further found that Schwartz died of a self-inflicted gunshot wound. Mrs. Schwartz was present at the inquest at the request of the authorities. During the inquest, she admitted for the first time that the charred body was not her husband and that the second body taken from the Nottingham Apartments was, in fact, her late spouse. Her somewhat bizarre behavior continued, however. She stated blissfully, "He seems beautiful to me in death."[28] Sheriff R. R. Veale had the last word, stating "This closes the case."[29]

It did not, however, end all speculation. A number of questions remained. One concerned the degree of involvement on Mrs. Schwartz's part in the murder hoax. It is likely that she played some active role, perhaps even a major one. Her early stubborn refusal to admit that the charred body was not her husband defied all logic. It is probable that she at least participated in stripping the Schwartz home of its personal effects and pictures. Certainly, her husband had no time to accomplish this after the murder, and even if he did, it would have been impossible without Mrs. Schwartz's knowledge and cooperation. Even when it was necessary for her to give the police a description of her husband to aid in the manhunt, it is likely that she misled them. She stated that he had a noticeably drooping left eye.[30] Photographs of Schwartz show no such physical characteristic.

Why would Alice Schwartz involve herself in such a bizarre and risky scheme? The life insurance policies, of which she was the main beneficiary, probably provide the most logical motive. But with the exposure of the true nature of Schwartz's death, most of the insurance money evaporated. Of the $190,000 in insurance policy benefits, only $25,000 was not automatically invalidated by Schwartz's suicide, and that smaller policy would be contested in the courts for years to come.

What were Schwartz's motives for the murder and attempted cover-up? They were probably numerous. The pending lawsuit by Miss Adam. The pressure being put on him by the shareholders to begin plant production. His desperate need for money and the double indemnity nature of his insurance policies. A desire to simply disappear and take with him all his mounting problems as a failed lover and a fraudulent businessman.

Whatever his motives, there can be no doubt that Leon Henry Schwartzhof, alias Mr. Stein, alias Harold Warren, alias Henry Orchard alias Charles Henri Schwartz was a singularly complex individual. On August 14, 1925, Alice Schwartz, through her lawyer, made a final and telling gesture. She offered her husband's brain to the University of California for scientific research. The university was quick to decline the opportunity.

Chapter Eleven

The Vengeful Valet—1930

*T*he Chinese house servant is more than a century-old institution
in San Francisco. As early as 1849, Jessie Benton Fremont wrote that
she was comforted during her visit by "admirable furnishings, fine car-
pets, French furniture, veranda, and Chinese servants."[1] The Chinese
were among the earliest immigrants to San Francisco. Denied most civil
liberties, they took menial jobs to survive. Soon they made up the entire
workforce in canneries, cigar factories, laundries, and fish-packing
plants. But homeowners quickly discovered that their placid natures, their
clean and mannered habits, and their willingness to work for low wages
made them ideal house servants. For the Chinese themselves, these were
desirable positions because they offered pleasant working conditions and
higher wages than were available elsewhere. Their loyalty and devotion
to the families they served soon became legendary. In the morning, cable
cars were frequently filled with Chinese on their way up to Nob Hill and
Russian Hill to begin their day's work in the homes of wealthier San
Franciscans. Often they "lived in," becoming almost a part of the families they served. To this day, many homes and apartments have an extra
room for the "Chinese houseboy." By the 1930s, the custom of having
and maintaining a Chinese housekeeper was almost universal among
well-to-do San Franciscans. Their loyalty to their households, their obe-
dience to their tasks, and their devotion to their employees were unquestioned. They were as much a part of the image of San Francisco as the

The low-lying skyline of San Francisco in 1930.

Bay itself. That's why San Franciscans found what happened on December 7, 1930, so hard to believe. It seemed almost contrary to the laws of nature, and it shook the city like an earthquake.

Rosetta Baker was a woman of indeterminate age. The city's newspapers would variously peg her at somewhere between sixty-five and seventy-five, although eventually they settled for referring to her as "elderly." One reporter solved the problem simply by noting her "desperate search for her long vanished youth."[2] One thing they could agree on: She was a woman of considerable means. Divorced by her husband in 1912, she had invested her divorce settlement in San Francisco real estate, and a string of apartment buildings on and about Nob Hill testified to the shrewdness of her investments. At the depth of the Depression, she had more than enough ready cash to indulge in her favorite hobbies.

One of her interests was the theatre. She regularly attended the opera and the city's major playhouses. She donated generously to amateur theaters, and in return she was given minor roles in productions. In the last year of her life, she appeared in Little Theatre productions of *School for Scandal, Lystrata*, and *Uncle Vanya*.[3]

Her other principal interest was young men. She was frequently seen in the company of escorts half her age, and she was rumored to have had several serious romances with eager young suitors. A vivacious and attractive woman despite her years, Mrs. Baker did nothing to conceal her penchant for younger men, and she spoke openly of it to her wide circle of friends. Her most recent swain permitted her to indulge both of

Mrs. Rosetta Baker, San Francisco socialite, property owner, sometime actress and patron of the arts. *San Francisco Chronicle*

her main interests. He was an actor named Walter Outter, who used the name Middleton for stage purposes. He was twenty-eight years old, tall and good-looking, sporting a trim moustache, and he talked constantly of going to Hollywood to break into the "talkies." By the latter part of 1930, Walter Middleton and Rosetta Baker had been keeping company for almost eight months, and she eagerly described him to friends as her "protege."[4] Mrs. Baker lived in one of her apartment buildings, at 814 California Street, just up the hill from Old Saint Mary's Church. Middleton was frequently seen by neighbors entering and exiting the building.

Mrs. Baker's closest friend was Mrs. Walker Coleman Graves, called Maude by her intimates. Maude was also a divorcee and a woman of means, and she frequently accompanied Rosetta Baker to social events, often, like her friend, in the company of younger men. So it was not an unusual foursome that gathered in the Baker apartment on December 7, 1930, even if it would have been somewhat eye-popping to the unknowl-edgeable observer: Rosetta Baker, in her seventies, with Walter Middleton, twenty-eight; Maude Graves, sixty-seven, and her date for the evening, Arthur Beale, twenty-three.[6]

Plans for the evening called for a delightful schedule of events. First there was conversation and sherry in the Baker apartment. Then the two couples climbed into Mrs. Baker's car and drove downhill to the Clift Hotel where they enjoyed a somewhat hurried dinner with wine. Then it was off to the Green Street Theatre where Mr. Middleton ap-peared in a starring role in the play, while Mr. Beale accompanied parts of the performance on the piano. Following the show and compliments for the two young men, all four then sped off to Polk Street, where they indulged in ice cream treats. It was now 11:30 P.M., and the foursome once again climbed into the Baker car for a trip to Maude Graves' apart-ment at 1100 Mason Street. There, the merrymakers had yet another round of cocktails, and at about 12:15 A.M., Rosetta Baker left with the two young men, with promises to call Maude later. Sometime after 12:30, Rosetta called Maude from her own apartment and the two ladies chatted joyously about the evenings' events and what enormous fun it had been.[7]

Before retiring, Rosetta Baker decided to read from her poetry book, as she frequently did after a satisfying day. One line of poetry especially caught her eye that evening. It read, "Sex is the curse of life." Rosetta quickly reached for her pen and wrote next to it. "This is true!"[10]

Liu Fook was a Chinese gentleman whose exact age also seemed to elude the city's reporters, who would variously describe him as sixty, sixty-three, and sixty-five. Attorneys, when it suited their purpose, would later refer to him as an "ancient Chinese." Liu Fook's exact history is lost in the dim mists of time, but it is known that he immigrated to San Francisco illegally as a cabin boy on a trans-pacific liner in 1920 from Hong Kong, leaving behind a wife and several children. Liu Fook was a slightly built man, weighing just 110 pounds and standing barely five feet tall.[11] He quickly learned enough English to become employed as a houseboy, a job he keenly enjoyed and valued. During his decade in America, he had led an unremarkable, quiet life, but he did manage in the course of events to father two additional children. For personal reasons, he never mentioned either his Hong Kong family or his later progeny to his employer of almost ten years: Mrs. Rosetta Baker of California Street.

Now, in the early morning of December 8, 1930, Liu Fook, clad in blue shirt and trousers, swept the front steps of Mrs. Baker's apartment building. Slight, stooped and moving slowly, he connected a hose to the front outside faucet and sprayed off the steps, then carefully watered the two small trees on either side. It was a chore with which he had started his day almost for longer than he could remember, and he performed the task somewhat automatically, pausing occasionally to wave at a familiar passer-by.

Liu Fook was next seen winding up the hose by the side of the building and entering the apartment building through a side door on Ellick Lane. Within minutes, all hell seemed to break loose.

Mrs. Ray Dix, the manager of the apartment building, suddenly was startled by a loud banging on her door, accompanied by shrieking and yelling. She quickly put on her housecoat and opened the door. There she found a frantic Liu Fook, yelling in Chinese, repeating the phrase "Boss Missy!" and gesturing wildly toward the open door of Mrs. Baker's apartment. Mrs. Dix entered the apartment, walked across the vestibule and turned into the bedroom. The sight that greeted her buckled her knees.

The wall-bed was pulled down, but the bedding was completely off the bed and lay on the floor to one side. At the foot of the bed lay the awkwardly contorted, blood-spattered, nude body of Mrs. Baker. Her nightgown and one of the bed sheets were tangled around her neck.

Mrs. Dix recovered her composure, hurried to the telephone, and called the police and the Harbor Emergency Hospital. Within a matter of minutes, San Francisco police officers rushed into the apartment and took over the scene.

They knew instantly that this was the scene of a terrible, horrific crime. There were signs of violence everywhere. It was clear that a ferocious struggle had taken place. Mrs. Baker's body had suffered massive trauma. A coroner's report would later detail the damage: three broken

The scene of the crime, Mrs. Baker's apartment building at 814 California Street. The murder took place in her flat on the first floor at the corner. *San Francisco Chronicle* teeth, indicating a vicious blow to the mouth; bruises on the right eye, forehead, and under the left eye; a crushed breastbone; eight fractured ribs; bruises on the throat and chest; and evidence on the throat of strangling. Under two fingernails of the right hand was coagulated blood, indicating that she had fought her assailant.[13]

Detective George Engler took his first good look at Liu Fook. His neck and chin bore deep scratch marks. When he was asked about them, Liu Fook mumbled incoherently. Police continued to search the apartment. They made three significant discoveries that would become important evidence in the case: a piece of skin about an inch square with a bit of flesh attached to it, a worn piece of leather from the sole of a shoe, and a button with a piece of blue cloth attached to it.[14]

The detective called Liu Fook forward again for a further examination. A look his shoes showed that the sole was missing from one of his shoes. The piece of leather fit it exactly. One of his fingers was missing a piece of flesh and was still oozing serum. The flesh found near the body fit the wound like a piece in a jigsaw puzzle. Liu Fook was wearing a suit made of blue cloth. There was no missing button, but a subsequent examination of a small room near the Ellick Lane entrance to the building revealed a metal pail full of water. Soaking in the water were a pair of trousers and a blouse, both belonging to Liu Fook and both made of blue cloth. Close examination showed that a button and a piece of blue cloth were missing from the right sleeve.[14]

The early evidence seemed conclusive. But why would a longtime Chinese servant want to kill his mistress? Liu Fook's protestations were loud and consistent. "No kill Boss Missy," he loudly repeated over and over to the detectives.[15]

A further examination of the body showed that robbery was certainly involved. The ring finger of the right hand had been nearly stripped of its flesh where her assailant had ripped off a ring. A search of the room revealed that other jewelry had been taken: a watch, a second ring known by Mrs. Dix to have been in the room, a necklace, and cash.

Then Mrs. Dix narrated a tale that seemed to remove any final doubt: The relationship between Mrs. Baker and her servant had often been strained. She had fired him several times in the past year for "insolence."[16] The point of contention had been her association with young men, especially Mr. Middleton. Liu Fook had been particularly upset to see Mrs. Baker kissing her suitor, "not like a mother, but like a sweetheart," and one evening he refused to cook dinner because Mr. Middleton was present. Even more damaging was Mrs. Dix's statement that Liu Fook had told her just days previous that if Baker didn't stop seeing Middleton, "someone is going to strangle her," and that he had dramatized this by placing his own hands around his throat.

To say that San Francisco was incredulous would be an understatement. How could this happen? Surely, no Chinese servant would ever be capable of such a crime; history and racial stereotyping simply didn't permit it. Maude Graves was quick out of the starting blocks, remarking, "I will never believe Liu Fook did it. It must have been someone else."[18] Other employers of Chinese housekeepers stepped forward with such pronouncements as, "It is absurd to accuse the Chinese" and "I have lived in China and the Chinese are completely trustworthy."[19] The Chinese community was equally incredulous. An official spokesman for the Chinatown's Six Companies publicly declared that "it could be declared emphatically, from a knowledge of the Chinese character, that Liu is not the murderer. It is an old Chinese custom that a murderer must flee from

The *Call-Bulletin* tells the city of the unspeakable crime.

the scene of a crime, otherwise he would be seized by the spirit of the victim in the form of a devil." Declared another, "It is inconceivable that Liu did anything of the kind. We don't believe it for a moment."[20]

However, it was an editorial in the *San Francisco Chronicle* that best summed up the sentiment. Entitled "Californians Cannot Believe Chinese Servant the Killer," the article went to say, "We believe (there is) a profound public sentiment that the crime is entirely out of tune with the character of an old Chinese servant. Never in all the years in which California has been used to this type of servant has there been a single case of murder with robbery or a crime of passion against an employer. Every

Liu Fook, the faithful Chinese servant and murder suspect.

The victim posing in her best society finery. *San Francisco Call-Bulletin*

one of those jewels would have been inhabited by a devil to pursue and torment Liu. He would have put as great a distance as possible between himself and his victim and her belongings. California public opinion cannot believe that it was Liu Fook who killed and robbed Mrs. Baker."[21]

Yet, just two days into the investigation, the missing jewelry was found under some old telephone directories in Liu Fook's janitorial room. Declared Captain Charles Dulles of the Detective Bureau, "We are going ahead and prosecute Liu."[21]

But it wouldn't be that easy. The Chinese community was now up in arms. It was announced that a large defense fund was being established for Liu Fook's defense, and a contingent of Chinese sleuths began tailing Middleton, whom they regarded as the real suspect in the case. Declared the Six Companies, the tongs that ran Chinatown: "We are not trying to interfere with the law, but we want to see justice done and we do not want the name of our people hurt."

And they did something else: They organized a team of top lawyers to defend Liu Fook, including Chan Chung Wing, "San Francisco's only Chinese lawyer."[23] It was an impressive and effective team and in the days leading up to the trial the team did its best to diffuse the evidence, dredge up other suspects, and drag some really pungent red herrings across the trail.

Wallace Middleton and Arthur Beale, the early suspects. *San Francisco Examiner*

Suddenly Liu Fook himself began speaking in full sentences and telling his own version of events with great effectiveness. From his jail came a cascade of theories and excuses. The cut on his finger was an earlier injury from a broken window. The scratches on his face were commonplace in his line of work. He and Mrs. Baker were the closest of friends at all times. She had trusted him with rent money and he had never stolen any. The night of the murder he had been asleep all night in his room in the basement. The police had beaten him to try to get him to confess, but he couldn't confess because he was innocent. A newspaper photo of Liu Fook showed him eating in his cell with chopsticks, looking scrcne and innocent.[24]

Meanwhile, his lawyers were raising questions and havoc whenever and wherever they appeared. They interrupted the inquest to the point that they were chastised by the judge. They dominated a visit by jurors to the crime scene with statements challenging the investigations. They held press conferences and street interviews with anyone who would listen.

The evidence? It was too perfect, they said, which meant that it had to be planted. Other suspects? They knew where they were and they claimed they were in constant pursuit of the true culprits. The jewels and the torn clothing found in Liu Fook's room? An obvious plant.

Blood evidence links Liu Fook to the crime. *San Francisco Examiner*

Judge Lazarus examines the cut finger of the accused.

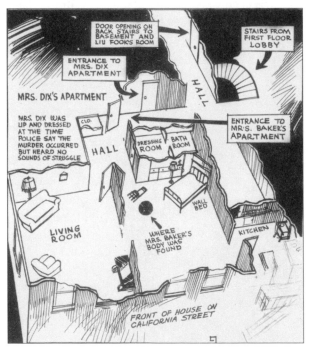

The *Chronicle's* diagram of the murder scene. Was the victim's body visible from the front door entrance?

The defense team propounded the theory that, since a tremendous battle had obviously taken place without anyone hearing it, the murder must have taken place outside the apartment building and her body then dragged by several unknown persons into the apartment.

Another theme that Liu Fook's attorneys dwelt on over and over again was that the accused was incapable of committing such a violent crime: He was small, frail, weak, and aged, and only a person of much greater size and strength could have wreaked such damage on the victim. It was more likely, they said, that the sturdy Mrs. Baker could have beaten up Liu Fook!

The case was front page news in all the San Francisco newspapers for weeks, with only a brief respite for the year-end holidays. Finally, on January 19, Liu Fook was brought before Superior Judge Harris to be arraigned and instructed for trial. Liu Fook took the stand, with a professional interpreter at his side. But when the judge asked him how he pleaded, Liu Fook ignored the interpreter, pounded his fists together and yelled, "I no guilty! I no kill bossy-missy. All time, somebody say, 'You guilty.' No. I no kill her!"[25]

Judge Harris set the trial date for February 24. San Francisco could hardly wait.

The trial itself was a replay of all evidence previously publicized and all the denials previously promulgated. There were, however, some electric moments.

The first was the real cause of death. Most had assumed that Mrs. Baker was strangled with the bed sheet, but the medical authorities stated that she had been strangled by hand, the larynx squeezed out of shape, and the bruises from the strangler's fingers were still visible on the throat of the corpse.

Liu Fook's claim that he had cut his hand on a window was blunted by testimony that the particular window he pointed out was unbroken and the spots of blood on the carpet near it turned out to be spots of paint.

Liu Fook had claimed that when he opened the door to Mrs. Baker's apartment he immediately saw Mrs. Baker's body from the vestibule. However, a diagram of the apartment demonstrated that the body could not be seen from that viewpoint.

But the most bizarre statement from Liu Fook was that the garment with the missing button was not even his. Mrs. Dix took the stand to state that it was in fact Liu Fook's, that she had seen him wearing it many times, and that she had mended a rip in it at his request just a few days before the murder. She even turned the garment inside out to show where she had mended it with purple thread. It made no difference: Liu Fook still maintained it wasn't his.

Liu Fook claimed the cuts on his face had been made while shaving that morning. Prosecutors showed pictures taken of him later in the morning that clearly showed him with a stubble of beard.

After two and a half weeks of testimony, the jury of ten men and two women retired to the jury room in possession of all these facts, as well as a shared conviction that no veteran Chinese houseboy could possibly murder his mistress. After twenty-one minutes of deliberation, they announced their verdict to the waiting city: "Not guilty."[26]

Liu Fook's face broke into a wide smile, as he leaped to his feet and shook the hand of each juror, all the while talking in a "half intelligible jibber-jabber."[27]

Outside the courtroom, he was greeted by a throng of jubilant well-wishers, and according to one account, "The little Chinaman was congratulated by Chinese and Americans alike."[28]

An acquitted Liu Fook shakes hands with City Jailer Thomas Kelly.

Jury Acquits Liu Fook in Baker Murder
Verdict in 21 Minutes, After Two Ballots

Chinese Houseboy Only Smiles at Decision of Deliberators

Liu Fook, acquitted yesterday of the murder of Mrs. Rosetta Baker, went from the courtroom to say good-by to his "host" for ninety-six days. Above he is shown shaking hands with City Jailer Thomas Kelly, who showed the old Chinese many kindnesses during his incarceration.

'THANK GOD THEY SET ME FREE!'

The words "Thank God They Set Me Free" in Chinese characters surround a beaming Liu Fook in a Chinatown pamphlet celebrating his acquittal.

Chinatown itself went mad with joy. Grant Street turned into a spontaneous carnival and Liu Fook was the star attraction. At dusk, he entered Grant Street flanked by his attorneys. Hundreds along the sidewalk cheered him as he walked the length of the street and his friends rushed up to shake his hand. His triumphal march ended at a restaurant where he and his attorneys enjoyed a celebratory banquet.[29]

In the meantime, the city's police department paid homage to the infallibility of the judicial system by announcing that they would now try to find Mrs. Baker's real murderer. Captain of Inspectors Charles Dulles had to admit that the search would be difficult. "I don't know where else to look," he said. "The evidence against Liu Fook is so overwhelming."[30]

Liu Fook seemed unconcerned about anyone trying to find the "real killer." On March 22, Liu Fook made an appearance at the famed Mandarin Theatre in Chinatown before an audience of more than two thousand cheering fans. He made a short speech in Chinese, during which he thanked his supporters and lauded the American system of justice.

Peter Wong, secretary of the Chinese Six Companies, summed up the entire incident for Chinatown. "On behalf of the Chinese people," he said, "I wish to compliment that American spirit that asserted itself during the trial that determined justice was done for Liu Fook. We Chinese are deeply appreciative of the fairness and high consideration which the people of San Francisco have always shown us."[31]

Like any good actor, Liu Fook knew how to make a timely exit. The next day he boarded the ship *President Johnson* and sailed off to Hong Kong and obscurity.

Chapter Twelve

The Last Lynchings—1933

The City of San Jose, some forty miles south of San Francisco and just beyond the southern tip of its great Bay, was proud of its humble origins. It had been founded in 1777 by the Spanish, but it quickly passed from Spanish to Mexican and then to American rule. In 1850, it was still only a small agricultural outpost when, for two years, it served as the capital of the state of California. The first meeting there of the state's rough-hewn legislature is remembered as "The Legislature of a Thousand Drinks."

But San Jose grew rapidly and prospered quickly, and by 1930 it clearly dominated the Santa Clara Valley, a fertile area fifteen miles wide and stretching more than fifty miles to the south. With pride, San Jose called itself "The Garden City," and "The Valley of Heart's Delight," and its 58,000 residents took their prosperity from the lush fields, vineyards, and orchards that surrounded it.

San Jose was by now far removed from its hard-drinking, gun-toting early days. Certainly no one could remember when San Jose had last seen a lynching, that product of vigilante justice more associated with its San Francisco neighbor to the north and with the gold fields of the lower Sierra. Impromptu hangings of the accused had once been commonplace in Northern California, and the truth is that they had not completely disappeared there, even with the advent of the twentieth century. In 1901, the good citizens of Mendocino County had lynched four men and a boy suspected of stealing cattle. And, as recently as 1920, three hoodlums had been strung up in Santa Rosa for murdering a San Francisco detective. But that was in another time and at another place, and no one in thriving San Jose would have believed that such lawlessness could now invade the city's pleasant environs. This was a law-abiding city, proud of the symbols of its culture: its twenty-nine schools, its forty-six churches, and its two institutions of higher learning. The people of San Jose were stable, God-fearing, respectful of the law, and certain of their destiny. In 1933, they had no way of knowing this was all about to change.

On September 1, 1933, the *San Jose Mercury Herald* carried a feature story with photographs of a festive banquet held the previous evening at the Hotel de Anza. In the presence of sixty-three family members and store employees, Alex Hart, owner of L. Hart & Company Inc., San Jose's largest department store, had conferred the title of vice-president upon his son, Brooke. He also declared, to the applause of the assembled, that Brooke was destined to succeed him as president of the company.[1]

University of
Santa Clara
photo of Brooke
Leopold Hart

The newspaper would probably have featured the story prominently even if the Hart Department Store had not been one of its largest advertisers, for the store was an important part of everyday life in San Jose, and the ascendancy of the younger Hart, just recently graduated from nearby Santa Clara University, constituted legitimate news. The photograph of the stout, balding Alex Hart, standing alongside his tall, handsome, blond son, was no doubt regarded with genuine interest and pleasure by most readers of the *Mercury Herald*. But for two of its readers, Jack Holmes and Harold Thurmond, the photo of the wealthy businessman and his handsome heir inspired a different thought: the prospect of easy money.

Jack Holmes and Harold Thurmond were a strange duo. Not close friends, they had, however, traveled similar routes to reach their current life of crime. They were both California natives from hard-working, middle-class families and products of the local school system.

Holmes was in his late twenties, an athlete of sorts, and a high school dropout. A good-looking man of medium stature, he was married and had

Hart (second from right) in a Hart Department Store photo.

Jock Holmes, instigator of the kidnap/murder. *San Francisco Chronicle*

two young children. Personable and charming, he earned his living as a salesman, but he seemed unable to hold any job for long. Consequently, he was usually short of ready cash and was invariably looking for ways to improve his fortunes. Friends said that his outward charm and easy-going personality masked a streak of rebellion and a nasty temper.

Harold Thurmond was one of five children of a religiously inclined family, and he was thought by his acquaintances to be something of a "dullard." Only a year younger than Holmes, he was light-years behind him in maturity and intelligence. Like Holmes, he had left high school to become a wage-earning laborer, and over the years he had drifted from job to job, but he was currently working as a gasoline station attendant. Unsuccessful in love and in his social life, he developed a reputation as a drinker, and it was agreed by those who knew him that he was easily led.

Holmes and Thurmond had known each other for only a year or so. They met in the gas station where Thurmond worked when Holmes came in for repairs to his car. Thurmond was eager for friendship, and Holmes was looking for someone to help carry out his schemes. The two began spending time together, and it was not long before Holmes convinced Thurman that they should "try something."[2]

Holmes' first plan was to highjack a Union Oil Company clerk while he was on his way to the bank with the day's receipts. Holmes had the dim-witted Thurmond do the risky work, running the clerk's car to the curb, entering his car with his gun drawn, and extracting the money bag before fleeing. Thurmond then drove his own car to where Holmes was waiting and handed him the money sacks. They contained $716 in small bills, which Holmes divided equally between the two of them. Holmes congratulated his grinning partner and did a little dance of joy. Their first escapade had been a great success.

Flushed with triumph, the two conspirators did not wait long for their next venture. Just a week later, Thurmond, on Holmes' instructions, highjacked a Shell Oil Company executive in his car, netting the pair of criminals $675 in cash and checks. They were on a roll now, confident that they were ready for bigger game.

On September 2, 1933, Jack Holmes sat down with Harold Thurmond and showed him the previoius day's copy of the *Mercury News*. There was the photograph of Alex Hart and his son. Holmes guessed that if Brooke Hart were kidnaped, he'd be worth as much as $40,000 to the father for his safe return. If anything, he probably guessed low, for Brooke Hart meant everything to his father. Brooke was his heir, his successor in business, and the future of the Hart family.

Brooke Hart was all a father could ask for in a son: handsome, intelligent, athletic, and personable. With wavy, ash-blond hair, a trim, well-muscled body, a confident stride, and a warm smile, he made friends wherever he went. He had just graduated from Santa Clara University where he had earned a bachelor of science degree in commerce, and now he had taken his place at Hart's Department Store as the "boss-in-waiting." Brooke worked hard at his assignments and was immensely popular with the store's employees.

Just before six-o'clock on the evening of Thursday, November 9, 1933, Brooke Hart walked out of the side entrance of the department store and headed for the parking lot where he kept his car, a light-green 1933 Studebaker roadster. He waved to a friend on the way, chatted briefly with the lot attendant, and then climbed into his car and headed back to the store where he was to pick up his father and sister.

Alex J. Hart, Sr. and his daughter, Aleese, waited patiently by the store for the promised ride home from Brooke. After fifteen minutes, they decided that something must have gone wrong or that Brooke had misunderstood their intentions. After another ten minutes, they gave up in baffled despair and asked an employee to pick them up.[3]

At eight o'clock that evening, the worried family gathered at the Hart residence. Brooke was nowhere to be found. He had failed to show up at a scheduled speaking class an hour earlier, and a check with several friends afforded no clue as to his whereabouts. Finally, in desperation, the family placed a call to San Jose's chief of police to report that Brooke was missing.

At 9:30 P.M. the phone rang and Brooke's sister, Miriam, picked up the receiver and identified herself. A quiet, controlled voice said, "Your brother has been kidnapped. You'll be hearing from us."[4] Suddenly, their worst fears were confirmed: Brooke had been kidnapped and was being held for ransom.

Kidnapping for ransom was already the fashionable crime of the decade. The Lindbergh tragedy was still fresh in the public mind. Ransoms recently paid by wealthy families were regular fare in the nation's newspaper: $700,000 for a child, Margaret McGrath, in Massachusetts; $40,000 for John O'Connell in Albany; $30,000 for Mary McElroy in Kansas City; and $200,000 for millionaire Charles Urschel in Oklahoma City.[5] The Hart family wondered what the terms would be for Brooke's return. They didn't have long to wait.

Just one hour later, at 10:30 P.M., the phone rang again, and once again Miriam answered. "We have your brother," a voice said. "He is safe, but it will cost you $40,000 to get him back. If you ever want to see him alive, keep away from the police. We will phone further instructions tomorrow."[6]

The next several days were a blur of bewildering phone calls and sad discoveries. At midnight, Brooke Hart's convertible was found on a country side-road, abandoned and with its lights still on. His wallet was discovered, having washed up in the San Francisco Bay. Demands for ransom came both in the form of phone calls and via letters sent to the department store. The substance of the demands was that Mr. Hart should put $40,000 in twenty-, ten-, and five-dollar denominations, into a satchel, and then to put the satchel into a Studebaker car and drive to Los Angeles on a prescribed route. The car would be intercepted by a man in a white mask, and after the satchel was handed over, Brooke would be released.[7]

At this point, the authorities were convinced that the kidnappers were true amateurs: It was common knowledge in San Jose that Mr. Hart did not know how to drive a car.

By now, the hunt for Brooke Hart and the kidnappers had taken on vast proportions. The local police, under the direction of Sheriff William J. Emig, and the sheriff's department were fully on the case. The F.B.I. had been called in on direct orders from Director J. Edgar Hoover.[8] Both the San Jose and San Francisco newspapers carried daily front page stories concerning the abduction and the ransom demands. Family friends and employees of Hart's Department Store scoured the city and the surrounding countryside. Tips of sightings of the kidnap victim were phoned in from virtually all corners of California. Authorities monitored every phone call coming into the Hart residence in the hope of tracing a ransom call quickly and nabbing the culprits. In one instance, the sheriff's men came close, missing the caller by only a few minutes.

Finally, on the evening of Wednesday, November 15, almost a full week after Brooke's disappearance, authorities got the break they were looking for. The telephone operator told them that two calls to the Hart residence had just been attempted. She was alerted to tell them immediately if another attempt was made, and Alex Hart was instructed to keep the caller on the phone as long as possible. Just before 8:00 P.M., the phone rang and Mr. Hart found himself talking to his son's kidnapper. He patiently responded to all the ransom demands, pretending to work out the details for the money delivery. Within minutes, Sheriff Emig was alerted that the call was coming from a pay phone in the Plaza Garage on South Market Street, not far from the police station.

It did not take the sheriff and his men long to get there. In the shadows of a corner of the garage, they saw a man with his back to them, talking on the phone. When the man saw the sheriff's men advancing on him, he hung up and turned around. He was a thin-faced young man with a stubble of beard covering his face. He was dressed in a pair of corduroy pants and a dark blue sweater.

"What's your name, mister?"

"Harold Thurmond," he said. "What's this all about?"

"Harold, you're under arrest," said Emig, as he locked handcuffs over the young man's wrists.[9]

Thurmond was hustled to a nearby F.B.I. outpost. There, he was interrogated by both the sheriff and the federal authorities. At first, Thurmond denied any involvement in the kidnapping, but eventually his bravado gave way, as his explanations became more and more implausible. Finally, he blurted out, "Brooke Hart is dead. We threw him off the San Mateo Bridge."[10]

Once Thurmond had confessed to murder, he eagerly named his co-conspirator in crime. It was, he said, Jack Holmes, who was currently staying at the nearby California Hotel. It was almost three o'clock in the morning before Thurmond's full confession was taken and recorded. When it was complete, Sheriff Emig and the F.B.I. agents hurried to the California Hotel, where Jack Holmes was rousted from his sleep and placed under arrest. Holmes howled out his innocence as he was taken in handcuffs to the courthouse where Thurmond was being held.

Holmes' accomplice, Harold Thurmond (center), at the time of his arrest by F.B.I. agent Reed Vitterli (left) and Sheriff Emig. *San Francisco Chronicle*

Holmes was a tougher nut to crack. He was surly and defiant, denying any knowledge of the Hart kidnapping. But when Thurmond's confession was read to him, Holmes crumbled, and soon he was giving his own version of events.

Although the two confessions differed somewhat in detail, they were consistent in the basic facts of the crime, and the story was one of repellent horror, of vicious criminality, and of mutual naiveté and stupidity.[11]

Thurmond and Holmes had known each other for only about a year. Both were short of funds and anxious to impress women they could not afford. After their first two robberies of employees carrying payrolls, they were emboldened to think of bigger game. It was Holmes who settled on Brooke Hart and the kidnapping scheme, but Thurmond was an eager convert and quickly became a strong advocate. In reality, they had no firm plan as to what to do with Hart once they kidnapped him. They talked vaguely of "taking him to an Oakland apartment or something."[12] Nor did they have any real idea as to how to extract a ransom from Alex Hart. Nevertheless, they agreed to proceed, and Thurmond was assigned the task of kidnapping Brooke at gunpoint, in the same manner in which he had commandeered the cars of the earlier robbery victims.

The day before the actual kidnapping, the two comrades-in-crime waited in Holmes' car for Brooke Hart to exit the department store at the end the workday, but that evening Brooke and his father left the store together and the kidnappers decided the time was not right. The next evening, as the two again waited in Holmes' car, Brooke and his father again exited together, but this time Brooke left his father at the store entrance and walked alone to the parking lot to get his car. Holmes decided the time had come for action, and he told Thurmond to get out and highjack Brooke Hart once he got into his Studebaker. He also instructed Thurmond to force Brooke to drive to a pre-determined place in the country, where Holmes would be waiting.

When Brooke stopped his car before entering the street from the parking lot, Thurmond quickly opened the passenger door, slipped inside the car, and pointed his gun at Brooke. The kidnapping was underway.

Thurmond ordered Brooke to drive to a country road in Milpitas. Brooke Hart obeyed the command, and within the hour the car rendezvoused with Holmes. Thurmond transferred Hart to the other car. Then the three of them headed for the San Mateo Bridge.

The kidnappers placed a pillowslip over Hart's head and told him that if he didn't make any trouble, he would not be hurt. The two kidnappers were still vague on what they were going to do with Hart. However, once they started over the bridge it dawned on them that, in Thurmond's words, "If we dump this guy, it would be slick and [we] write a note and get a quick turnover before they get too worried."[12]

When they got to the middle of the bridge there were no other cars around, so they ordered Hart out of the car, telling him that he was being transferred to yet another automobile. Holmes then opened the trunk of the car, took out a concrete block, and smashed Brooke Hart over the head with it. Hart fell to the ground, bleeding and unconscious. Then the two kidnappers got out a spool of wire and tied two concrete blocks onto his feet. They carried Hart to the railing of the bridge and threw him into the water. At the last minute, Hart had shown signs of life and they heard him splashing about in the water below. So Thurmond took out his gun, leaned over the railing, and emptied the cartridge, firing into the growing darkness in the direction where he thought Hart's body might be.

Holmes, in the meantime, turned the car around and picked up Thurmond, and the two men, satisfied that their victim was properly disposed of, headed back toward San Jose. On the way, they decided the ransom demand should be $40,000, and Holmes directed Thurmond to make the phone calls to the Hart home.

All in all, it had been a clumsy affair, poorly thought out and awkwardly executed, but the kidnappers were pleased with their work and confident they were on the brink of attaining their fortune.

News of the arrests and the confessions of the two men swept through San Jose and the Peninsula like a prairie fire. Headlines in the San Jose papers shrieked at the infamy of the crime. Sympathy for the Hart family was surpassed only by the outrage that the citizenry felt over the nature of the murder. People wanted justice—and they wanted it fast.

Newspaper coverage of the event was, if anything, inflammatory. The headline and editorial in the *San Jose Evening News* was especially provocative:

"HUMAN DEVILS---If mob violence could ever be justified it would be in a case like this and we believe the general public will agree with us. There was never a more fiendish crime committed anywhere in the United States, and we are of the belief that unless these two prisoners are kept safely away from San Jose there is likely to be a hanging without waiting for the courts of justice. To read the confession of both of the criminals...makes one feel like he wanted to go out and be a part of that mob."[13]

Just a few hours after that *News* editorial appeared, the San Jose city council adjourned its business meeting in respect for Brooke Hart's memory, after passing a resolution: "It is hoped that justice will be sure and swift and that the subterfuges and technicalities of law that frequently thwart or delay justice will not be taken in this instance. We rail at the inefficiencies of the police department, at the waste of time in trials, at the release of dangerous criminals after they are convicted."[14]

Anger in San Jose over the murders was almost palpable. People talked of little else in their homes, on street corners, and in bars. The next day, Jack Holmes' father came to visit him in the Santa Clara County jail. He had to push his way through a growing throng of five hundred people to reach the jail door. "What is this crowd gathering for?" he asked. "What do they intend to do?"[15]

No one was quite sure, but the growing anger of the community seemed so dangerous that Sheriff Emig and the F.B.I. agents involved took the precaution of spiriting Thurmond and Holmes out of San Jose and up the Peninsula to the quieter confines of the F.B.I. offices in San Francisco.

Now that the two kidnappers were in their city, the San Francisco newspapers felt obligated to take up the cry. Wailed the *Chronicle*:

"There is only one thing to do with the murderers of Brooke Hart. That is to hang them legally but promptly. The guilt of the culprits is unquestioned. They have confessed. There is no defense or litigation. The crime was cold-blooded, premeditated. At the earliest legal date, the gallows should end two lives which have forfeited all rights except to be executed by the law. Something is owed to public feeling."[16]

The *San Jose Mercury Herald* added its own voice for swift punishment: "It is hoped that the trivialities which are so often resorted to by attorneys for the one and only purpose of clogging the wheels of justice will not be permitted."[17]

In Washington, D.C., F.B.I. chief J. Edgar Hoover kept in touch with the activities of his men on the case and quickly caught the tenor of the times. He wrote his assistant this note:

"Please call agent Vitterli at once and tell him to stop taking these two criminals out of jail. If they should be lynched while in our custody it would be terrible."[18]

Still, the time came when Thurmond and Holmes had to be returned to San Jose. It was done under the cover of darkness and with intense security. No one was anxious to have the word out that the two prisoners were back in town.[19]

In San Jose, rumors flew everywhere, and the theme of many of them was that these two fiends had a chance of getting off. The case, it was said, was not as sure-fire as people were being led to believe, and the workings of the legal justice system might not be so simple after all.

The time sequences reported in Holmes' and Thurmond's confessions were at variance, and Holmes' relatives claimed that his appearances before and after the murders did not allow enough time for him to have committed the crime the way the police conjectured it was carried out. In fact, Holmes now repudiated his entire confession, claiming he had been tricked and abused into confessing. There was a question as to which one had actually committed the murder: Was it Holmes when he hit Hart over the head or Thurmond when he emptied his revolver at the victim? There was also the question of jurisdiction: San Jose authorities felt the trial should be held in the city where the kidnapping took place, the district attorney felt the suspects should be tried in Santa Clara County, and, if the confessions concerning the killing were correct, the homicide jurisdiction might actually rest in Alameda County.

To complicate these matters, there was no *corpus delicti*. A thorough search for Hart's body had been underway ever since the confessions, but the combined efforts of the sheriff's search team dragging the waters of the Bay, together with a host of volunteers combing every corner of the water's edge, had produced nothing.

Slowly, but surely, a fear arose in San Jose that there was a chance that Holmes and Thurmond might not get what was coming to them, that the intricacies of the law and the cleverness of defense attorneys might get the charges against them reduced. There was even fear in some quarters that they might get off. A tide of outrage began to sweep the city. On Friday, November 17, the *San Francisco Examiner* reported, "The temper of San Jose citizens is at white heat."

In the midst of all this speculation, another trial for murder was actually taking place in San Jose. A farmhand named Ray Sousa had killed a well-known and popular farmer in a dispute over money, and the case was going to the jury following an impassioned plea by the accused's lawyer. The district attorney demanded the death penalty, but after deliberating for twenty-eight hours, the jury returned a verdict of manslaughter, carrying a maximum sentence of ten years in San Quentin. This meant that Sousa could possibly get off with an even shorter jail term, allowed by probation. The unfortunate timing of the verdict served to further inflame the citizenry, which was already fearful that Thurmond and Holmes would slip the noose.

The *Chronicle* reported on November 25 that a vigilante committee was being formed in San Jose, and between sixty and seventy citizens had signed a secret agreement stating they "stood ready to take adequate action against the kidnappers of Brooke Hart if the court failed to do its duty."[20]

Then, on Saturday, November 25, the final catalyst occurred to ignite the fury of the citizens of San Jose. The decomposed body of Brooke Hart was found.

Early that morning, two duck hunters had set out through the fog in a rowboat from Alameda Creek, several miles north of the San Mateo Bridge. They headed north toward the mouth of Mt. Eden Creek into some shallows a mile off shore, where ducks were known to gather. Suddenly their boat bumped into something. At first, they thought it might be a dead seal. When they looked more closely, they saw that it was the body of a man. The body had been almost destroyed by the waters of the Bay and the creatures that live in it. From the waist up, it was scarcely more than a skeleton. The face and hair were eaten away. The hands were gone. Only remnants of a shirt remained, but the lower part of the body was still clothed. After the authorities were notified, they were quick to identify the remains as those of the kidnap victim. News of the discovery ran through San Jose like a flash flood.[21]

The discovery of the body had occurred early in the morning hours of the day. By 10:00 A.M., it had become common knowledge in the city. By 11:00 A.M., one of jailers at the county jail, where Thurmond and Holmes were being held, looked out of the window and discovered to his astonishment that the driveway and the area around the jail doors were filling up with people. By noon, the crowd had become immense.

The news of the discovery of Hart's body was being flashed throughout the county, via the city's radio stations. The announcer at station KQW went beyond mere broadcasting of the news to proclaim, "The crowd is gathering tonight in Saint James Park!"[22] For various reasons—revenge, curiosity, thrill-seeking—people for miles around began piling into their cars and heading for downtown San Jose and the park next to county jail. It was Sunday and people had time on their hands and were eager to be in on the excitement.

Sheriff Emig, realizing that major trouble was brewing, rushed to the scene. He was relieved to find that some defenses had been built up around the jailhouse and that, though the crowd was large, it did not seem in an especially ugly mood. Nevertheless, Emig immediately requested reinforcements from a variety of sources, including the California Highway Patrol and the national guard. By late afternoon, ten members of the highway patrol had arrived as reinforcements, but Governor Rolph refused to send the guard. In fact, the governor was quoted as saying, "If they lynch those fellows, I'll pardon the lynchers!"[23]

The local constabulary was now, for all practical purposes, on its own. The crowd began to become louder and more menacing. It was made up of people of all ages, including women and even children. But in the main it was youthful, and it included an increasing number of men coming from nearby bars. As the sun began to fade and darkness crept across the park, the crowd took on an added militancy and began moving closer to the jail.

Sheriff Emig now had a decision to make. The guards were heavily armed, but they needed instructions on how to react in case of violence. Emig, balancing the need to protect the prisoners against the horror of killing perhaps hundreds of San Jose citizens, issued an order that no guns would be fired. Tear gas would be used to disperse the crowd.

By nine o'clock, the crowd began to act. They rolled away a truck that had been employed to block the driveway. The front ranks of the crowd pushed through some wooden barriers that had been set up. A dozen or so officers behind the barricade stood together with locked arms, and for a moment they seemed to hold back the crowd. Then one of the deputies in the building hurled a tear gas cannister at the crowd, and all hell seemed to break loose.

The crowd retreated briefly, then surged forward again. The police, sensing disaster, retreated into the jailhouse and barricaded themselves behind its massive metal doors. More gas grenades were hurled, but now individuals in the crowd picked them up before they could explode and hurled them back through the windows of the jail. A cry of, "Lynch 'em, lynch 'em!" went up. People began chanting, "Brook-ie Hart! Brook-ie Hart."[24]

The mob was now out for blood. Mob members threw themselves against the jail doors, but the doors would not budge. Then someone remembered that a new post office was being built next to the courthouse. A group of men rushed to the site to see what could be found there, and they returned carrying a large metal beam. A constant barrage of rocks and bricks now pelted the jailhouse and most of the windows were shattered. Someone cut the electricity to the jail, so that the only light in the area came from the headlights of the cars outside. Fumes from the gas grenades cast an eerie pall over the scene. Men screamed and cursed, and the crowd was in a frenzy.

The mob uses a battering ram to force its way into the jail. *San Jose Mercury News*

Inside the jailhouse, the police and the guards realized there was little they could do. On command from Emig, the men hid their weapons so that they could not be used against them.

A dozen men began using the beam as a battering ram against the doors. Over and over, the men lunged against the doors until they finally gave way. Twenty or so men, some with handkerchiefs masking their faces, rushed into the jail and headed for the staircase. An undersheriff and a deputy blocked their paths. "Don't do this, boys! Let the law take its course!" one of them pleaded.[25] But the invaders knocked these men aside in their headlong rush up the stairs to the jail cells. Sheriff Emig stood resolutely at the top of the stairs. "You're not going to get them, men!" he yelled, but Emig was quickly felled by a blow to his head from a metal pipe.[26]

One of the ringleaders grabbed the cell keys and the group headed for what they believed would be Holmes' cell. When they opened it and burst into the cell, it appeared empty. Then they discovered a man cowering in the toilet room.

"Holmes?" one of them demanded.

"I'm not Holmes," the prisoner yelled. "I'm Jack Pearson from Evergreen."[27]

The invaders shined a light into his face. "The hell you're not Holmes," one of them yelled as he slammed his fist into the man's face.[28] Then other men stepped forward and hit him until he fell unconscious. They slapped him awake and continued hitting him until his face was a bloody pulp. Then they tied a rope around his neck and dragged him down the stairs headfirst.

Others began to search for Thurmond. It didn't take them long to find his cell, but he didn't seem to be in it. Finally, he was located in the shadows of his toilet stall, upside down and clinging to the grating in the ceiling with his fingers, "like a treed racoon," as one newspaper reported.[29] When he was pulled down from his hiding place, his head smashed on the toilet and he was knocked unconscious. The men put a rope around his neck and soon led him, stumbling, down the stairs, still only semi-conscious.

When the men emerged from the jail with the two prisoners, a wild cry went up from the crowd. Holmes fought like a tiger against his abusers but it was to no avail. They ripped off his clothes and dragged him across the park, while people jumped on him and smashed his face with rocks until he was almost unrecognizable.

Thurmond was carried along behind Holmes, but he showed few signs of consciousness. "Wake him up," someone yelled. "We want him to know what's happening to him."[30] However, the mob didn't seem to care about such refinements, and when they reached the park, they carried Thurmond's limp body to a mulberry tree in the corner of the park. There, a red-headed youth tightened a rope around Thurmond's neck and threw the end over a sturdy branch. "Remember Brookie Hart!" someone yelled. "Let him have it,"[31] yelled someone else, and with four or five men on the end of the rope, they pulled the kidnapper up in lurches. Thurmond's legs went stiff and his eyes opened. The crowd yelled out in jubilation and triumph. A young girl yelled out, "How do you like it, you bastard? How do you like it, up there?"[32] Someone pulled off Thurmond's pants, and the crowd let out a shriek of joy and approval. Several women, old and young, jabbed cigarettes into Thurmond's exposed thighs. Someone held a match to his pubic hair. It took Thurmond several minutes of spasms and convulsions to achieve death. His face turned black and his tongue hung out as his body slowly twirled at the end of the rope.

Now the crowd turned its attention to Holmes. The leaders decided he needed his own tree, so they dragged him to an elm tree some distance away. Holmes was still fighting for his life, but it was a losing battle. Several youths, some swigging booze from flasks, beat him with their

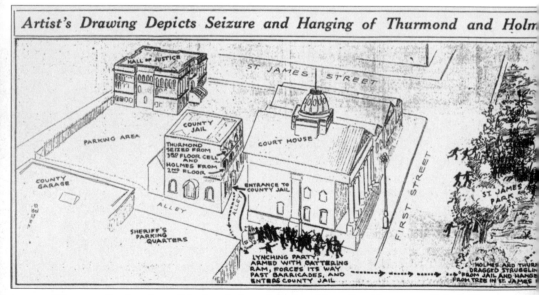

Diagramatic drawing of the break-in and the lynching. *San Francisco Call-Bulletin*

fists, and women lit matches against his flesh. It was as if the mob had turned into a herd of savage jackals. Holmes continued to struggle as they placed a noose around his neck. "Let him see what we've done to his buddy!" someone yelled.[33] So the lynchers pulled on the rope and lifted him well off the ground to give him a look at Thurmond as he dangled from the tree. Then they dropped Holmes to the ground, where he was beaten again. Again they hauled him high into the air, while Holmes struggled vainly to grab the rope and get it off his neck. The mob lowered him again and broke his arms. Then they hauled him up for a final time, as he screamed in pain and desperation. Holmes kicked in the air several times and finally went limp. A stream of urine signaled the fact of his death. The mob let out a lusty roar of satisfaction, and some in the crowd even held their children aloft for a better view. It was over. The mob had slaked its thirst for vengeance. The hangmen gradually melted back into the crowd, which was already beginning to disperse.

The two men hung from the killing trees for about forty minutes before the authorities arrived to cut them down. Their battered, naked bodies were placed in a hearse and, in a final irony, they were taken to

Harold Thurmond hangs from a tree in the city park. *San Jose Mercury News*

the same mortuary that held the mortal remains of Brooke Hart. It was only the second time that the three men had ever been together—once in life and now once in death.

News of the lynching dominated the news, not only in California, but also across the nation. There was not so much outrage as a feeling that justice, however crude, had been done. Governor Rolph personally hailed the lynchings. Said the governor, "This is the best lesson California has ever given the nation! We have shown the country that California will not tolerate kidnapping."[34] And he renewed his vow to pardon anyone involved who was convicted of a crime.

There was, of course, an attempt to investigate the lynchings and to prosecute the perpetrators, but it was perfunctory at best. The governor's pledge of pardons made the investigation seem an empty exercise, and there were few, if any, witnesses willing to testify. A conspiracy of silence settled over the community. All too quickly the entire incident faded into history, and came to be referred to simply as "the last lynchings."

In fact, this was not the last lynching in California. Just twenty months later, a mob in Siskiyou County seized the confessed slayer of a police chief and hung him from a pine tree. But these sad incidents, taken together, put a permanent end to the long custom of vigilante justice in the state. The lingering memory of the frenzy of the mob, the lust for blood, and the horror of human viciousness brought this chapter in California to its conclusion.

Cartoon showing Governor Rolph "pointing with pride." *Baltimore Sun*

Chapter Thirteen

The Alameda Enigma—1955

*C*apital punishment in California has, at best, an uncertain history. We will never know, for instance, how many Californians were executed for crimes during the first forty-one years of the state's history. Over that period, executions were performed by county authorities, and no one took the trouble to count heads—or, more specifically, bodies. But, in 1891, the state took over the onerous task of putting criminals to death. Proclaimed the legislature: "A judgment of death must be executed within the walls of one of the State Prisons designated by the Court by which judgment is rendered." Hanging was the sole method of dispatching criminals at that time, and all hangings were subsequently performed at Folsom and San Quentin prisons. Between 1891 and 1938, a total of 498 convicted felons were dispatched at these two institutions. Then, in 1937, lethal gas was adopted as the official means of state-inflicted death. However, those already convicted were "grandfathered," and the last legal hanging in California took place on May 1, 1942, when a Major Raymond Lisenba was hanged for murdering his wife by sticking her foot into a box full of diamondback rattlesnakes.

Albert Kessell, a convicted Sacramento murderer, had the honor of being the first to perish in the gas chamber at San Quentin, the institution then designated as the sole locale for California executions. In the years that followed, an average of eight Californians were executed every year, after spending an average of less than two years on death row.

But while executions had became more or less routine in the state, by the mid-1950s there was a growing anxiety about the appropriateness and morality of state-sponsored death. Then in 1955, an event occurred across the Bay from San Francisco that would serve as a catalyst to bring the issue to the forefront of California's political life.

By all accounts, Stephanie Bryan was a very ordinary fourteen-year-old girl. A student at Willard Junior High School in Berkeley, she was attractive without being especially pretty, intelligent but quite shy, not really a little girl anymore, but far from being a woman. She was an honor student, but so reticent to speak in class that her teachers seldom called on her.

She had several close friends but only a very limited social life. She had not yet discovered boys, and boys had not yet discovered her. She had just begun wearing her first brassiere. Standing five feet, three inches tall, weighing 105 pounds, and with brown hair and brown eyes,[1] she was barely distinguishable from her dozens of classmates.

Stephanie's home life was also quite ordinary. She lived in a modest middle-class home with three younger sisters and an even younger brother. She had been conservatively raised by her father, a radiologist at a hospital in Oakland, and by a religious and caring mother. Every morning her father drove her to school before heading off to work, and every afternoon she walked home on a prescribed route laid out by her mother.

April 28, 1955, seemed like another ordinary day in Stephanie's life. Wearing a blue pleated skirt, a white pullover sweater, and a dark blue cardigan, she arrived at school on time and attended all of her classes.[2] Promptly at three-thirty in the afternoon, she left school with a girlfriend and started for home. She was carrying her French textbook in anticipation of studying that evening for a French test the next day. On the way home, the two girls stopped at a pet store where Stephanie bought a book on parakeets. They also stopped at a library where Stephanie checked out two teenage novels. They then stopped briefly at a bakery where each girl purchased a doughnut. Stephanie and her friend parted as they approached the tennis courts at the Claremont Hotel, the great white luxury resort situated on the hill above their path. Stephanie headed down Eucalyptus Path, a shortcut she always took that led straight to Alvarado Road where she lived.

And then something very out of the ordinary happened to Stephanie: She completely disappeared.

When Stephanie had not arrived home by 4:30 P.M., her mother became concerned and decided to walk out and meet her daughter. She walked the route that Stephanie always took and eventually arrived at the now deserted school. She quickly retraced her steps, thinking that perhaps her daughter had taken another route. But when she arrived back at the house, Stephanie was not there. At 5:30 P.M., Mr. Bryan arrived at home from work. The two parents decided to call some of Stephanie's friends. They did so, but none of the friends knew where she was. At 6:30 P.M., Mr. Bryan drove to the police station and reported his daughter missing.

The police had received no report on the girl. For a day, they theorized that she might have simply run away. The local newspaper, however, did not hesitate. "Berkeley Girl May Be Kidnap Victim" read the next day's banner headline. And, the search for Stephanie Bryan got underway.

Just before midnight on the day that Stephanie's disappearance was made known, the Bryans received a troublesome phone call. The caller informed them that Stephanie had been kidnaped and that she could be ransomed for $5,000. A meeting place was arranged for the next day, and at the appointed time, police arrested an eighteen-year-old mental patient who, it was quickly determined, had nothing to do with Stephanie's disappearance.

HAVE YOU SEEN THIS CHILD?

The *Oakland Tribune* pleads for information on the missing Stephanie Bryan, fourteen-year-old daughter of a Berkeley radiologist, pictured here with her dog "Hoagy."

Other false leads followed. Several people identified Stephanie as a girl who had spent several hours in the San Rafael bus station on the day of her disappearance. The girl's clothing, however, did not match what Stephanie had been wearing. Other sightings were reported, one from as far away as Massachusetts. Police, however, put considerable stock in a report from a motorist who reported seeing a man struggling with a young girl in a car on Broadway Tunnel Road, east of Berkeley. Within another day, five more drivers called Berkeley police to say that they had also witnessed a similar event on that part of the highway. The car was described as a grey, early fifties Pontiac or Chevrolet sedan.[3]

Now the search for Stephanie attained full steam. Teams of Berkeley police checked gas stations in the area in the hope that an attendant might have seen the car bearing the struggling girl. Circulars with a picture and description of Stephanie were sent to law enforcement agencies in eleven states. Five off-duty policeman voluntarily scoured the Berkeley hills and were startled to find the body of a female stuffed into a concrete pipe. It was not Stephanie, but the corpse of an older woman whom police were unable to identify.

The *Berkeley Daily Gazette* sketches out the known details: the last sighting at the Claremont Hotel in Berkeley, the screaming girl near the Broadway tunnel, the mystery car sighting and the discovery of Stephanie's French book on Franklin Canyon Road.

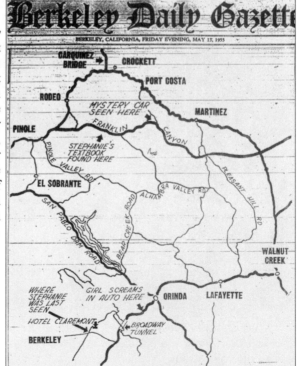

Then, on May 2, the first viable clue was discovered. Stephanie's French textbook was found by the side of the road on Franklin Canyon Road, three miles east of Pinole, several miles south of the Carquinez Bridge, and about an hour's drive from where Stephanie had disappeared. This discovery was deemed to be proof positive that Stephanie had been kidnaped. In the days that followed, hundreds of volunteers searched the area. The Federal Bureau of Investigation immediately entered the case, making its full services available to local police. The National Guard and the Boy Scouts volunteered their services. Reconnaissance planes flew over the surrounding hills and valleys. A week later, police investigated the ominous presence of buzzards circling a spot over Lemont Canyon, and twenty officers were dispatched to the area. They found the body of a dead deer.[4]

On May 15, police announced that, unless further clues were found, the searches would be deemed unproductive and would be discontinued. The case of Stephanie Bryan's disappearance would be kept open, but it would be necessary to reassign the officers involved in the case. In the weeks, and then the months, that followed, the investigation simply dried up and it seemed that the sad case of the missing girl would remain unsolved and eventually forgotten, except by those who had known and loved her.

But on July 15, the case cracked wide open. Electrifying news arrived from a neat stucco house at 1408 San Jose Avenue located on the small residential island of Alameda which sits in the San Francisco Bay just west of Oakland. This was the residence of Georgia Abbott, a young housewife and beauty parlor operator, and her twenty-seven-year-old husband, Burton Abbott, a student at the University of California in Berkeley, who was studying accounting on the G.I. Bill of Rights.

Mrs. Abbott told police that she had gone to the basement that evening to look through a box of old clothes for something to wear in an amateur theatrical appearance. While rummaging in the box, she came upon a red handbag she did not recognize. Out of curiosity, she examined the contents. Inside were Stephanie Bryan's student identity card, her Junior Red Cross membership card, a picture of her dog and several schoolmates, and a letter to a friend.[5]

Family friends Otto and Leona Dezman were visiting the Abbotts at the time. All of them agreed that the purse must have belonged to the missing girl they had read about. Mr. Dezman picked up the phone and called the police. After the police arrived and took possession of the purse, Burton Abbott and Otto Dezman resumed playing chess. According to later reports, Abbott showed no signs of fright, stress or even concern. Police made a brief examination of the premises, noting that Abbott's car was parked in the garage. It was a grey 1950 Chevrolet sedan.

The Abbott home at 1408 San Jose Avenue. Note the 1950 Chevrolet sedan, shown parked in the driveway. *Alameda Times Star*

The big break in the case: Stephanie's purse is found in a box of old clothes in the garage of a house in Alameda.

The next morning, the police and the FBI arrived at the Abbotts' house with picks and shovels. They dug up a garden near the garage, but found nothing. Next they began digging in an unexcavated part of the garage floor, and within minutes, they hit paydirt. Buried in the dirt were Stephanie's school books, her two library books, her eyeglasses, and her brassiere.[6] The Abbotts professed to be dumbfounded.

Police pressed Burton Abbott for details about his whereabouts on the day of Stephanie's disappearance. He told them that on April 28 he had left his house at about 11:00 A.M. and driven to Sacramento to file a property claim but, after being unable to find the right building, he decided to continue on up Highway 40 to a family-owned cabin in the mountains of Trinity County for the opening of the fishing season the next day. Skeptical, police asked Abbott to submit to a lie-detector test and a psychiatric examination. Abbott took both tests voluntarily. The results, authorities said, were "inconclusive."[7]

While police were pondering what to do next, two *San Francisco Examiner* reporters drove up to Abbott's cabin in Trinity County, hired a local tracker and two bloodhounds, and conducted a search of the grounds around the cabin. The dogs led them to a spot on a hill about three hundred yards behind the cabin. There they found a shallow grave, which appeared to have been recently prepared. In it was the decomposed body of a young girl, naked from the waist up. The rest of the girl's body was clad in a blue-green skirt and white saddle oxfords. A pair of panties were tied around her neck. Her skull had been dented by a series of savage blows. This, it turned out, was all that remained of Stephanie Bryan.

Burton Abbott was immediately placed under arrest for the kidnapping and murder of Stephanie Bryan. When told of the grisly discovery, Burton said, "I don't know how it got there. I don't know anything about it. I'm staying with my story that I don't know anything about it."[8]

The authorities began an intensive investigation of Abbott and his background. He certainly didn't seem like the kind of person who would be capable of such a crime. He was a veteran of World War II, and he had been honorably discharged. While in training camp, he had developed double pneumonia and later tuberculosis. As a result, he had one lung and seven ribs removed, leaving him permanently disabled after spending two full years in a military hospital. Even after his discharge, his health problems continued. He developed an abscess on his chest that required constant medication. He was slight and skinny and he had trouble breathing. At 130 pounds, he seemed to have little energy or strength. His brother, Mark, remarked at the time of Abbott's arrest, "He is in constant pain. He is so weak that he can't even lift his four-year-old son."[9] How could a man of such limited physical ability have overpowered a teenager only some twenty pounds lighter than he was? And how, it was asked, could he have ever dragged her up a steep hillside and then buried her?

Abbott's social history also indicated him to be an unlikely murderer. His wife, his family, and his friends all said that he was gentle and kind, never became angry, and was easygoing in temperament. He had no known history of anti-social behavior, and he had no prior arrests for any crime. He seemed to be happily married and was not known to have demonstrated interest in other women. He had a young son on whom he doted, and he was studying hard to develop the skills necessary to support his family.

Nevertheless, the evidence seemed overwhelming, and on July 30 a grand jury returned an indictment of kidnap-murder. Burton Abbott was bound over to the Alameda County jail in Oakland to await his trial set for November 7, 1955.[10]

Abbott continued to deny, quietly but forcefully, that he had committed the murder or had any knowledge of it. He made a formal plea to

Burton W. "Bud" Abbott
The Oakland Museum of California

be able to meet and confront Stephanie's parents, but his request was dismissed by the district attorney as a publicity stunt.[11] Abbott spent the weeks and months before his trial reading, consulting with his attorneys, and denying his guilt over and over again.

During that time, however, a second portrait of Burton Abbott began to emerge. Doctors gave him a complete physical examination and were surprised at his excellent physical condition, virtually normal for a man his age. He was also described by some who knew him as an ardent sportsman, capable of hiking over the roughest terrain for long periods of time. Police discovered that Abbott had a juvenile record of sex offenses and that his car had been identified by several girls who complained that he had tried to entice them into the back seat of his car. One Berkeley housewife complained that Abbott had once followed her and tried to flirt with her, an allegation that Abbott vehemently denied. A thirteen-year-old girl made a charge that Abbott had tried to pick her up some weeks after Stephanie had disappeared. Abbott was known as a loving and devoted

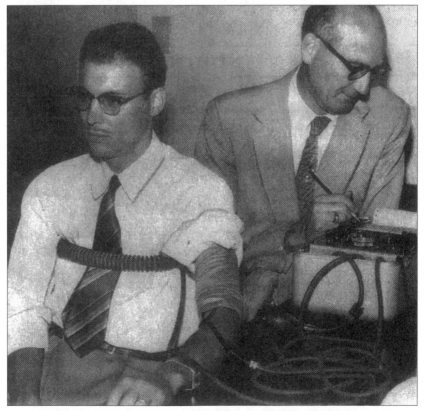

Abbott takes his lie-detector test. The results were "inconclusive."
Oakland Tribune

father, but his cellmate testified that when he was given in jail some drawings made for him by his four-year old son, he glanced at them indifferently and then threw them aside without comment.[12]

In short, Burton Abbott was an enigma, a conundrum, a puzzle that no one could quite figure out. His family thought him to be a loving and devoted husband and father. On the other hand, one examining psychologist stated that Abbott had no real feelings or emotions for anyone other than himself. His friends believed him to be an intelligent and sound individual, but he was described in court as having "an infantile personality compatible with this sort of crime."[13] His wife stated under oath that since his lung operation "he has not been highly sexed and for the past two years we have practically ceased having marital relations."[14] Yet, there was specific evidence of a dangerous sexuality in his character. Perhaps, no one really knew the real Burton Abbott. It is possible that he had a dual personality, and that even he was not aware of the chasms in his life and the way he lived it.

Whichever was the real Burton Abbott, both sides of his personality went on trial on November 7, 1955, in the courtroom of the Alameda County courthouse. The presiding judge was Charles Wade Snook, a jurist with a reputation for fairness and firmness. The prosecution was in the hands of District Attorney J. Frank Coakley, noted for his vigorous prosecutorial style and for his tough cross-examinations. He was assisted by Assistant District Attorney Folger Emerson, another experienced prosecutor. Abbott selected two immensely capable defense attorneys, Stanley Whitney, a former Alameda city attorney, and Harold Hove, an Alameda city councilman and an ex-FBI agent.

In one of his statements to the press before the trial, Folger Emerson remarked, "If ever there was a crime that fitted the punishment of death, this is it." And, at the opening of the trial, the prosecutors asked for convictions for both kidnapping and murder. A jury of seven men and five women proceeded to sit patiently through fifty-four days of testimony and deliberation. Before it concluded, this would become the longest murder trial in California history.

All the evidence against Abbott was circumstantial. Witnesses testified that Abbott probably knew who Stephanie was. They were both regular patrons of Pring's Doughnut Shop, which was located near Stephanie's home and on Abbott's route to the university. It was known that Stephanie had made a purchase there on the fateful day. Three witnesses testified to seeing Abbott in Berkeley on the afternoon that he claimed he had spent driving up to his cabin. One of them was a patron of Mrs. Abbott's beauty

Before the trial, Abbott professes his innocence, flanked by his wife, Georgia and his lawyer, Stanley Whitney.

salon, and she testified that Burton had visited the salon at about 2:30 P.M., just an hour and a half before Stephanie disappeared.

Three motorists who saw a man struggling with a girl in a car similar to Abbott's on the highway he would have taken to Trinity County provided testimony. The discovery of Stephanie's possessions in the Abbott garage was recounted, as was the unearthing of her body behind Abbott's cabin. The prosecutors also made it clear to the jury that they believed this had been a sex crime. Said Emerson, "The defendant kidnapped the girl for a sex motive. How else can you explain the brassiere and the fact that her panties had been cut from her body." And then he hypothesized, "They were also used as a gag or for strangling the girl, or tied around her neck and used for dragging the body up the hill."[15]

A great deal of the prosecutor's time and energy was devoted to refuting Abbott's alibi. He claimed that he had stopped on the way to his cabin at a Shell station in Corning and then, later, at a restaurant in Red Bluff and, still later, at a bar in Wildwood. No one at the gas station was able to recall Abbott being there that day, and Abbott claimed he had paid cash and thus had no receipt. Several people claimed to have seen Abbott at the Red Bluff restaurant, but under cross-examination they admitted it could have been someone else and they weren't sure. Abbott's appearances at the Wildwood bar on or near the night of the murder were more complicated. The owner and a friend of Abbott both remembered Abbott being there for an extended period the next day and one witness thought he might have seen him the day before. But Abbott's friend remembered the owner saying to Abbott on the second night, "Why, Bud Abbott, what the hell are you doing here this time of year?"[16] The impact of this testimony on the jury was visible to the thirty or so reporters covering the trial.

Abbott's claimed route on the day of the abduction and murder. His side trip to Sacramento had few believers.

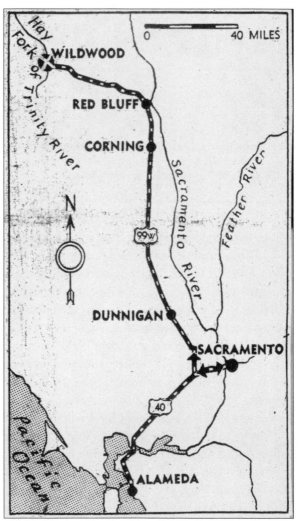

Georgia Abbott took the stand briefly and supported her husband wholeheartedly. It was evident that she simply couldn't believe the man she thought she knew so well could be capable of such a heinous crime. Then Burton Abbott took the stand—and he stayed there for four days. He recounted his tale of innocence. He denied any knowledge of how Stephanie's effects came to be in his garage, offering the possibility that almost anyone could have put them there, especially since the garage had been used weeks earlier as a polling place. Nor did he have any explanation as to how Stephanie's body came to be buried behind his cabin. He denied having made earlier statements attributed to him by police. In four days, he never yielded in his insistence that he was not guilty of the crimes for which he was on trial. He remained calm, poised, soft-spoken, and deliberate. He never presented the image of a psychopath or a madman.

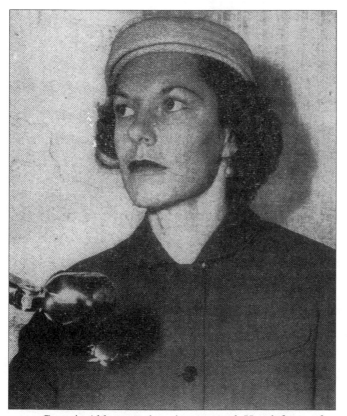

Georgia Abbott on the witness stand. Her defense of her husband was unyielding. *Oakland Museum of California*

Perhaps the most electrifying moments of the trial came during the testimony of a prosecution witness, Dr. Paul L. Kirk, a highly respected criminologist from the University of California. Kirk testified that he had found fibers in Abbott's car that matched those from Stephanie's sweater. He said he had also discovered hairs in the car that came from Stephanie's head, as well as evidence of blood buried deep in the fabric of the seats. He also had examined particles of clay and dirt on a pair of Abbott's boots. They matched, he said, samples taken from around the grave site. It was, everyone agreed, a pivotal point in the trial.

The defense ripped savagely into the state's case, claiming in no uncertain terms that Abbott had been "framed" by the police. Police, said Defense Attorney Whitney, "grabbed a patsy and moved heaven and earth to pin it on him while ignoring any search for anyone else." Every bit of evidence, he went on, "points to Abbott's innocence." "How," the defense asked, "could a man in the defendant's condition of ill health and physical weakness have carried a body and made it up that hill which had a six-foot vertical wall between the wall and the slope, and why would Abbott, a reasonable, intelligent man, bring back the victim's personal possessions to his home, leaving a trail to his front door?" Whitney also referred to the disposition of his client. "You have seen him for two months now," he said to the jury. "You know he is not stupid, idiotic or unbalanced." And he concluded, "This was a frame-up!"[17]

Defense attorney Whitney holds forth on the subject of Stephanie's belongings, claiming they were planted in the garage by parties unknown. *Oakland Tribune*

But the defense saved its final assault for Dr. Kirk: "Kirk knows what type of evidence the DA wants and he will deliver it for a price! He is too careful to lie. He holds to the truth, but with variations!"[18] And then the defense offered its own counter-witness, Lowell Bradford, director of a crime laboratory in Santa Clara County. Bradford rebutted many of Kirk's findings, and he attempted to blunt those he could not dispute.

Through it all, Burton Abbott sat calmly, almost stoically, giving little hint that he was disturbed or even especially concerned. Only when two witnesses testified he was in Berkeley on the afternoon of the crime did he "hunch down in his seat and look with astonishment."[19]

Prosecutor Coakley closed by reading to the jury the letter Stephanie had written to a friend on the last day of her life, the letter that was found with her effects in the Abbott garage:

"Dear Teddy,

I am writing this letter on notebook paper because I am at school with some extra time and no letter paper...

I have had my hair cut fairly short. I like it better this way. It's much easier to take care of.

How are you doing in school? I won a gold pin for being on the superior scholarship during the time I have been here. Fifteen other people got them. We are planning our summer trip.

We had hoped to come home until we found out the cost of transportation. I wish we could have come. We are planning a camping trip to different places in California.

The news reports say there have been big storms in the East.

It's Spring here. It has been dry for a couple of months but the spring rains are here. The first trees have all bloomed and the trees that lose their leaves are budding.

This hasn't been a very eventful winter. So I can't think of anything to say now."[20]

When he finished reading, Coakley was choked with emotion and tears ran down his cheeks.

On January 19, the case went to the jury. The jurors had a lot to think about, and they took their time. The transcript of the trial ran to thirty-five bound volumes and more than 1,400,000 words.[21] After six days of deliberation and fifty hours behind closed doors, the jury finally announced its verdict: guilty on both counts of kidnap and murder, without a recommendation of mercy.

A sober and attentive jury weighs the evidence during the closing arguments. *Oakland Tribune*

Burton Abbott showed no emotion at the announcement and, after the attempt at a brief press conference during which he refused to answer any questions, he returned to his jail cell and a game of bridge with his cellmates. Days later, he gave a press interview and announced that someone had "framed him." He remarked, "I now have a theory on the frameup but still have no idea as to why the person would want to frame me. My theory may be pertinent later. All I can tell you is that I'm innocent." When asked what kind of person would commit such a brutal crime, Abbott reflected a moment and then replied, "A vicious person."[22]

On February 3, Abbott was sentenced to die by lethal gas in the gas chamber at San Quentin on March 5, 1957.

The intervening months were filled with increasingly desperate appeals and maneuvers to save Abbott's life. There was an appeal to the California supreme court, which failed. Abbott's mother, who had been in hiding during the trial, suddenly surfaced, proclaiming her son's innocence and paying for newspaper advertisements in which she offered $2,500 for information leading to a reversal of the court verdict. As the date for execution drew near, an appeal was made to Governor Goodwin Knight for executive clemency. It was refused. A petition went to the United States Supreme Court for a stay of execution and a new trial. It was also refused. An appeal was made directly to Supreme Court Justice William O. Douglas, who had often intervened in capital punishment

Abbott Shaken By 11-to-1 Guilty Verdict Rumor

The superior court jury deliberating the fate of Burton W. Abbott entered its sixth day this afternoon as tension mounted throughout the building.

Speculation was touched off that the seven men and five women weighing the case might be nearing their first ballot as Jury Foreman Harry Whitehead called for legal tablets and paper clips shortly after noon.

Meanwhile, an informal report that the jury stood 11 to 1 for conviction left the slender defendant "stunned" and visibly worried in his jail cell, observers said.

REPORTED 'SULKY'

When informed that press sources indicated an 11-to-1 stand, Abbott reportedly told a jailer: "Oh, in my favor of course."

The defendant's demeanor changed rapidly when informed that the report had it for conviction. Sheriff H. P. Gleason reported Abbott has "been sulky" since he was told.

Meanwhile, the defendant's mother, Mrs. Elsie Abbott, who broke down and sobbed hysterically for the first time in public yesterday, today denied that she and Abbott's wife, Georgia, had

Minor Storm Appears To Be Passing

Beyond a few scattered light showers, the latest storm to bring new rainfall to California appeared to be passing today with predictions for partly cloudy and clearing skies. The U. S. Weather Bureau forecast clearing skies in northern California this morning and this afternoon with partly cloudy

When Abbott heard the rumor of a 11-to-1 verdict, he told his jailer, "In my favor, of course!"

cases. Douglas also refused on the grounds that no federal issues were involved. Two days before the execution date, Abbott's lawyers flew to Washington to apply directly to the Supreme Court for a writ of certiorari. Again, the Court denied the request.

The day before the date of execution, Abbott's mother and brother paid him a final visit. Later, his wife, Georgia, comforted him alone in his cell. Abbott himself was reported to be calm and resigned, playing solitaire and reading books and magazines. Though he was a Protestant, Abbott asked to be visited by a Roman Catholic priest. He ordered an elaborate last meal, with precise instructions as to the way he wanted it prepared and the kind of sauces it should include.

Abbott's lawyers made another desperate appeal to Judge Walter Pope of the Ninth U.S. Circuit Court of Appeals. Once again, the court refused. There was now only one last hope of halting the execution: an order of stay from the governor. But Governor Knight was not readily accessible. He was in Oakland at a reception on board the aircraft carrier *USS Hancock*. Execution was set for 10:00 A.M., and at 9:00 A.M. the ship finally arrived at the Alameda Air Station. After hearing from Abbott's lawyers, who claimed that additional appeals were being made to the courts, Knight granted a one-hour delay. The lawyers quickly went to the California supreme court for one last attempt at appeal. This was also refused. Shortly after 11:00 A.M., Abbott was taken from his cell and led toward the gas chamber.

Still, the lawyers would not give up. They tried again to contact Governor Knight, but by this time he was cruising the Bay on the *Hancock*. The ship-to-shore radio was occupied and they couldn't get through. Finally, they made contact and pleaded with the governor for more time. Knight contacted Joseph G. Babich, his clemency secretary in Sacramento, to see if another delay should be granted.

Abbott walked unaided into the chamber at 11:15 A.M., wearing blue denims and a white shirt, open at the collar. To the thirty-seven people viewing the proceedings behind a glass wall, Abbott seemed calm and in control. As he was strapped into the apple-green death chair, he looked at the attendant and said, "It's all right." A slight smile crossed his face.

California Governor Goodwin Knight boards the *U.S.S. Hancock*, where his inaccessibility added greatly to the drama of Abbott's execution. *The Bancroft Library*

Babich got through to San Quentin and finally reached the warden. "Did it start?" he asked "Yes," was the reply. "Can you stop it then?" Babich asked. "It's too late," replied the warden.[23] The gas pellets had already been dropped. Burton Abbott was declared dead at 11:25 A.M.

Controversy surrounding the case did not end with Burton Abbott's death. Questions still haunted those who had followed the case. Why would such a seemingly normal person as Abbott, from all outward appearances a good family man and an industrious university student, commit such a horrifying crime? Why would Stephanie Bryan get into his car when she was so close to home and when she had been carefully coached by her parents never to do such a thing? How could Abbott, with one lung and seven missing ribs, haul a 103-pound girl up a steep, slippery slope for more than three hundred yards and then dig a grave? Why would Abbott bring all of her personal effects back to his own home and then carelessly conceal them in his garage? Why did Abbott show such little concern when her purse was found and then readily agree that the police should be called? How could Abbott have remained so serene and virtually unaffected by everything that was happening to him right up to the moment of his death? These are questions that still haunt students of the case.

They may also have been on the governor's mind the next day when he declared himself opposed to the death penalty. But, he was also motivated by the lawyers' last-minute machinations to frustrate the course of the law. Said Knight, "It is not in keeping with the high principles of the legal profession to make a mockery and a circus of legal proceedings in connection with a death case."[24] Knight then promised to sign a bill placing a moratorium on the death penalty in California.

Assemblyman Lester McMillan quickly announced his sponsorship of bills to suspend and abolish the death sentence. "The present law is all wrong," said McMillan. "Executing Abbott is no deterrent to other criminals. In my opinion, the state has no right to take a life."[25] California State Attorney General Edmund G. Brown, later elected governor of California, issued a statement calling for a five-year moratorium on capital punishment in the state.

There are two sad postscripts to the case. An insurance company denied the payment of Burton Abbott's $10,000 G.I. insurance policy to his five-year-old son because of an exclusion for any policy holder executed for murder. And on March 16, 1957, the remains of Stephanie Bryan were finally released to her family for burial. She was interred far away from the horrifying events of her murder, in a family plot in Massachusetts.

Chapter Fourteen

Labor in the Crosshairs—1966

San Francisco has been a strong labor union city from its very beginning. Noted one historian, "There is so much evidence of early trade union activity in San Francisco that one is tempted to believe that the craftsmen met each other on the way to California and agreed to unite."[1] As early as 1849, the city's carpenters went on strike over a wage dispute, and both sailors and musicians walked out on their jobs before another year was out.

Over the next century, almost every phase of human occupational endeavor in San Francisco claimed union representation. The building trades, manufacturing workers, and dock workers were among the earliest workers to be organized, but eventually there were also unions for stablemen, dishwashers, fish cleaners, poultry dressers, wool sorters, gravediggers, janitors, and chorus girls! By the turn of the century, San Francisco had acquired a reputation as the most unionized city in the United States. The city claimed more than a hundred and eighty different unions, forty-two of them in the building trades alone.[2]

Along with this intense union activity came a full share of union violence. Before 1900, much of the violence, initiated by the unions themselves, was directed at Chinese laborers, especially in the cigar-making, shoe manufacturing, and clothing industries, where Chinese workers were regarded as a threat to both wages and working conditions. Chinese in these fields were routinely threatened, attacked and even murdered. Strike-

breakers were routinely imported into San Francisco and their presence invariably provoked conflict. In the general city-wide strike of 1901, five people were killed and more than three hundred were injured. In 1907, during a strike of the city's streetcar operators, clashes between unionists, strikebreakers, and the police resulted in six deaths due to gunshot wounds, as well as twenty-five deaths and more than a thousand injuries from hand fighting.

San Francisco union violence was occasionally directed at non-union workers. In the early 1920s, the iron-moulders union was accused of using a roving wrecking crew that "regularly shot down or otherwise assaulted in the most cruel and brutal manner other defenseless foundry workers."[3] In the waterfront strife of the 1940s and 1950s, there were more than a dozen deaths as the longshoremen clashed over and over again with both strikebreakers and police.

But, accustomed as San Franciscans were to mayhem in their union life, they were scarcely prepared for what happened in the spring of 1966, for this would be union violence of a different kind. And, it would leave a scar on the city's psyche that would be visible for years to come.

It was a scene straight out of a Raymond Chandler novel. The date: April 5, 1966. The time: one o'clock in the morning. The place: Sixteenth Street near Valencia in the Soma district of San Francisco. Three men left the B & E bar and headed toward the corner. The red neon sign above the bar blinked through the early morning mist as they reached the corner. Two of the men said goodbye to the third, got into a car, and drove off. The third man crossed the street and headed toward his own car, parked nearby on South Van Ness.

As the man approached his car, he failed to notice another car, dark and idling quietly, sitting at the curbside directly across the street. The man took out his keys and proceeded to unlock his car door. The window on the other car slid silently down and the muzzle of a shotgun protruded. Suddenly, the roar of a 12-gauge split the nighttime silence and the man took the blow in the right side of his back, spinning him around. A second blast sent a pellet through his right eye and into his brain. The man fell heavily to the street, face down, as the car sped off into the night, tires squealing.

This was no commonplace, random murder of the kind to which San Francisco had become all too accustomed in recent times, and the city's newspapers made this point ever so clear in the following days. The dead man was Dow Wilson, the leader and recording secretary of Painters Local #4 and one of union's most controversial figures.[4] Wil-

Dow Wilson, head of Painters Local #4, and victim of the first murder. *San Francisco Chronicle*

son, forty years old and instantly recognizable from his flame-red hair and beard, was a man who had as many enemies as he had friends. The number of suspects was almost beyond reckoning, and the police inspectors knew they would have their hands full.

Wilson had been a controversial figure for most of his adult life. A high school dropout, he had moved up quickly in the union ranks even as a young man because of his outspoken and confrontational style. He seemed continually at war with his superiors, his employers, and, frequently, his co-workers. Said the president of his local, "He was a tough boy and he didn't care whose toes he stepped on."[5] Wilson struggled constantly for greater autonomy for his 2,600-man local, fought against what he felt to be "sweetheart deal" contracts, and railed against corruption and thievery by both local and international union officials. Of late, his crusades had reached new heights of volume and audacity. Just two years earlier, Wilson had engineered a merger of San Francisco's two painters' unions into a single union, over the strong opposition of the International Union leadership. Then, he announced his intention to run against these same leaders in 1968, calling them "fakes and phonies," "high class pimps," and "sellout artists."[6] Even earlier, he had earned the enmity of East Bay District Council secretary Ben Rasnick, when he claimed a contract Rasnick had negotiated was a sellout to management. Wilson and some followers actually burst into a meeting at one point and physically dragged Rasnick out of a room where the contract was being finalized.

Wilson was equally unpopular with the area's painting contractors, who claimed that he kept the union members in a state of constant agitation. And Wilson even managed to arouse the passions of union leaders in his own state, claiming that the welfare fund in Sacramento was being mismanaged and pillaged. In short, the choice of suspects in Wilson's murder was wide and varied.

Police first questioned the two men who had been with Wilson in the B & E bar. They turned out to be union friends who had been drinking and conversing following a hall meeting. They had driven directly home and were removed from the list of suspects. That left everyone else.

Homeowners along Van Ness and Sixteenth streets were questioned. The bartender at the B & E bar was interrogated, as were a number of its customers. Leaders, as well as rank-and-file members, of Local #4 were grilled. In the possibility that out-of-town hit men had been employed, investigators searched airline passenger lists for the days preceding and following the murder in search of known assassins. The local union itself posted a reward of $10,000 for information, and then, in an action that revealed its own suspicions, it ran an advertisement proclaiming the reward in New York, where the International Union was located.

At the same time, others had their own say. Morris Evans, one of the local's business representatives, announced dramatically, "This was an assassination. It looks to me like a paid operation."[7] Edgar Hammer, the business agent of Wilson's local, received a phone call during which the caller asked, "How do you like what our union creep got?"[8] Jessica Mitford, author of the best-selling book, *The American Way of Death*, received a more ominous call: "Your husband's on that list too!" Mitford, at the time, was married to Robert Trenhaft, a lawyer running for district attorney of Alameda County.[9] Joseph Belardi, president of the San Francisco Labor Council, was told in a phone call that he would meet "the same fate as the other labor leader."[10] Despite these threats, John Burton, a longtime California politician, eulogized Wilson as "a man who worked for the betterment of mankind."[11]

As for the police, they seemed to be at loose ends. Lieutenant Barnaby O'Leary offered lamely, "Wilson was a caustic sort of character. Apparently, everywhere he went, he made enemies." And then to add to the confusion, he added simply, "It could have been some kind of nut."[12]

The weeks drug by with no apparent progress in the case. Then on May 7, a startling development occurred. After a late night meeting of Painters Local #1178 in Hayward, a San Francisco bedroom community, Lloyd Green, financial secretary of the union, retired to his office with an associate to talk over the meeting. As he paused in front of the office window to open a can of beer, a 12-gauge shotgun exploded the window and Green took the force of the shot full in face. It nearly tore his head off and he fell to floor with a sickening thud, the second labor leader to die by shotgun blast in a month.

Panic took over the Painters Union. Demanded one member, "What are they going to do? Let all us be murdered?"[13] Wallace Rood, a business agent for Local #500 in Richmond, demanded police protection, as did Morris Evans, who had succeeded Dow Wilson in the leadership of Local #4. Union leaders pushed the reward for information up to more than $40,000.

Police drawing of the shotgun murder of Lloyd Green in his Hayward union office.

The authorities now stated publicly that they believed both killings to be the work of "imported hirelings." Said Charles O'Brien, the deputy attorney general in San Francisco, "We believe these to be out-of-state contract killings."[14] However, this was really a ruse to keep the real killers from becoming suspicious. The truth was that police inspectors suspected, almost from the beginning, that the murders were the result of local inter-union conflict and that the assassins were homegrown.

The previous February, a thirty-four-year-old ex-truck driver named Wallace Charleston sat at a bar in the San Francisco Tenderloin area, celebrating his release on bail for his participation in a recent bar brawl. The owner of the bar, Richard Rock, sat down next to Charleston and asked him if he would be interested in "dumping" someone for his brother-in-law, Carl Black. Charleston, eager for some easy money, said he was interested, and Black later came by and picked Charleston up in his car. Charleston found himself seated in the back seat with "a big guy with hard eyes who looked like a judge."[15]

The man asked Charleston if he would "dump" someone from the Painters Union at Local #4. He gave Charleston the name of the victim, but Charleston was later able to recall only that the name started with the

The union raises its reward to more than $42,000 for the arrest and conviction of the killers.

letter "D." As payment for the killing, the man said he was willing to pay $5,000, and he gave Charleston an envelope with $2,500, the other half to be paid when the victim's obituary appeared in the paper. But Charleston got cold feet, handed the man back the money, left the car and called the police.

Detectives conducted an investigation, then reported back to Charleston that there were no officials in Local #4 whose last name started with "D." As a result, they decided that the whole thing was probably some kind of scam. But on the morning of April 7, Charleston read in the newspaper that Dow Wilson had been murdered, and he realized right away that he had misunderstood the recitation of the intended victim's name. What he thought had been a long last name was actually a combination of a first and a second name. He had been asked to kill Dow Wilson. He immediately called the police again.

The detectives on the case were now anxious to have Charleston re-contact Carl Black. Eager to bargain away the charges against him for the bar brawl, Charleston agreed. Then the detectives got a major break in the case. Police in Sacramento informed them that members of Local #478 had been complaining about the administration of the union's welfare fund. The principal complainant: Dow Wilson. The accountant for the fund: Carl Black.

Wallace Charleston, principal witness for the prosecution, gives his telling testimony. *San Francisco Chronicle*

Norman Call, the Sacramento painting contractor who arranged the murders. *San Francisco Chronicle*

242

Detectives went through the California department of motor vehicles files and pulled out the license photo of every person who was involved in the administration of the welfare fund in question. Detectives sat down with Charleston and went through the pictures one by one. Just as they reached the end of the stack, Charleston suddenly laid his finger on one of the photographs. Without hesitation, he said, "This is your boy."[16] He was pointing to the photo of Norman Call, a forty-six-year-old painting contractor in Sacramento who sat on the administrative committee of the welfare fund at Local #4. Call had been the man in the back seat of the car, the man who tried to talk Charleston into killing Wilson.

Now it was Call, not Black, that the police wanted Charleston to get back in touch with. By tracking Call's movements, they were able to arrange for Charleston to "accidentally" encounter Call on a Sacramento sidewalk one afternoon in mid-May. Charleston had a radio transmitter concealed under his coat. Police surrounded the area with audio recorders and with motion picture cameras to record the event. The conversation that ensued was an eye-opener.

Charleston: *I see you got your man "dumped." How many were in on it?*

Call: *There's only three of us knows—the guy that gives the order and me that set it up, and the two that done it. Well, that's really four then, I mean, putting it that way. And there's another in the make right now.*

Charleston: *How much is it?*

Call: *It's a cheap one, but I mean....*

Charleston: *How much is a cheap one?*

Call: *Huh? Two.*

Charleston: *Two thousand?*

Call: *Yeah. He's just a....*

Charleston: *Who is he?*

Call: *Well....*

Charleston: *Another labor guy?*

Call: *Yeah. He's just a...it'll be a relief. No big shot. Just some mouthy son of a bitch. Just a couple of strong arm boys are needed. There's one down in Oakland real, real ready to go.[17]*

This was just what the police needed, except for two things. They didn't get the name of the trigger man—and they didn't yet know who the next victim was to be. So they set Charleston up two more times with Call, who now regarded Charleston almost as a confederate. But these two subsequent conversations still did not yield the names they wanted. The second encounter did, however, give the detectives something else to work on. It took place in a hotel bar in Sacramento, and Call brought with him, for the first time, another man who was obviously in league with him. The new man didn't participate in the conversation, but instead sat silently off to the side, looking on. He was quickly identified by police as Max Ward, thirty-seven years old and small in stature, a contractor in Sacramento. Ward, police quickly learned, was also listed as a member of the union's welfare fund.

The People Involved

These are the people in the Painters Union shotgun assassinations:

Killed

Dow Wilson, secretary of Local 4 in San Francisco. who was gunned down near the Labor Temple on April 5

Lloyd Green, financial secretary of the Painters Union at Hayward, killed last Saturday at the union offices

Arrested

Norman Call, 46. a Sacramento painting contractor and employer member of the Sacramento Local 478's trustee and welfare fund.

MAX WARD, 47. of Carmichael, also a painting contractor, who joined Call at the TowneHouse minutes after Call talked of another local man who "had to go."

CLYDE SIMMONDS. 75 an office employee of Call and secretary of the Painting and Decorating Contractors Association in Sacramento

RICHARD ROCK, 33. owner of the Square Chair bar at 246 Leavenworth street in San Francisco, who allegedly acted as go-between for two men trying to recruit a killer.

Sought by Police

CARL MOSES BLACK, 47. an Oakland accountant and Rock's brother-in-law. Black, also known as Schwartz, is on probation for income tax evasion and is believed to be in Miami.

Informant

WALLY CHARLESTON. 34 who refused $2500 last February to kill Wilson and then cooperated with police after reading of Wilson's assassination.

The *San Francisco Chronicle* sorts out the principals in the first trial.

Max Ward, the gunman, who pulled the trigger in both murders. *San Francisco Chronicle*

Green's murder now gave the entire project new urgency. No one could guess how many other union officials were marked for death. The time had come to move—and to move fast. On May 11, less than a week after the second shooting, San Francisco detectives, working with Sacramento police, broke into Call's house and rousted him out of bed. While Call protested his innocence and bellowed his outrage at the invasion, police searched his house and his garage. The search yielded a number of incriminating items—several spent shotgun shells and hand-drawn maps of both Lloyd Green's home and office. The maps indicated possible shooting sites, as well as escape routes. And that wasn't all. On the maps were the fingerprints of little Max Ward.

Ward's home was next to be visited in the police sweep. Rousted out of bed, Ward looked even more diminutive than he had when he accompanied Call to the meeting with Charleston. Police quickly surmised the reason: He didn't have on the specially designed "lift" shoes that he always wore when in public. The evidence from the Ward residence was also impressive—shotgun shells and a 12-gauge shotgun. Ward was hauled off, loudly protesting his innocence and demanding to see his lawyer. He would be seeing a lot of his lawyer—and of other lawyers—in the months ahead.

The roundup continued. Richard Rock, the owner of the Tenderloin bar and the man who first approached Charleston about a "dumping," was taken into custody on the street in front of his bar. Carl Black, the man who drove the automobile at the original meeting, was arrested in a phone booth in Miami while frantically calling his wife after reading about the other arrests.

With the alleged assailants in custody, San Francisco detectives on the case breathed a sigh of relief. Their respite did not last long. On May 18, they once again went into action. Sture Youngren, the administrator of the painters' welfare fund, put a .45 automatic to his temple and pulled the trigger. He left behind a note that read, "The coward's way out, but I'm taking it."[18] When police removed the body, they also took the precaution of removing the fund's books. They got them out just in time. Only a few hours later, the sheriff's seal on the door was broken, the door was battered down, and the place was torn up in a frantic search for the records that were already in the hands of the police.

The welfare fund books were examined for the authorities by accountant James W. P. Conway. At the conclusion of his analysis, Conway made a dramatic announcement—more than $100,000 had been embezzled from the fund, more than 20 percent of the total assets. Norman Call had made a total of ninety-three fraudulent claims on the account. Max Ward had illegally extracted funds from the fund on twenty-four occasions.[19]

At the first trial, attorney Lois Prentice, Max Ward and attorney Melvin Belli consult. *San Francisco Chronicle*

Carl Black, the original go-between, nervously awaits his sentencing. *San Francisco Chronicle*

The trial of Call, Ward, Black, and Rock got under way on August 8, and from the outset it gave every sign of being a circus. Each defendant had his own defense attorney. Black's attorney, George T. Davis, ostentatiously withdrew himself from the area occupied by the other defendants and set up his own table in the courtroom, saying, "My client is pretty much defending himself without regard to whose toes he steps on!"[20] Little Max Ward was defended by the massive and bellicose Melvin Belli. Belli asked for special consideration for his client, stating, "I think it is exemplary that he stole a mere $3,000."[21] All the lawyers tried to have Judge Norman Elkington disqualified on various grounds. As for the judge himself, he admonished the various attorneys, "You are to make no more shouting statements!"[22]

Finally, after almost two weeks of wrangling and the vetting of more than a hundred and sixty prospective jurors, a jury of five men and seven women was empanelled. Prosecutor Walter Ginbinni tried to eliminate some of the confusion by deciding to try Norman Call first, and by himself. He calculated that the evidence against Call was the strongest and that a conviction might persuade him to turn state's evidence.

The trial went Ginbinni's way from the start. It began with no fewer than twelve accountants and financial experts trooping to the stand to portray Call as the principal looter of the union's welfare fund. Said one, "He used it like a personal bank."[23]

Next came the really damning evidence: the tape recordings in which Call described to Charleston the details of the killings. Robert Scott and Baird McKnight, the attorneys for Call, fought vigorously to have the tapes excluded. The previous evening, the two had argued in the judge's chambers that the tapes violated Call's right to due process. The judge ruled against them, and the tapes were played for the jury the next day. One newspaper called them "a chilling story of murder."[24]

The final tape was especially damning. Call had asked Charleston to bring a .38 revolver to their meeting. Said Call, "I like the noise. I guess I'm a little sadistic."[25] The defense attorneys did their best to discredit Charleston as a scoundrel and a felon. But he was a superb witness in his own right. He remarked that he had only one regret: "If we tried harder, we might have saved a man's life."[26] After just one day of deliberation, the jury found Call guilty of murder in the first degree.

Prosecutors didn't have to wait long for Call to buckle. Faced with death by electrocution, he decided not to take the whole rap by himself. Within the week, Call asked for a meeting with Deputy Chief Neders. In his high security cell, Call made a full confession and named all the others involved. Said Call bitterly, "The bastards didn't even send me cigarettes."[27]

His confession was a revelation, and it contained some real surprises for both the prosecutors and the detectives who had worked on the case. Call was not only the "go-between" who hired and paid the killer, he was also the driver of the car in both murders. The hit man himself, far from being an out-of-town hired assassin, was none other than the little Sacramento contractor Max Ward. And, the biggest shock of all: Both murders had been carried out under the orders of Ben Rasnick, the leader of the district council of the Painters Union, the man who had been dragged bodily out of a union meeting by Dow Wilson more than a year before. Rasnick's motive for the murders was not the pillaging of the welfare fund, said Call, but rather union politics. He explained that Rasnick and his district, as well as the International Union, were fearful of Wilson's and Green's ambitions for higher union office. They just wanted them out of the way.

The trial of Max Ward got underway in mid-November, and it injected into the mix the one element that had so far been missing that would make the murders perfect fodder for the tabloids: sex.

Ward's attorney, Melvin Belli, realized that Call's testimony that this client was the actual hit man would be damaging, if not conclusive. So he decided to try to discredit Call, while at the same time creating

Ben Rasnick, the union's East Bay District Council secretary, who ordered the murders. *San Francisco Chronicle*

sympathy for Ward by introducing Ward's wife, Donna, into the proceedings. His thesis: Call had been having an affair with Donna and was in love with her. His allegations against Ward were Call's way of getting him out of the way. But when Belli put Donna on the stand, he got more than he bargained for.

Three days into the trial, Donna Ward, a petite, attractive, red-headed woman, told a dazzling story of sex, blackmail, and intrigue. Call, she said, had gotten her drunk, seduced her, and then, by threatening to expose her as an unfit wife and mother, had coerced her into a long-running affair. Later, he introduced her to Ben Rasnick, whose trial was scheduled to follow Ward's. Rasnick had also fallen in love with her, she said, had given her expensive gifts and then persuaded her to move from Sacramento to Hayward, where he would have more ready access to her favors. All this must have been unsettling to poor Max Ward, who suffered in silence during his wife's testimony.

Donna then testified that she knew from "pillow talk" that only Rasnick and Call were involved in the killings, and that her husband had not been involved.

"Shortly after Dow Wilson was killed," she testified, "Rasnick told me did I know Lloyd Green and I said no, and he said Green would be next."

"Why didn't you go to the police?" asked Belli.

"Are you kidding?" Donna responded in astonishment.[28]

However, Donna's testimony wasn't enough to save her husband from Call's testimony which, combined with a totally inept appearance on the stand by the defendant ("Why had you drawn a map of Green's office showing escape routes?" followed by the response, "How do I know what my reasons were?"), convinced the jury that the authorities had the right man. In less time than it took to convict Call, the jury announced its verdict on Max Ward: guilty of murder in the first degree.

Now, suddenly, Donna Ward became the key witness against Ben Rasnick, whose trial was up next. She had not only failed to free her husband, but she had also incriminated Rasnick. It almost cost her her life.

Just three days before Rasnick's trial was set to commence, Donna entered the kitchen in her new Hayward home and set an armload of dishes onto the counter. As Donna turned back to continue clearing the table, a blast shook the house. The full load of a 12-gauge shotgun blasted through the window and smashed into the wall beyond, just missing Donna's head. Donna screamed, ran to the phone, and demanded immediate police protection. The courts were all too happy to give it to her. They had come within inches of losing their star witness.

The trial of Ben Rasnick as the perpetrator of the murder of Dow Wilson took place in the Hall of Justice in San Francisco. It looked to the prosecution like a piece of cake. Norman Call would testify that Rasnick had ordered the murders. Donna Ward would testify to Rasnick's admissions to her. However, they hadn't counted on the brilliant defense staged by Ed Merrill, Rasnick's experienced and clever trial lawyer. When Call testified concerning Rasnick's involvement, Merrill simply shredded him with a barrage of questions about his own background and involvement in the crimes. He portrayed Donna Ward as a sleep–around floozie bent on vengeance against her lover. By contrast, Ben Rasnick made a splendid witness on the stand, well-dressed and groomed, articulate and poised. He was everything Call wasn't.

But Merrill's crowning achievement was the testimony of Rasnick's wife, Mary. Just as her husband had contrasted perfectly with the disheveled Call, so Mary was the perfect counterpart to Donna: dignified, controlled, beautifully dressed, and perfectly coifed. And she played the role of the loyal and trusting wife to the hilt. Even better, she had a great story to tell. Donna Ward, she said, had telephoned her before the trial, saying, "I don't want to testify against your husband, and if you'll give me five thousand dollars I have a foolproof way of getting out of it." Mary's wonderful reply? "I told her that would be morally wrong."[29]

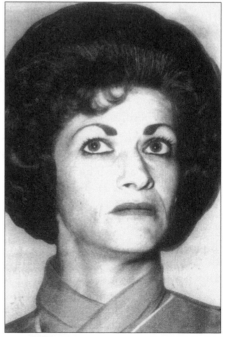

Donna Ward, wife of the triggerman, who injected into the second trial the one main ingredient it was missing: sex.
San Francisco Chronicle

At least some of the jurors bought it, and Rasnick benefited from a hung jury.

Rasnick's joy was short-lived however. Early in the following year, Rasnick went on trial for the murder of Lloyd Green. This time, the trial was held in Alameda County, where the Green murder had taken place. The jurors listened to essentially the same testimony by the principals in the case, but this time they came to a different conclusion: Rasnick was guilty as charged.

Rasnick was sentenced to life in prison and, after the standard appeals were attempted and denied, he was finally admitted to San Quentin, where he spent the remainder of his life. Little notice was taken at his death there in 1992.

Carl Black, who drove the car during the initial meeting between Call and Charleston, was tried and acquitted. Charges against Richard Rock, the bar owner who first approached Charleston about the "dumping," were eventually dismissed. Norman Call was given a commuted sentence in reward for his testimony against Max Ward and Ben Rasnick, and he served out a twenty-five-year sentence. Little Max Ward, disappeared into the prison system and was never heard from again.

Chapter Fifteen

The Sign of the Zodiac—1970s

It was only in the last century that any accurate record of mass murderers was kept. And only in recent decades was the concept of the "serial killer" recognized—that is, the individual who over and over murders a particular kind of person or dispatches multiple victims in a certain way or for a particular reason.

The United States, with less than 5 percent of the world's population, has produced the overwhelming majority of these brutal psychopaths, and the Federal Bureau of Investigations estimates that at any given time thirty-five to fifty serial killers are at work in this country.[1]

There is no doubt that multiple murderers played a part in the history of San Francisco and the Bay Area. The first may well have been the "Hounds" who roamed the city's streets in 1849. A loose confederation of young men who stole property and extorted money, they murdered at will any citizens who did not give in to their demands. San Franciscans finally rose up in July of that year and, after a brief series of trials, imprisoned some of the "Hounds" and drove the others out of town.

"Shanghai" Kelly, the city's legendary provider of seamen to outgoing ships, might well also qualify as an early serial killer—as witness the bodies that frequently floated ashore after Kelly had done his night's work.

More recent California history is rich in serial killer legends, many with colorful but terrifying names such as the Sunset Slayer, the Freeway Killer, and the Hillside Strangler. Yet, no such murderer ever so captured the public's attention or inspired such deep-set fear as the man known as "the Zodiac Killer." For almost a decade, he terrorized the Bay Area with his ghastly crimes and his obsession with notoriety. To this day, he haunts the minds of those who read about him regularly in the city's newspapers—as well as the memories of those who sought to stop him.

David Faraday was seventeen years old, a good student, an Eagle Scout, and a five-sport athlete. He lived in Vallejo, some twenty miles north of the Golden Gate Bridge. Late in the autumn of 1968, he met and became enamored of a pretty, dark-haired, sixteen-year-old schoolmate named Betty Lou Jensen, who lived on the other side of town. Although David made the trip over to her house regularly to see Betty Lou, they did not have their first real date until one Friday evening late in December.

David borrowed his mother's car for the occasion, and a little before 8:00 P.M. he picked up Betty Lou, who had told her parents they were going to a Christmas concert at the school. Instead, the young couple drove to a friend's house, where they stayed about an hour. After that, they went to a drive-in, where they ordered Cokes, and then David headed the car toward Lake Herman Road and drove to a spot known as a "lover's lane." At about 11:00 P.M. David shut off the motor and locked all four doors. Together, the two young people looked at the moon and talked. After only a few minutes, another car pulled up alongside them. A heavy-set man got out, walked up to their car, and demanded that the couple get out. When they refused, he drew a revolver and fired two shots through the driver window.[2]

In a panic, David and Betty Lou fled out the passenger door. As soon as they had exited, the stranger shot David just below the right ear, killing him instantly. Betty Lou screamed and began to run down the road. The gunman followed her and shot her five times in the back. She fell dead just twenty feet from the car. The killer, without robbing or molesting either of the youngsters, then got into his car, backed up and drove slowly away. The date was December 20, 1968.[3]

Some six months later, a young Vallejo housewife named Darlene Ferrin left her home on Virginia Street late in the evening and drove her car to a friend's house on Georgia Street. Even though Darlene was married and had a baby at home, she frequently dated other men, including Mike Magean. Darlene was twenty-two years old; Mike was several years her junior. Together, they drove to a parking lot at the Blue Springs Golf Course, an area frequented by young lovers. No sooner had they parked the car than another vehicle, a Ford Falcon, pulled into the parking slot next to them. The lone occupant of the car looked at them a moment and then drove off. But a few minutes later, the car returned. Suddenly, a powerful and blinding light was beamed at them from the other car, and the driver jumped out of the door and advanced toward them. Then the light went out. The man went to the driver side of the car and once again blinded them with his powerful flashlight. Then they heard the click of metal against the frame of the open window, followed by the blast of a gunshot. The roar deafened them, and the stranger proceeded to pump a fusillade of bullets into the car. Darlene slumped forward, hit by bullets that had passed through Mike's body as well as by bullets meant for her. Then their assailant turned and walked back to his car. Before he re-entered his vehicle, he looked back to see Mike Magean staring at him in panic. Calmly, he returned to the Corvair to finish the job. The tall, stocky man coolly leaned through the driver window. Mike, desperate to escape, leaped backward into the rear seat, his legs thrashing. The stranger fired two more shots directly at Magean, aimed two more at Darlene and then returned to his own car and slowly drove away.[4]

Darlene had been hit nine times. Two bullets caught her right arm and two hit her left arm. Five bullets hit her in the right side of the back, piercing both her lung and her heart. Mike was badly wounded in the left arm, right arm, and in the neck. One bullet had entered his right cheek and exited the left cheek, ripping a hole in his tongue and jawbone.

A caretaker at the golf course heard the shots and reported the incident to the police, who arrived some fifteen minutes later. Mrs. Ferrin died on the way to the hospital. Mike Magean went into emergency surgery, where doctors labored to save his life.[5]

One half hour after the shooting, a call came into the Vallejo Police Department. A man with no discernible emotion in his voice said, "I want to report a double murder. If you will go one mile east on Columbus Parkway to the public park, you will find two kids in a brown car. They were shot with a 9-millimeter Luger. I also killed those kids last year. Goodbye."[6] The date was July 4, 1969.

The signature of the Zodiac on his letter of August 1, 1969.

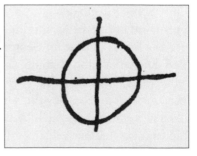

Three weeks later, envelopes postmarked in San Francisco were received by three different newspapers in the Bay Area: the *San Francisco Chronicle*, the *San Francisco Examiner* and the *Vallejo Times Herald*. Inside each was a letter and a cryptogram comprised of symbols. Each letter said the same thing:

> "Dear Editor, This is the murderer of the two teenagers last Christmas and the girl on the 4th of July near the golf course in Vallejo. To prove I killed them I shall state some facts which only I and the police know.
> Christmas
> 1.Brand name of Ammo Super X
> 2.10 shots fired
> 3.The boy was on his back with his feet to the car
> 4.The girl was on her right side feet to the west
> 4th July
> 1.Girl was wearing patterned slacks
> 2.The boy was also shot in the knee
> 3.Brand name of ammo was Western
> (Over)
> Here is part of a cipher the other 2 parts of this cipher are being mailed to other papers.
> I want you to print this cipher on the front page of your paper. In this cipher is my identity.
> *If you do not print this cipher by the afternoon of Fry (sic) lst of Aug 69, I will go on a killing rampage Fri. night. I will cruse (sic) around all weekend killing lone people in the night then move on to kill again, until I end up with a dozen people over the weekend."*[7]

All three papers printed the letter, although at police request they did not publish the last paragraph for fear of creating panic. The *Examiner* was the last to publish and it printed all three ciphers together. Following is just the *Chronicle* portion:[8]

One third of the cipher block which baffled the experts but was solved by amateurs.

The combined ciphers were sent immediately to Naval Intelligence on Mare Island for decoding, but the experts were unable to crack the code.[9] Fortunately, a number of amateurs took a shot at the cipher and, incredibly, a husband and wife team living in Salinas solved the puzzle. Donald Gene Harden, a forty-one-year-old high school teacher, and his wife, Bettye, worked on the strange symbols all weekend. By Monday, they had the solution and phoned the *Chronicle*. The newspaper, in turn, sent the Hardens' answer to Naval Intelligence, which agreed they had solved it. The now confirmed interpretation read (retaining the spelling and grammatical errors):

I LIKE KILLING PEOPLE BECAUSE IT IS SO MUCH FUN. IT IS MORE FUN THAN KILLING WILD GAME IN THE FORREST BECAUSE MAN IS THE MOST DANGER- OUS ANAMAL OF ALL. TO KILL SOMETHING GIVES ME THE MOST THRILLING EXPERIENCE. IT IS EVEN BET- TER THAN GETTING YOUR ROCKS OFF WITH A GIRL. THE BEST PART OF IT IS THAT WHEN I DIE I WILL BE REBORN IN PARADICE AND THE I WILL BECOME MY SLAVES. I WILL NOT GIVE YOU MY NAME BECAUSE YOU WILL TRY TO SLOI DOWN OR STOP MY COLLECTION OF SLAVES FOR AFTERLIFE. EBEORIETEMETHHPIT1.[10]

The Hardens said that they had broken the code by looking for four letter patterns that would fit the word "kill," in the belief that it would be the most frequently used word. The killer had made the cryptogram more diffi- cult by using eighteen different symbols for the letter "e," which is the most commonly used letter and the letter that analysts first look for. The eighteen characters at the end of the message might well be the killer's name, but no one could come up with a solution to that part of the cryptogram.

The police and the authorities in Vallejo and San Francisco now began working together to solve the crimes. It was clear that they were dealing with a psychopathic killer, one who murdered without conscience and enjoyed taunting the police and publicizing his crimes.

They also had a description of the murderer, for one of his victims had miraculously managed to survive. Young Mike Magean, despite his grievous gunshot wounds, had pulled through in surgery and had been able to describe his attacker. He was, said Magean, between the ages of twenty-five and thirty. He had short, wiry, light-brown hair worn in a military-style crewcut. He had a thick body, weighing about two hundred pounds. He guessed the man's height at about five feet, eight inches tall. He had a large face and a slight potbelly.

No sooner had the investigation gotten underway than a second letter arrived at the *Chronicle*. It seemed to be in response to open speculation that perhaps the first letter was from someone only trying to claim credit for the crimes. This letter left no doubt that it was the killer himself. And this time he gave himself a name—"Zodiac."

"Dear Editor.

This is the Zodiac speaking. In answer to your asking for more details about the good time I have had in Vallejo, I shall be a happy to supply even more material. By the way, are the police having a good time with the code? If not, tell them to cheer up; when they do crack it, they will have me.

On the 4th of July, I did not open the car door. The window was rolled down all ready. The boy was originally sitting in the front seat when I began firing. When I fired the first shot at his head, he leaped backwards at the same time thus spoiling my aim. He ended up on the back seat then the floor in back thrashing out very violently with his legs; that's how I shot him in the knee. Did not leave the cene of the killing with squealling tires and racing engine as described in the Vallejo papers. I drove away slowly so as not to draw attention to my car. The man who told the police my car was brown was a negro about 40-45 rather shabby dressed. I was in the phone booth, haveing some fun with the Vallejo cops when he was walking by. When I hung the phone up the dam thing began to ring—that drew his attention to me & my car.

Last Christmass In that episode the police were wondering as to how I could shoot & hit my victims in the dark. They did not openly state this, but implied this by saying it was a well lit night & I could see silouets on the horizon. Bullshit that area is srounded by high hills & trees. What I did was tape a small pencel flash light to the barrel of my gun. If you notice, in the center of the beam of light if you aim it at a wall or ceiling you will see a black or darck spot in the center of the circle of light about 3 to 6 in. across. When taped to a gun barrel, the bullet will strike exactly in the center of the black dot in the light. All I had to do was spray them. No address."[11]

If there was ever any doubt that the original letter writer, who now identified himself as "the Zodiac," was the real killer, the second letter erased it. A full-fledged manhunt was now underway.

Five weeks after the Zodiac's second letter arrived, two young people were on their way in a white Carmen Ghia for an outing at Lake Berryessa, some thirty miles above Vallejo. They were Cecelia Ann Shepard, a college student at Pacific Union College in Napa County, and a fellow student, Bryan Hartnell. Bryan, a tall, good-looking, pre-law student, had helped his pretty friend Cecelia pack up her belongings for shipment to the University of California at Riverside, to which she was transferring. After completing the task, they decided to reward themselves with a trip to the lake where they would relax and do some reading.

When they arrived at the lake area, they parked the car and walked to a clearing by the lake. There they spread out a blanket and sat down with their books and admired the beginning of what promised to be a beautiful sunset.

They had not been there long when Cecelia noticed the figure of a man approaching them across the clearing. The man was stocky and well built and seemed to be wearing a bizarre costume. As he came closer, Cecelia cried out to Bryan, "My God. He's got a gun!"[12] As he came closer, he looked like an eerie and evil apparition. He was dressed all in black. His baggy trousers were clamped tightly around his ankles. His dark jacket was partly concealed by the large square-shaped hood that hung down almost to his waist. The hood had two eye holes and a slit for the mouth. On the front of the hood at chest level was emblazoned a large white circle with a cross intersecting it. From his left side hung a bayonet-type knife about a foot long. On his right hip was a black holster with its flap open. As he approached the young couple, he pointed his gun directly at them.

The man in the strange costume spoke softly to the terrified couple. He told them he was an escaped convict and that he wanted their money and their car keys. He threw down two pieces of rope and ordered them to tie each other up. They obeyed, tying each other's hands and feet. The hooded intruder put his gun away and pulled the knife out of its sheath. Then he said calmly, "I'm going to have to stab you people."[13]

"Then stab me first," said Bryan.

The killer replied, "I'll do just that."[14] He dropped to his knees and plunged the dagger into Hartnell's back six times. Then, laughing, he walked over to the girl, knelt down beside her, and stabbed her ten times in the back. When she rolled, screaming, onto her back, he stabbed her four more times in the chest.

Drawing of the Zodiac costume at Lake Berryessa
on September 27, 1969. *Illustrated by artist Alan Brooks
from the police description*

The hooded assassin then rose to his feet and, without robbing or molesting the unconscious young people, walked slowly back to the area where he had parked his own car next to Bryan's Carmen Ghia. There he knelt down next to the driver door of his victims' car. With a black felt-tip pen, he wrote the following on the side of the car:

"Vallejo
12/20/68
7/4/69
9/27/69 - 6:30
by knife "[15]

One hour later, the phone rang at the Napa Police Department. The caller said, "I want to report a murder—no, a double murder. They are two miles north of park headquarters. They were in a white Volkswagen Carman Ghia. I'm the one who did it."[16]

In the meantime, both Cecilia and Bryan had regained consciousness. Bryan managed to free himself and screamed to a fisherman who was in a boat out on the lake. The fisherman came ashore to investigate, and, seeing the horribly wounded couple, he hurried to notify authorities. Finally, a park ranger and the owner of a nearby resort arrived and wrapped the two in blankets. Together, they put the two victims, screaming in pain, into a car and sped them to Queen of the Valley Hospital where, two days later, Cecelia Ann Shepard died of multiple stab wounds to her neck, chest and abdomen. Bryan Hartnell, however, proved to be a survivor. Despite the grievous nature of his wounds, he responded well to emergency surgery. One of the stab wounds had come within a fraction of an inch of the aorta of his heart, and another had barely failed to penetrate his lung. But Hartnell pulled through and was able to give the police a detailed description of everything that had happened. Hartnell described the attacker as about five feet, ten inches tall, stocky and powerfully built, weighing at least two hundred pounds. A pot belly was visible under his bizarre costume.[17]

Three different police authorities were now on the case of the Zodiac killer. Detective Sergeant Kenneth Narlow headed the investigation in Napa. In Vallejo, Detective John Lynch was on the case. And, because the letters had come to San Francisco newspapers, Detective David Toschi was assigned to the case by the San Francisco police department. Toschi would not have to wait long before his involvement became much more intense and personal.

On the evening of Saturday, October 11, 1969, just two weeks after the slaughter at Lake Berryessa, a stockily-built man, wearing a black parka-type jacket, hailed a taxi cab on Geary Street in San Francisco's theater district. The man climbed into the rear seat and instructed the driver, a twenty-nine-year-old graduate student at San Francisco State College named Paul Stine, to take him to the corner of Washington and Cherry streets, a destination in the quiet residential district known as Presidio Heights. The journey took about ten minutes, and when Stine pulled to a stop at the corner, his passenger instructed him to go one block farther. When Stine finally parked his cab against the curb, the passenger in the dark parka leaned forward, pressed the muzzle of a gun against Stine's head just below his right ear, pulled the trigger, and blew his brains out.

The killer then quickly exited from the back seat and slipped into the front passenger seat. He held Stine's bleeding, shattered head in his lap as he took Stine's wallet from his pants pocket and tore a piece out of his shirt. He then exited the car and began wiping down the handles of the car doors and the rear view mirror. Then he turned and walked off toward the darkness of the Presidio park.

Directly across the street, a young girl heard the shot, rushed to her window, and witnessed the strange happenings on the street below. She called police headquarters and reported that the gunman was wearing black. Tragically, when the call went out to police cars in the vicinity, this was translated into a description of the killer as a "black man." A police car was quickly on the scene and its two occupants saw a stocky white man in a black jacket headed for the Presidio. They shouted to the stranger and asked if he had seen a black man in the area. He replied that he had seen a black man running in the other direction. Had the police been a little closer to the stranger, they would have seen that the entire front of his jacket was covered in blood. Instead, they drove off in the other direction.[18]

The police had no reason to connect Stine's murder with the Zodiac murders until three days later when an envelope arrived at the offices of the *Chronicle*. Inside was a piece of cloth and the following letter:

> *This is the Zodiac speaking. I am the murderer of the taxi driver over by Washington St. & Maple St. last night to prove this is a blood stained piece of his shirt. I am the same man who did the people in the North Bay Area. The s.f. police could have caught me last night if they had searched the park properly instead of holding road races with their motorcycles seeing who could make the most noise. The car drivers should have just parked their cars & sat there quietly waiting for me to come out of cover.*[19]

The killer then closed his letter with a threat that would haunt the police and the authorities for months to come: *"Some children make nice targets. I think I shall wipe out a school bus some morning. Just shoot out the front tires and then pick off the kiddies as they come bouncing out."*[20]

There was no doubt that this was the same Zodiac, and the piece from Stine's shirt was verified by detectives. The newspaper published the letter, but without the last paragraph. It was now evident that Zodiac presented a massive threat to the area. San Francisco assigned eight additional detectives to work with Detective Toschi. Thousands of tips flooded police departments throughout Northern California. Many communities put armed guards on their school buses. In Napa County, sheriff's patrol planes flew over school bus routes. Drivers of school buses were alerted to keep their vehicles moving even if their tires were shot out.

October 14, 1969 letter to *The Chronicle,* which contained a swatch of Stine's shirt.

On October 20, twenty-seven detectives from seven police agencies met in San Francisco for three hours, trading information, theories, and suspicions. They had a wealth of information to go on. The suspect was about five feet, ten inches tall, weighed about two hundred pounds, and had a full head of dark hair. He was about thirty years old, stocky and strong. He knew a lot about weapons, possibly from military service. His misspellings might indicate that he had only a limited education, and it was likely he had at least some training in cryptography. He knew the Bay Area well, its back roads and its parks and city streets. He killed on weekends, usually in or near recreational areas. He spoke in a calm, unemotional manner. Psychiatrists speculated that he was someone who "broods about cutoff feelings, about being cut off from his fellow man…comparing the thrill of killing to the satisfaction of sex…and has feelings of inadequacy."[21]

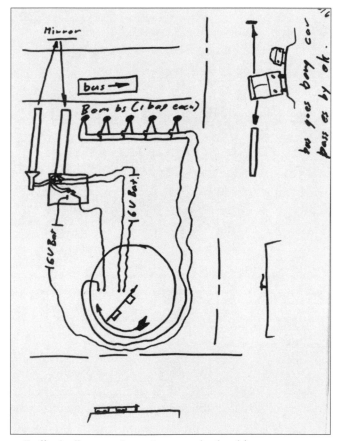

Zodiac's diagram for a threatened school bus massacre.

Ballistics tests showed that he used a different gun every time. Gun dealers throughout California were questioned about purchases of .22-caliber and 9-millimeter handguns, and signatures on hand-gun regulations were compared to the Zodiac's writing. Witnesses and survivors, with the aid of a police artist, drew up a composite sketch of the killer which was sent to all neighboring police departments. Still, no good leads developed.

Wanted poster of Zodiac distributed by police after the Stine murder.

Then on November 10, 1969, the *San Francisco Chronicle* received two new pieces of correspondence from the Zodiac. One was a greeting card containing yet another cryptogram and another small piece of Stine's shirt. The other was a long, seven-page letter.

"This is the Zodiac speaking

Up to the end of Oct 1 I have killed several people. I have grown rather angry with the police for telling their lies about me. So I shall change the way the collecting of slaves. I shall no longer announce to anyone when I commit my murders, they shall look like routine robberies, killing of anger & a few fake accidentes, etc. The police shall never catch me because I am too clever for them."[2]

Z

The Zodiac letter went on to say that he only looked like the police description of him when he was doing the killing, that he always wore transparent finger-tip guards when he committed his crimes, that all of his "killing tools" were purchased through the mail. He went on to taunt the police for not catching him in the Presidio park and made specific reference to the police who stopped him to ask if he had seen anyone suspicious. He concluded: *"Hey pig doesn't it rile you up to have your nose rubbed in your booboos?"*[23]

Terrifyingly, his letter continued, describing a "death machine" that he was making and detailing all of the ingredients he had assembled for its construction. Finally, he stated what he planned to do with his home-made bomb: *"I think you do not have the manpower to stop this one by continually re roat* [re-route] *& re-schedule the busses because the bomb can be adapted to new conditions. Have fun! By the way it could be rather messy if you try to bluff me."* The Zodiac ended his letter by demanding that certain parts of it be printed in the newspaper or *"I shall do my thing."*[24]

On the postcard that accompanied the letter, the Zodiac had printed: "Dec. July Aug. Sept Oct = 7." Authorities knew of only five people killed by the Zodiac, and none had been killed in October. Did this mean that there were two additional victims they did not know about? A search of Bay Area police records did not reveal any likely victims, and the police were inclined to put the Zodiac's new claim down either as a boast or as an attempt to confuse.

The *Chronicle* obediently reprinted Zodiac's latest correspondence, but once again left out the threat to bomb buses.

In the ensuing weeks, police in three counties followed every lead that came in, pursued new clues, and pleaded with the Zodiac to give himself up, all to no avail.

The next major development was an odd one indeed: a letter to San Francisco lawyer Melvin Belli. Belli was a celebrated attorney, known primarily for his tort cases, but also for defending well-known figures in court. A letter postmarked December 20 arrived at Belli's office while the famed lawyer was in Germany at a legal conference. An aide opened the letter and found inside a piece of a shirt stained with blood and a letter with the following hand-printed message:

"Dear Melvin: this is the Zodiac speaking, I wish you a Merry Christmass. The one thing I ask of you is this, please help me. I cannot reach out for help because of this thing in me wont let me...Please help me because I am drownding. At the moment the children are safe from the bomb because it is so massive to dig in & the triger mech requires much work to get it adjusted just right. But if I hold back too long...I will loose all control of my self & set the bomb up. Please help me I cannot remain in control much longer."[25]

A photocopy of the letter was rushed to Belli. The lawyer responded to the Zodiac through a statement in the *Chronicle* that said, "I will do anything in my power to provide you with whatever help you may need or may want."[26] Belli offered to meet with the Zodiac any time and any-where, but the killer never responded to Belli's appeal.

On March 17, 1970, Kathleen Johns was making the journey from San Bernardino to Petaluma, a dairy-farming community about thirty miles north of San Francisco. With her in her car was her ten-month-old daughter. When she reached Modesto, she turned west onto highway 132, a seldom-traveled road. She had been driving all day and it was close to midnight when she noticed in her rear-view mirror that a car seemed to be following her. Suddenly, the driver of the car began to blink his lights and sound his horn. The car pulled alongside and the driver yelled to her that one of her rear wheels was wobbling.

Wary of the stranger, she pulled off the smaller road and out onto a better traveled highway, where she stopped. The stranger pulled up directly behind her car, got out, and volunteered to tighten the lugs of the wheel which he claimed was wobbling. Kathleen stayed in the car but accepted his offer to help. She noted that the man was well-dressed, about thirty years old, heavy-set and with a noticeable stomach bulge. He wore a dark jacket.

Dear Melvin

This is the Zodiac speaking I wish you a happy Christmass. The one thing I ask of you is this, please help me. I cannot reach out for help because of this thing in me wont let me. I am finding it extreamly dificult to hold it in check I am afraid I will loose control again and take my nineth & posibly tenth victom. Please help me I am drownding. At the moment the children are safe from the bomb because it is so massive to dig in & the triger mech requires much work to get it adjusted just right. But if I hold back too long from no nine I will loose complet all controol of my self & set the bomb up. Please help me I can not remain in control for much longer.

Zodiac's letter to Melvin Belli claiming new victims.

The man worked on the wheel for a few minutes and informed Kathleen that it should now be fine. Kathleen thanked the man and drove off, as the stranger's car followed her. Suddenly, the left rear wheel fell completely off and spun noisily into the weeds by the side of the road.

The heavy-set stranger pulled in behind her, walked up to Kathleen's car, and offered to drive to an Arco gas station that was visible just up the road. Reluctantly, Kathleen gathered up her infant daughter and got into the other car's front passenger seat. The stranger drove off but, when he came to the Arco station, he kept going. Kathleen was speechless with fear. He continued down the highway past several exits, then turned down a deserted farm road. After driving for about half an hour, the driver turned to Kathleen and said, "You know you're going to die. You know I'm going to kill you."[27]

Several times, the man pulled over to the side of the road, but then continued driving, as if he were looking for a certain kind of area. Kathleen was in a panic, but she retained an outward calmness, so as to not upset the man. The next time the man stopped his car, Kathleen jumped out with her baby, dashed across the road, and hid in an irrigation ditch near a field of high grass.

The man got out and came looking for her, shining a flashlight into the field, and calling out for her to return. Just then, a truck came by, stopped, and the driver demanded to know what was going on. The man in the dark jacket hurried back to his car and sped off down the road. Kathleen was taken to a nearby police station where she relayed her astonishing story. As she was interviewed by a policeman, Kathleen happened to look up on the wall at a "wanted" poster. "Oh my God," she yelled. "That's him! That's him right there!"[28]

She was looking at the composite portrait of the Zodiac. When the police went to recover Kathleen's car, they found that it had been burned beyond recognition.

On April 19, another letter from the Zodiac arrived at the *Chronicle*:

"This is the Zodiac speaking. By the way, have you cracked the last chapter I sent you? My name is [symbol]"[29]

This thirteen-character symbol was obviously presented as yet another taunt to the police. Since it contained numerals as well as symbols, it was generally regarded as meaningless and undecipherable, and it has never been successfully decoded.

The letter also stated that the Zodiac was no longer interested in killing children, because *"there is more glory in killing a cop than a kid."* The letter writer also claimed he had now killed ten people and stated, *"I hope you have fun trying to figure out who I killed."* The letter then signed off with an insulting:

"ZODIAC 10 SFPD - O"[30]

The police asked the *Chronicle* not to publish this latest letter from the Zodiac to see if this would provoke him and to determine how important publicity was to him. It didn't take long to get an answer. Just ten days later, another Zodiac missive arrived on the desk of the editor of the *Chronicle*. In it was a request that people in the city should start wearing Zodiac buttons!

> *"If you don't want me to have this blast you must do two things: 1 Tell everyone about the bus bomb with all the details. 2 I would like to see some Zodiac buttons wandering about town. Everyone else has these buttons like (peace symbol), black power, melvin eats blubber etc. Well it would cheer me up considerably if I saw a lot of people wearing my button. Please no nasty ones like melvins. Thank You. Signed* (sign of the Zodiac)"[31]

Two months later, still another letter from Zodiac turned up in the *Chronicle* mail, the eleventh letter confirmed to be from the killer. In it, the Zodiac professed his unhappiness:

> "This is the Zodiac speaking. I have become very upset with the people of San Fran Bay Area
> They have not complied with my wishes to wear some nice Zodiac buttons. I promised to punish them if they did not comply. I shot a man sitting in a parked car with a .38.
> *ZODIAC - 12S FPD - 0 "*[32]

A map accompanied the letter that indicated an area near the peak of Mount Diablo. Also included was a new cipher with thirty-two symbols.

Then just a month later, on July 29, the twelfth and thirteenth Zodiac letters arrived at the *Chronicle*, each indicating a new level of frustration and frenzy. In one of the letters, Zodiac claimed thirteen victims, and he described in terrifying detail how he would torture them in the afterlife. He then went on to describe the kinds of people he would like to kill in the future, and in the oddest twist of all, he did so paraphrasing Ko Ko in Gilbert and Sullivan's *The Mikado*:

> "As some day it may happen
> that a victim must be found
> I've got a little list. I've
> got a little list of society
> offenders who might well be
> underground who would never be
> missed. There is the pest -
> ulential nucences who whrite
> for autographs, all people who
> *have flabby hands and*
> *irritating laughs, etc.*"[33]

The plagiarized poem went on for forty-five more lines, and, if produced from memory, as the many mistakes, misspellings, and transpositions would indicate, it meant that Zodiac had some real familiarity with Gilbert and Sullivan. Police added it to his official description, and they interviewed members of the Lamplighters, a local Gilbert and Sullivan performing group, but wound up none the wiser.

"Dragon" greeting card sent by Zodiac to *The Chronicle* on April 28, 1970.

The other letter read:

> *"this is the Zodiac speaking I am rather unhappy because you people will not wear Zodiac buttons. I now have a list starting with the woeman & her baby that I gave a rather interesting ride for a coupple of howers on evening a few months back that ended in my burning her car where I found them."*[34]

This was the Zodiac's way of bragging about a crime while clearly authenticating his identity as the Zodiac. The kidnapping of Kathleen Johns and her baby girl had never been publicized.

The Zodiac was quiet for the next several months. There were no Zodiac killings as far as anyone could tell, and no more letters arrived. But on October 6, the *Chronicle* received a Zodiac postcard. It was a white, three-by-five file card on which the Zodiac had constructed a message by pasting words and letters from the *Chronicle* of the previous day. It read, *"Dear Editor You'll hate me, but I've got to tell you. The pace isn't any slower! In fact it's just one big thirteenth 13. Some of them fought. It was horrible."*[35]

The editors, in concert with the police, decided not to publish the card. The prevailing opinion was that the Zodiac was now simply boasting, but, for some reason, had ceased his crimes. Then, just a few weeks later, the fifteenth Zodiac correspondence landed on the desk of Paul Avery, the *Chronicle* reporter who had written most of the Zodiac stories for the paper. It was Halloween time, and the Zodiac sent him a garish letter with a dancing skeleton on it. The number "14" was written over the skull. It was addressed to Avery, "From Your Secret Pal." The letter was a taunt: *"I feel it in my bones. You ache to know my name. And so I'll clue you in...But then why spoil our game! BOO! Happy Halloween!"* On the back he had lettered, *"Paradise Slave. By fire. By knife. By gun. By rope."*[36]

The police considered the letter to be threatening, as no other correspondence to a newspaper had ever been addressed to an individual. Avery was issued a gun permit by the department and encouraged to practice at the police target range. Avery's fellow reporters, mostly but not entirely in jest, began wearing tags that read, "I am not Avery."[37]

The next development in the case came by way of an anonymous letter to Avery from Southern California, claiming that there might have been an earlier Zodiac killing in Riverside in Orange County. Avery checked it out with the Riverside police and learned of the Zodiac-type murder of a Riverside City College freshman named Cheri Jo Bates. The

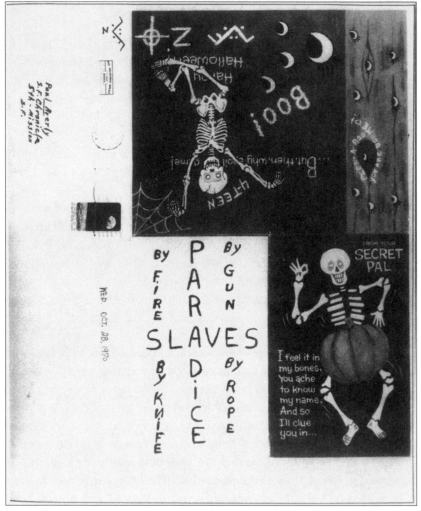

Zodiac's death threat card to reporter Paul Avery on October 27, 1970.

murder had occurred on the evening of October 30, 1966, prior to any of the known Zodiac murders in the Bay Area.

On that evening, Miss Bates had driven to the school library to get some books she needed for class the next day. When she left the library at about 6:30 P.M., her car would not start. A man approached the car, offered to help, and persuaded her to go in his car, either for a trip to a service station or to her home. Just a short distance away, he produced a knife and stabbed her twice in the chest, then slashed her throat so viciously that he severed her jugular as well as her voice box, almost decapitating her. Then he plunged the knife into her back.

She had not been robbed or sexually violated. Ten feet from her body, police found a Timex watch with a band presumably broken in the struggle. When police examined Cheri Jo's car, they found that the distributor and condenser wires had been ripped out.

Following the murder, letters had been sent to the local newspaper, the Riverside police, and to the father of the murdered girl. The first letter read:

> *She was young and beautiful, but now she is battered and dead. She is not the first nor will she be the last. I lay awake nights thinking about my next victim...When we were walking from the library, I said it was about time. She asked me, "About time for what?" I said it was about time for you to die...I am not sick. I am insane. But that will not stop the game...I am stalking your girls now."*[38]

A second letter said simply, in large letters: *"Bates had to die. There will be more."* At the bottom of the paper was scrawled the letter "Z."[39]

Avery obtained copies of the letters and submitted them to Sherwood Morrill, the documents expert for the State Criminal Investigation and Identification Department. Morrill, who had become the authority on the Zodiac's handwriting, examined both letters against all earlier Zodiac correspondence. His verdict: They were "unquestionably the work of Zodiac."[40]

This put a new complexion on the already baffling criminal life of the Zodiac. It meant that he had been active prior to any of the Bay Area killings. Yet, in his first letter he had not counted Cheri Jo Bates among his victims. Had he included her in his later totals? Were his claims of subsequent victims merely a taunt to the police, or were they real? Investigators in San Francisco, Napa, and Solano counties continued to follow every piece of evidence and to track down each of the hundreds of tips that came in from private citizens. But still they could not identify a single viable suspect.

On March 15, 1971, the Zodiac sent another letter, this time to the *Los Angeles Times*. It was postmarked in the Bay Area town of Pleasanton. It was filled with insults and boasts:

> *"This is the Zodiac speaking. Like I have always said I am crack proof. If the blue meanies are ever going to catch me, they had best get off their fat asses & do something... I do have to give them credit for stumbling across my Riverside activity, but they are only finding the easy ones, there are a hell of a lot more down there. The reason I'm writing to the Times is this, They don't bury me on the back pages like some of the others."*[41]

Then he added this chilling ending to his letter: "*SFPO - 0 Zodiac - 17+*"[42]

Just one week passed before the next Zodiac communication. It was a common four-cent postcard, addressed to Paul Avery at the *Chronicle*, and it was filled with words cut from newspapers. The card hinted that his latest victim was buried "around in the snow" somewhere in the Sierra. It included such nonsense phrases as "pass Lake Tahoe areas" and "Peek through the pines."[43] On the opposite side, he had pasted a drawing of a structure at Forrest Pines, a condo development near Incline Village on the north shore of Lake Tahoe.

The March 22, 1971, postcard that referred to the disappearance of Donna Lass the previous year.

A call to the police there revealed that a pretty young nurse named Donna Lass had been missing since September. Her car had been found near her apartment. A call from a man that day had informed Donna's landlord that she would not be returning because of an illness in the family. It was a lie; no one in Donna's family had been sick. Because of heavy snowfall in the area, it was difficult to conduct a meaningful search. Donna Lass's body has never been found.

After the Zodiac card in the spring of 1971, three years passed with no further correspondence and no real breaks in the case. There had been a stabbing of a legal secretary in San Francisco after she got off a bus in Tamalpais Valley. A man in a white Chevy stopped and offered her a ride. When the young lady refused, he leapt out of his car and began stabbing her, only to be scared off by the lights of another car. The man was in his early forties, five feet nine or ten inches tall, and husky. The victim recovered from her wounds and the Zodiac made no claims of being the assailant. However, police suspected at the time that he might have been the Zodiac.

The police department in San Francisco still maintained a "Zodiac squad," an extensive file of all his letters and clues, as well as a record of all the possible suspects it had unearthed and all the tips it had received. Just as the police were about to give up on the case, another Zodiac letter surfaced. In the morning mail at the *Chronicle* on January 30, 1974, was an envelope bearing the sign of the Zodiac. The letter inside reached a new level of strangeness, even for the Zodiac:

> *"I saw and think 'The Exorcist' was the best satirical comedy that I have ever seen. Signed, yours true. He plunged himself into the billowy wave and an echo arose from the suicides grave, titwillo, titwillo, titwillo Ps. If I do not see this note in your paper, I will do something nasty, which you know I'm capable of doing."*

At the end of the letter Zodiac made a new boast: *"Me - 37 SFPD - 0"*[44]

Police were dumbfounded by the letter, until someone pointed out that the poetic lines were taken once again from a song sung by Ko-Ko, the Lord High Executioner in *The Mikado*. The revelation was of little help to members of the Zodiac squad. They weren't any farther along in tracking him down now than they had been six years earlier when he first surfaced.

A final, braggadocio Zodiac letter was received in 1978—and that was the last that anyone ever heard from the Zodiac. No one knows if he still lives in the Bay Area. No one knows whether he is still at large or is imprisoned for some other crime. No one knows whether or not he is still alive.

This is not to say that there are no theories as to who the Zodiac was.

In the early seventies, the Vallejo police questioned a man in connection with the Darlene Ferrin murder and actually developed a seventeen-page document concerning this man and his proximity to a number of the other murders. They followed the man's travels and activities closely for a number of years but were never able to gather sufficient evidence to make an arrest.

Robert Graysmith, who was the editorial cartoonist at the *Chronicle* during the Zodiac years, became deeply involved in the case and developed his own theories and successfully decoded one of the Zodiac ciphers. His pursuit of the Zodiac lasted the better part of a decade and resulted in the most definitive and best-selling book on the subject. He eventually settled on two primary suspects. One, whom he identified as "Don Andrews," originally lived in Southern California and later moved to the Bay Area. "Andrews" is described in Graysmith's book as "nervous, frantic, and temperamental and often exhibited hostility toward sex." He is also purported to be a Gilbert and Sullivan fan, and he once showed a friend a school bus bomb—based on plans in a book he owned.

The last letter from the Zodiac, April 24, 1978.

Graysmith's second suspect was identified in his book as "Bob Hall Starr." "Starr" lives in Santa Rosa and has, according to one psychologist, five distinct personalities. He often carries about with him a small metal box which he will permit no one to look into. Of all the suspects, he is the only one that can be placed at all the murder scenes at the time of the crimes. He is, according to Graysmith, "the gut-feeling choice of most detectives."[45]

A writer and cipher analyst named Gareth Penn has an entirely different theory. He has made an exhaustive study of all the Zodiac documents and has come to the conclusion that the Zodiac is a visiting professor at Harvard University named Michael O'Hare. Penn has written and published a 375-page treatise to prove his contention that O'Hare traveled from Massachusetts to commit the Zodiac killings, although he believes there are only seven Zodiac murders, whereas Graysmith believes the total could be as high as forty-nine.[46]

The Zodiac murders continue to mystify and fascinate crime afficionados, police reporters, and the public in general. The case has inspired several movies, including Clint Eastwood's *Dirty Harry*, in which the hero chased down a Zodiac-type murderer named "Scorpio." A number of books have been written on the case, including a novelization of the murders called *The Zodiac Killer*.[47]

There have been a number of amateur attempts to catch the Zodiac. The most bizarre occurred shortly after the arrival of the last Zodiac letter when some followers of the case produced a low-budget movie entitled *Zodiac* in hopes of ensnaring the murderer. They opened their film at the Golden Gate Theater and, during the week it ran, they placed a large box in the lobby, offering a new motorcycle to the person who wrote the best answer to the statement, "I believe Zodiac kills because…"[48] The answers were to be dropped into a slot in the large box, where they were immediately read by a man with a flashlight who was crouching inside the box. If one of the answers indicated the writer was the Zodiac himself, the man was instructed to immediately alert a policeman who was standing by. Nothing came of it, and police eventually studied all of the handwritten answers. Their conclusion: The Zodiac had skipped the movie.

The passage of time has dimmed the ardor of most Zodiac sleuths and enthusiasts. The last letter was received three decades ago, and the killer would probably now be well into his sixties, or early seventies, if he is, in fact, still alive. Yet, even today, the spectre of the Zodiac killer can conjure up fear and frustration in the people who were involved. One of the Zodiac survivors moved far away from the area, changed her name, and, to this day, remains incommunicado. Most experts on the subject believe the Zodiac will never be heard from again.

Former San Francisco Police Inspector Jim Deasy, who was assigned to the Zodiac case for years, recently posited the following:

"An elderly lady someday may call us up and say, 'You know, my upstairs tenant just passed on, bless his soul, and he left behind a box full of strange things that I think you ought to look at,' and we'll go down and take a look. The hood that the Zodiac wore at Lake Berryessa will be there, and the .22 automatic that he used on the couple at Lake Herman Road, the missing piece of Paul Stine's shirt—all of it will be packed away in that box. Sometimes I think that's the only way we'll ever solve the case."[49]

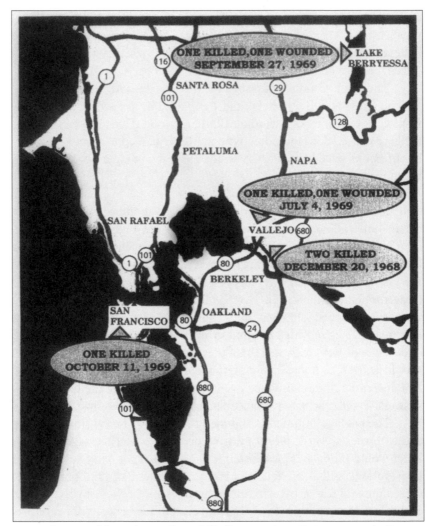

A map of the only confirmed Zodiac murders. Some experts believe they represent only the tip of the iceberg. *Map by Alan Brooks*

Chapter Sixteen

The City Hall Murders—1978

*O*n April 15, 1850, the state legislature of the State of California
*approved San Francisco's first city charter. Among its many provisions
was a stipulation that the city's chief executive would no longer be entitled "alcade," a Spanish term used since the city's founding some years
earlier. The charter proclaimed that a "mayor" of San Francisco should
be popularly elected on the fourth Monday of April of each year. So it
was that the following year 3,425 citizens cast their votes and elected
John White Geary the first mayor of San Francisco.*

*Since that time, San Franciscans have trooped to the polls more
than seventy times and have chosen forty-one different people to serve as
their mayor. These forty-one mayors have come from all kinds of back-
grounds and experiences—and have demonstrated the full panoply of
human virtues and frailties.*

*There have been successful mayors. James Phelan, the twenty-fifth
mayor, was elected to three terms and then went on to serve in the United
States Senate. Washington Bartlett, mayor number nineteen, and James
Rolph, Jr., mayor number twenty-nine, both went on to become gover-
nors of the State of California.*

*There have been mayors who were scoundrels. Ephraim Burr, mayor
number eight, was convicted of accepting a commission on government
loans. Eugene Schmitz, mayor number twenty-four, was convicted on
twenty-seven counts of graft and bribery and given the maximum prison*

sentence. On a smaller scale, Charles Boxton, mayor number twenty-six, was thrown out of office for petty theft after just seven days as mayor.

There were mysterious mayors. No one has any idea where George Wilson, mayor number seven, came from before he became mayor, and no one knows where he went after his term expired. After Frank M. McCoppin, mayor number twelve, was elected, it was discovered that he had lied about his date of birth, his place of birth, and even the fact that he was a citizen of the United States.

There were mayors who were builders. Henry Coon, mayor number eleven, oversaw the installation of the city's first electric fire alarm system as well as its first telegraph line. Andrew Bryant, mayor number seventeen, built the first city hall, which was later put to shame by the construction under "Sunny Jim" Rolph, mayor number twenty-eight, of the most imposing city hall ever built for any American city. Angelo Rossi, mayor number thirty, was the city's great bridge builder. During his tenure, both the Bay Bridge and the Golden Gate Bridge were completed.

Yet, it is doubtful that any San Francisco mayor will ever have a firmer place in the history books than the city's thirty-seventh mayor. Had he served out his full term, he might well be remembered for his accomplishments or for the style he brought to the office. Tragically, he did not—and so he will be remembered, instead, as the victim of one of the most outrageous single acts in American civic history.

On a fog-filled morning in early January of 1978, the first board of supervisors elected from individual city districts during the twentieth century stood in the great oak-walled chamber of the second floor of San Francisco City Hall for the official swearing-in ceremony.[1] The members represented an eclectic cross-section of the diverse city, as well as a dazzling array of partisan politics. They included a black woman, a Chinese American, a single mother, a wealthy Jewish woman, a young Irishman, and an avowed homosexual. On hand to swear them in was the City's first truly liberal mayor.

It was as combustible a collection of elected officials as was ever chosen to govern a major city. Even so, there was no hint of the catastrophe that would result from this collision of diverse and conflicting personalities. The ceremony went smoothly and it was followed by mutual congratulations, polite conversation, and the usual pledges to work in harmony for the good of the city.

The mayor, George Moscone, had come to this office by relying on his easy-going charm, his intense ambition, and his constant good luck.

A native San Franciscan, he had grown to maturity during the hectic years of World War II in a town largely devoid of young men, except for the soldiers and sailors passing through. He was a good athlete, an indifferent student, and a magnet for the young women the war had left behind. Good-looking and intelligent, Moscone floated effortlessly through high school, went to college on a basketball scholarship, and then glided easily into Hastings Law School.[2] It was here that Moscone found his calling—politics. He discovered he had a way of persuading people to his point of view, he loved to give speeches, and he enjoyed the give-and-take of political argument.

Shortly after graduating, George married his high school sweetheart and started a family that would eventually include two sons and two daughters. But Moscone never gave up his bachelor ways. He was frequently seen in the company of other women and was known to occasionally visit the City's red-light districts.

As a promising young attorney, a conspicuous man-about-town, and a confirmed Democrat, it was only a matter of time before Moscone caught the eye of political king-maker Phil Burton. Burton was in the process of building a liberal political organization, and he persuaded George to run for the California state assembly. Moscone lost, but he did get more votes than any Democrat had ever received before him in his district. He had made his mark. In the words of one observer, George had "the right politics, the right church, the right spirit, even the right teeth."[3] In 1963, he ran again, this time for a seat on the San Francisco Board of Supervisors, and this time he won.

The newly elected Board of the City Supervisors of San Francisco. (Harvey Milk is on the extreme left, Dan White is third from left.) *Photo courtesy of John L. Molinari*

Moscone quickly made his mark as a supervisor, fighting for the underdogs of society, battling the developers, and spreading charm and good will over the electorate. His success emboldened him to try for bigger things. Just three years later, he submitted himself to the voters as their candidate for state senator. The voters liked what they saw and swept him into office in a landslide.

Moscone spent eight years in Sacramento, making deals and friends, enhancing his reputation as a protector of the underprivileged, and battling Governor Reagan's conservative agenda. But he missed the hurly-burly of San Francisco politics, and he decided it would be more fun being a bigger fish in a smaller pond. He ran for mayor of San Francisco and, propelled by the favor of the City's poor, its minorities, and its gay population, he narrowly beat his principal opponent in a runoff.

As mayor, Moscone catered to the constituencies that put him in office. The changes in the City's makeup over the previous decade had been dramatic. The Irish and the Italians, so long the backbone of the political establishment, had given way to a growing population of blacks and Hispanics. Even more significant was the growing influence of the gay population. Moscone was quick to show where he stood with these new political power blocks, appointing blacks and community activists to the police commission, environmentalists to the planning commission, and gays to the housing commission. Moscone was pleasing his backers, but he wasn't making everyone happy.

On the list of unhappy San Franciscans was City Supervisor Dianne Feinstein. Though still in her forties, Feinstein clearly represented an older, more traditional San Francisco. She even looked the part—always well dressed and carefully coifed. Dianne was even rumored to occasionally wear the white gloves that marked the City's women of wealth and good breeding. A middle-of-the-road Democrat, Feinstein was philosophically opposed to Moscone's liberal agenda and rarely voted for his recommended programs. A third term supervisor, she had twice made unsuccessful runs for the mayor's office and now her political ambitions had ebbed. She confided to friends that she no longer had any desire for higher political office.[4]

Also on the list of those unhappy with the mayor were most members of the San Francisco's police department. Already under a judicial order to hire more minorities, the department seethed with animosity against the liberal agenda. Moscone threw fuel on the fire with his appointment of Charles R. Gain as the new chief of police. Gain was a reformer, with a reputation for conflict with the men under his command in every city in which he had worked. Worse, he had never even lived in San Francisco. There was also a rumor that Gain had received his appointment as a result of having suppressed one of George Moscone's sexual escapades. He was, in short, a living provocation to the men in blue. Among Gain's earliest actions was to initiate a program to recruit homosexuals for the police force. Hatred in the police ranks for Moscone and his police chief reached a new level when Gain attended the notorious Hooker's Ball, a celebration established by the City's prostitutes to mock the Policeman's Ball. Worse yet, the police chief's picture appeared in the newspapers the next day with his arms around both Margo St. James, head of the prostitute's association, and a transvestite called Wonder Whore.[5] San Francisco police now felt shame as well as anger.

The infamous photo of Police Chief Charles Gain with Margo St. James and Wonder Whore.

And, there was someone else who resented Mayor Moscone, even though the two had never met. He was a popular young fireman named Dan White. White was a native San Franciscan, born in the south Market area known as "Visitation Valley." When Dan was a youngster, the area was populated by hard-working Irish and Italian families, and their modest houses were trim and neat, with carefully mowed lawns. But now Vis Valley had changed. The streets weren't clean anymore. Youngsters with dark skins idled on the street corners. Dope was sold openly on the streets, and wrought iron bars protected the windows of the houses.

Dan White in full campaign mode for the office of City Supervisor.

Much of this change had occurred while Dan had been away. As a youngster out of high school, he enlisted to fight in the Vietnam War. After three years, he returned, a strong, handsome and restless young man. He traveled to New Orleans and later to Alaska to find his future, but he couldn't seem to discover what he was looking for. Finally, he came back to San Francisco and joined the police force, doing undercover work and riding patrol in the Outer Mission district. He was a good cop, but he had a strong, almost overpowering sense of right and wrong. He could hardly stomach the thefts, rapes, and murders that filled his day. He was equally unforgiving of the shortcomings of some of his fellow officers, even filing charges against them for what he regarded as prisoner abuse.

In the long run, Dan White decided he wasn't cut out to be a cop, and he applied to be a member of the San Francisco fire department. At last, he seemed to have found his milieu. He aced the entrance exam, came close to a perfect score on the physical agility test, and was elected president of his class at the Fire College.[6] As a fireman, he won respect for his courage and leadership, and his superiors marked him for rapid advancement. Dan finally felt free to marry his girlfriend, Mary Ann, and soon he became the proud father of a handsome baby boy. Still, Dan was not happy. He was not happy with San Francisco, and he wanted to change it.

In Dan's firehouse on Moscow Street, there was talk of the upcoming elections. For the first time in almost a century, city supervisors would be elected by districts instead of by citywide ballot. That set Dan to thinking. The district he was raised in, where he had policed and fought fires, was District Eight. Who knew it better than he did? Who was more upset than he about what had happened to it? With almost no more thought than that, he drove down to City Hall and declared his intention to run.

White was so politically naive that he didn't realize that he was no longer living in District Eight. But he learned fast, changed his residence, put together a campaign team, and went out shaking hands and giving speeches. White had a lot of work to do: He was one of fourteen candidates for the seat. However, his speeches left no doubt as to where he stood in the political spectrum:

> "For years, we have witnessed an exodus from San Francisco by many of our family members... alarmed by the enormous increase in crime, poor educational facilities and a deteriorating social structure. These malignancies will erupt from our city and engulf our tree-lined, sunbathed communities... unless we who remain can transcend our apathy. Individually we

are helpless... yet there are thousands of people waiting to un-leash a fury that can and will eliminate the malignancies which blight our city. A recent headline proclaimed "San Francisco; a Cesspool of Perversion." Should we continue to be maligned and shamed throughout the nation? I say NO! I am not going to be forced out of San Francisco by splinter groups of radicals, social deviates and incorrigibles!"[7]

His call to arms and his endless energy campaigning in the neigh-borhoods, the beer halls, and bowling alleys carried the day. His campaign slogan, "Unite and Fight," seemed to strike just the right note. And, Dan had the good fortune to become a public hero exactly in the middle of the campaign. Responding to a fire alarm at an apartment building in Hunter's Point, White and a fellow firefighter found a woman on a high balcony, screaming for help as smoke poured out of the door behind her. Dan and the other fireman rode the elevator to the seventeenth floor, battered down the door with sledgehammers, subdued the fire enough to find their way to the balcony, crawled out onto the balcony, and finally reached the dis-traught woman, who held a baby in her arms. They swaddled the baby in a blanket and led the mother and child out through the smoke to safety. The next day, the *Chronicle* ran the story of Dan's heroism under the banner: "Candidate for Supervisor Saves Two Lives."[8]

When the votes were counted on election day, Dan White had car-ried every neighborhood in District Eight. He was just thirty-one years old and he was on top of the world. He had won by standing up for what he believed in, and now he would be an important voice in the running of the City. He didn't know much about being a supervisor, but that wasn't important. He was certain that, somehow, he would make his mark on the history of San Francisco.

Just as Dan White had found an ideal electorate in District Eight, so the makeup of District Five seemed tailor-made for a budding politician named Harvey Milk. Harvey was a transplanted New Yorker, attracted in the early sixties by San Francisco's famed hippie lifestyle. With long hair, faded blue jeans, and a necklace of love beads, he had easily merged with the homosexual lifestyles of the Haight-Ashbury. He made one trip back to New York to make sure that his affection for the City by the Bay was genuine, but he soon returned, this time with a lover named Scott Smith. Milk and Smith spent the better part of a year living on their joint unem-ployment checks, then they impetuously opened a camera store in the Castro. Business was slow, but life outside the store was vibrant and exciting.

The corner of Castro and Eighteenth was in the process of becoming the homosexual capital of the world. Nothing like it had ever happened before in the history of the country. The entire area was being resettled by openly homosexual men and woman, gays and lesbians who flocked in from all corners of the world. Men and woman with no children to feed, with no need for schools, with only themselves to worry about, were transforming the neighborhood in a way that stunned much of San Francisco.

Harvey Milk poses at the door of his campaign office during the 1977 campaign.

Harvey Milk decided the Castro needed representation in City Hall, and twice he offered himself to the citywide electorate, with pathetic results. But now in 1976, it was a whole new ballgame. Supervisors would be elected by district, and Milk knew that this was his chance to gain a political entrance to the mainstream. Four neighborhoods had been stitched together to create District Five: Haight Ashbury, the Duboce Triangle, Noe Valley, and the Castro. The gay population dominated two of the neighborhoods, but Milk knew that to win he would need to appeal to a wider audience. He shaved off his goatee, tied his long hair into a neat ponytail, and bought some new, more conservative clothes. He even gave up marijuana during the campaign.

Harvey knew he would have to campaign hard: Sixteen other candidates were vying for the supervisor's seat that Harvey lusted after. He decided to simply outwork and out-campaign all the others. He made the rounds from dawn to dusk, attending every gay gathering and every church event he could find. He led a well-publicized parade through San Francisco advocating gay rights, and he put on such an intense and successful campaign that he won the endorsement of the *Chronicle*.[9]

His victory on election day was every bit as impressive as Dan White's. But Harvey was both thrilled and sobered—sobered because he felt that, as the country's first openly gay elected official, he was vulnerable to assassination. He decided to write a political will, a letter in which he stated his preference for his successor in the case of his death. At the end of the letter he wrote, "If a bullet should enter my brain, let that bullet destroy every closet door."[10]

Throwing caution to the winds, Harvey Milk, with his arm around his new lover, Jack Lira, led an Inaugural Day parade from the Castro to City Hall, where he was to be sworn in as a new supervisor of the City of San Francisco.

Harvey Milk and Dan White were not the only newly elected supervisors. Carol Ruth Silver, a feminist attorney, who saw herself as an ally of Mayor Moscone and Harvey Milk, was newly elected from a district just south of the Castro. Also serving for the first time were Ella Hill Hutch, a black woman, and Gordon Lou, a Chinese American, both of whom had a liberal bent. It was clear that Dan White would be a swing vote in close decisions on which the supervisors disagreed. On the first vote taken, Dan voted to elect Dianne Feinstein the new president of the board. The vote was 6 to 5. The struggle to run the City was on.

In the early days of 1978, Milk and White seemed to get along well on a personal basis, even though they disagreed on most political matters. Each had his own personal agenda. Milk's primary goal was the passage of a gay rights ordinance which would give the City's gays and lesbians a special protective status in hiring and in hate crimes. Dan was already on record as having called homosexuals "social deviates" and was expected to oppose the ordinance.[11] Dan's initial goal as a supervisor was to kill something called a "Youth Campus," which was scheduled to be built in his District Eight. White regarded it simply as a potential headquarters for young thugs and hoodlums, and he had no desire to see it established in his neighborhood. The vote would be close on both issues, and White went to Milk to discuss both matters. He came away with what he felt was an excellent arrangement: Dan White would vote for the gay rights bill and Harvey Milk would, in turn, vote against the youth center.

In these early days, White remained something of an idealist. He believed that all the supervisors would "always do what was right for the city." Supervisor Quentin Kopp felt a little sorry for White, because he thought he was politically naive. Said Kopp to one of his colleagues, "White hasn't got a clue."[12]

When the gay rights legislation came before the committee, Dan White cast a deciding vote and the action received national publicity. It was Harvey Milk's first major triumph and a cause for celebration throughout the gay community. At the suggestion of Harvey Milk, the mayor signed the bill in lavender ink.

It was not long before the matter of the youth center in White's district came before the supervisors. Dan invited a number of his friends and key constituents to the meeting, confident that they would witness his first triumph as a supervisor. But when the vote was taken, Harvey Milk voted to keep the center in White's district, thereby defeating Dan's initiative by a single vote. White was incredulous. He stared over at Milk who, it seemed to White, smirked back at him. White became visibly emotional and left the meeting. It was his ugly baptism into San Francisco City Hall politics.

Over the next months, White continued to be the swing vote between the conservative and liberal wings of the board. Even though his relations with Harvey Milk were outwardly cordial, there was no doubt that they were political rivals. And, Dan White became increasingly frustrated because some of the supervisors were not acting for what he continued to think of as "the good of the City."

But City Hall politics was not White's only problem. He was out of money. His salary as supervisor was a paltry $9,200 a year, hardly enough to support himself and his family.[13] He had used all of his reserve cash in

Milk and Mayor George Moscone after signing the Gay Rights Bill.

the campaign, and he had, in fact, taken on campaign debts of $8,500.[14] During the spring of 1978, Dan became friendly with an entrepreneur named Warren Simmons, who was in the process of creating the restaurant and shopping wharf at Pier 39. Simmons liked Dan White and sympathized with his financial problems. He came to White with a proposition: For some $20,000, White could own a concession at the wharf called "The Hot Potato," an open-air snack stand that would, Simmons said, easily return its original investment every year. White talked it over with his wife, Mary Ann, mortgaged his house, and took on the franchise.

On June 12, Mary Ann went into labor. Dan drove her to Children's Hospital where she presented Dan with a handsome baby boy. They named the baby Charles, after Dan's own father, and Dan couldn't have been prouder. He presented a bottle of Chivas Regal to every supervisor and invited them all to the christening. Milk came along with the others, and the ebullient White introduced Harvey to one of his friends as "one of the greatest guys I know."[15] Over the summer and into the early fall, Dan White's problems continued to close in on him. He didn't really enjoy being a supervisor, handling all the political pressures and balancing his sense of what was right against the needs of political expedience. The opening of "The Hot Potato" had gone well, but soon it became a time-consuming monster for both himself and his wife.

Mary Ann had to spend most of the day at the stand serving customers, and Dan would drive to Pier 39 after a full day at City Hall, help count the receipts, and then peel potatoes far into the night. He rarely got a good night's sleep, taking the 3:00 A.M. feeding of baby Charlie so that Mary Ann could get some rest.

And something else had happened that upset him even more. The downtown business community and the City's real estate interests had decided to help Dan out with his campaign debts. They held a political fundraiser for him that was attended by a list of what one commentator called "a liberal activist's worst nightmare." Dan's political adversaries began a rumor that Dan White was getting into the pocket of the business community. Unfortunately for Dan, he soon found himself voting against Mayor Moscone's new business tax package that was expected to yield some $30 million in new revenue for the City. White devoutly believed the tax was the wrong way to go, but his deciding vote in the 6 to 5 decision against the new tax looked to many like a payback for the financial support he had recently received. The attack on White's integrity drove him to distraction.

As the year moved into autumn, pressures on Dan White seemed to go from difficult to unbearable. He wasn't sleeping well, and his eating habits became erratic. He lived for days on junk food, and his appearance began to disturb his associates. One friend ran into White at a merchant's luncheon, and he later called Dan's former campaign manager. "You better go see your friend Dan White," he told her. "He looks terrible."[16]

White continued to go downhill in the months that followed. He was inattentive at board meetings, restless in his office, irritable at home, and quick to anger when things went wrong at "The Hot Potato." He became convinced that he wasn't serving his constituents well, that he was short-changing his family, and that he was being unfairly persecuted by his enemies. Finally, on the morning of November 10, he left his office, drove to Pier 39, and said to his wife, "I'm going to resign. I can't take it anymore."[18]

After a brief conversation with Mary Ann, he drove back to his office and met with his assistant, Denise Apcar. He told her he was going to resign as city supervisor, but he didn't know how to do it. Together, they decided he should write a letter of resignation to the mayor. White took pen in hand and wrote the following letter:

> "Dear Mayor Moscone, I have been proud to represent the people of San Francisco as their elected Supervisor from District Eight for the past ten months but due to personal responsibilities which I feel must take precedent over my legislative duties, I am resigning my position today. I am sure that the next representative to the Board of Supervisors will receive as much support from the people of San Francisco as I have. Sincerely, Dan White"[19]

Denise delivered the letter to Moscone, who then requested that White visit him right away. Moscone wanted to make certain that Dan was sure he knew what he was doing. When Dan assured the mayor that he had thought it through carefully, the mayor shook his hand and wished him good luck.

Word of the resignation ran through City Hall like wildfire. White held a brief press conference and announced his decision to an astonished press corps. Harvey Milk was with his new lover, Doug Banks, when he got the news. "This is terrific, " he exclaimed. "Now I've got my sixth vote!"[20]

The City was shocked at White's unexpected resignation. Most of Dan White's supporters were horrified. The Chamber of Commerce exhorted him to reconsider. Paul Chignal, president of the Police Officers Association, was especially chagrined. White, a former policeman, had been the main voice of support for the police department. The department would now be at the mercy of the liberal mayor and their hated police chief. Over the next two days, a procession of supporters called on White at his home in an attempt to convince him that he had made a mistake. Their appeal was a telling one: He had reneged on his promise to represent the people who voted for him. He had a moral commitment, they told him, to soldier on. Gradually, White began to come around. It was true that he had acted in a moment of desperation and haste. Perhaps he had made a mistake. White picked up the phone and called the mayor. He reported he would like to come over and see him, that he had changed his mind and would like to have his letter of resignation back. Moscone told him to come right over, that he understood.

Dan White drove over to City Hall and hurried to the mayor's office. Moscone had already given the letter to his secretary, who returned it to White. White returned to his old office, waved the letter, and said to his assistant, "Well, I guess you can call me a supervisor again!"[21]

Unfortunately, it wasn't quite that simple, as Dan White would soon learn. White's letter had not always been on Moscone's desk. In the intervening days, Gilbert Boreman, secretary to the board of supervisors, had made a copy of the letter, and, in the ordinary course of events, had placed it before a meeting of the supervisors for acceptance. It was a routine matter, and the supervisors, believing it expressed Dan White's wishes, voted unanimously to accept it. So now, a legal question confronted the city government. Dan White had successfully retrieved his letter, but in the meantime, the letter had become part of the official record. Was Dan White a supervisor or wasn't he? The City's district attorney would have to decide. The attorney guessed that it might take as long as a week to resolve what had become a complicated legal issue—a week during which Dan White would be twisting in the wind.

Several days later, the opponents of Dan White, most of whom had run against him just a year earlier, organized a rally in District Eight. With a crowd of several hundred in attendance, White was denounced as a puppet of the business and real estate interests. White himself tried to take the stand and speak, but, after saying just a few words, he was shunted aside. Everyone agreed that Dan White looked terrible.

Finally, the legal ruling was made: The acceptance by the supervisors of White's letter of resignation meant that he was officially out of office. White's name was removed from his door at City Hall. Still, everyone recognized that all George Moscone had to do was to reappoint White and he could resume his seat on the board.

Being restored as a supervisor now became an obsession for Dan White. It was a matter of pride and of principle. As far as White was concerned, he had a commitment from Moscone that he would be permitted to keep his seat. But White also knew that others, especially Harvey Milk, did not want him back.

Harvey was hard at work to make sure that White was replaced with a supervisor more to his liking and to his politics. He visited the Mayor's office several times over the next two days to make sure Moscone understood what was at stake. Moscone would be standing for re-election in a year and Harvey made it clear that, if White was re-seated, Moscone would not get the gay vote.

City Hall was filled with rumors that Moscone was considering several District Eight politicians as possible replacements for White. On Thanksgiving Day, an occasion when Dan White was hoping for some peace of mind from his daily tortures, the *Chronicle* ran an article that the mayor would probably appoint Helen Fama, one of White's political enemies, to take his place. The article went on to say: "White has only himself to blame for his troubles. If he has any gift for self-appraisal, he must be kicking himself."[22]

White spent the following weekend in solemn silence. Mary Ann was out of town attending a wedding. Dan spent most of the time in bed. He was exhausted, but he couldn't sleep. He wondered if he was having a nervous breakdown. He had virtually stopped eating. He felt beaten and humiliated. He had been betrayed by George Moscone, stabbed in the back by Harvey Milk.

On Monday morning, November 27, Dan White put on his best suit and his best pair of shoes. He walked over to his bureau and pulled out his old police revolver and put bullets into each of its five chambers. He strapped on his leather holster and clipped it onto the back of his belt. Then he took down a box of Remington .38 cartridges, removed eight bullets, and folded them into his handkerchief. His assistant was scheduled to pick him up for the drive to City Hall for a pre-arranged meeting with George Moscone, and Dan wanted to have everything ready for the meeting.

White hurried up the steps of City Hall and was about to open the front door when he remembered the metal detector that awaited him inside. He turned away and walked toward McAllister Street and down the side of the building to another entrance that supervisors sometimes used. That door was locked, but White noticed an open basement window. He stepped inside, walked through a testing laboratory, and then climbed a back stairway that led to a corridor outside the mayor's office. [23]

White entered the mayor's office complex through a side door and found himself standing in front of Cyr Copertini, the mayor's secretary. White asked to see the mayor. Cyr went into the mayor's office and George Moscone said he would see White in a minute or so, even though he was not looking forward to the encounter. Finally, Dan White was admitted to George Moscone's formal office. Moscone was sitting at his big walnut desk, and he gestured for Dan to take a chair.

White came right to the point. "What I came for," he said, "was I want to know if you're going to reappoint me."

The mayor was equally direct. "No, Dan, I'm not going to reappoint you."[25]

White demanded an explanation, claiming to have the support of the voters of District Eight. White said he had been a good supervisor. As he spoke, his voice rose and he seemed very emotional. Moscone tried to be soothing. It was just a political decision, he told White; it was nothing personal.

Moscone was anxious to end the meeting, but he felt sorry for Dan, who looked absolutely terrible. He invited Dan to come into the back room with him to have a drink, even though it was only mid-morning. As he gestured White toward the room, he walked over to the other door, stuck his head out and said, "Cyr, hold my calls."[25]

Dan White slumped down into the couch, while George Moscone carried two drinks into the room. He handed one to Dan and lit a cigarette. As he turned to face White again, he found himself staring at the short barrel of White's revolver. Dan stood up and fired the first hollow-pointed slug into Moscone's chest. Moscone toppled forward. As he fell, White fired a second slug into the back of the mayor's shoulder. Moscone hit the floor heavily, his lighted cigarette falling to the carpet. White straddled Moscone's fallen body and leaned down, putting the gun close to Moscone's right ear. He pumped two more shots into the head, severing the brain stem. Blood spattered everywhere and covered Moscone's upper body. Dan stepped back and reloaded his gun. He had more work to do.

White stepped out through the sitting-room door, back into the corridor. He ran down the corridor until he came to the back entrance of the supervisors' office. He opened the door and moved quickly down the hall. He passed Dianne Feinstein's office, where her assistant called to him. White stopped for just a moment and replied, "It'll have to wait. I have something to do first."[26]

White walked over to Harvey Milk's office and found Harvey and his assistant, Carl Carlson, looking over some papers. "Harvey, can I see you a moment?" White asked. Harvey looked up, somewhat surprised, "Sure," he replied.[27]

Milk followed Dan into his old office, now deserted except for a desk and two chairs. White closed the door behind them.

"What the hell are you doing to me?" White demanded. "Why do you want to hurt me... my family..."[28] Then, Dan freed his gun and squeezed off the first shot.

Milk had risen from his chair at the sight of the gun. The shot tore into his bowels, spinning him to the right. White fired again, and the bullet grazed Milk's arm, entering and exiting the flesh of his chest and spinning him further. As Milk toppled to the ground, White fired two more shots, one entering Milk's back and another penetrating the base of his skull. Blood and tissue splattered the wall. White stepped forward, pressed the gun against Harvey Milk's bleeding skull and fired one final shot. Milk's body jumped and lay still, bathed in blood.

White reholstered his gun, then walked out into the hall, slamming the door behind him. Several staffers stared, speechless, as White ran past them toward the stairway. On the way, he passed an aide he knew. "Hi, Anne," said Dan White, and then he plunged down the stairs and hurried out of the building.

The front page of *The San Francisco Examiner* on
Monday, November 27, 1978.

Dianne Feinstein was sitting in her office when she heard the first shot. It flashed through her mind that Dan White must have killed himself. But, when she heard other shots, she knew it must be something else, equally terrifying. She rushed to Dan White's old office, and with Milk's aide, Carl Carlson, she entered the office. She rushed to Harvey Milk's body and tried to find a pulse, but the profusion of blood made it impossible. It didn't make any difference, as Harvey Milk was obviously dead. Feinstein asked Carlson to call the police department, but Carlson was almost hopelessly distraught and unable to dial the telephone. Feinstein took the phone from his trembling hands and dialed Chief of Police Gain. She reported to him that Harvey Milk had been shot to death. Gain quickly informed her that George Moscone had also been murdered.

As news of the killings reached the police officials on the fourth floor of the Hall of Justice Building, scattered cheering broke out. One inspector who had not yet heard the news wondered what all the cheering was about. After all, he thought, the World Series had wrapped up long ago and the 49ers weren't playing for another five days.[29]

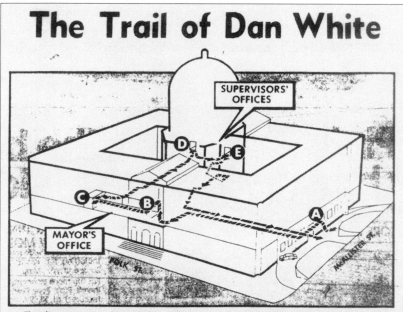

The Trail of Dan White

This diagram traces the probable movements of the suspect through City Hall on Monday. The suspect enters through basement window on the McAllister street ramp (A); takes elevator to mayor's office on second floor (B); walks down inner corridor to the mayor's private sitting room, where Moscone was killed (C); leaves through sitting room door and walks across building to supervisors' offices (D); where Harvey Milk was slain; then walks to aide's office (E); for car keys, hurries down two flights of stairs to first floor, around pillars to basement stairs and out to aide's car on McAllister ramp.

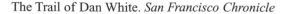

The Trail of Dan White. *San Francisco Chronicle*

297

Dan White drove to a nearby diner, placed a call to his wife, Mary Ann at "The Hot Potato" and asked her to meet him right away at Saint Mary's Cathedral. Then he drove the five blocks to the cathedral, went in, and knelt down to pray. Within fifteen minutes, Mary Ann was at his side. "I shot the mayor and Harvey," he said.[30] Then, together, their arms around each other, they left the church and walked toward the Northern Police Station. Dan White wanted to turn himself in. He wanted to tell the authorities what he had done. Even more importantly, he wanted to explain why he had done it. He wanted them to understand.

News of the assassination swept the City like a firestorm. People heard the news in stunned disbelief. City Hall was quickly filled with reporters, eager for any scrap of information. Dianne Feinstein, now the mayor of San Francisco under provisions of the city charter, stood in the hallway outside the supervisors' offices, supported by Chief Gain, who stood at her side. She spoke slowly and emotionally, as flashbulbs popped all about her.

Feinstein began to speak: "As president of the board of supervisors, it is my duty to inform you that both Mayor Moscone and Supervisor Harvey Milk have been killed." Gasps and cries interrupted her. She wavered slightly and then continued, "The suspect is Supervisor Dan White."[31] Now in tears, the new mayor was escorted back into her office.

The bodies of Milk and Moscone, in body bags, being placed in the ambulance at City Hall.

By that time, Dan White was at police headquarters making a full confession to an inspector. White talked for almost fifteen minutes in a voice that alternated between eerie calm and uncontrollable sobbing. He talked of his honor, his family, and his own personal tragedies. He described the betrayal by Moscone and Milk. He described his actions in both killings in considerable detail, saying he hadn't really planned to shoot them, and he hadn't really intended to kill them. He spoke of "a roaring in my head."[32] When he was through speaking, he wept. It had been only an hour and a half since he fired the first bullet into the body of the mayor of San Francisco.

The events following the murder were, if anything, even more remarkable and more historic than the killings themselves.

That night 30,000 people, many of them carrying candles, marched from the Castro area to City Hall. It was an eerie and moving sight as the throng moved slowly, chanting, in a huge and solemn procession through the streets. When the marchers arrived at their destination, they were met by the new mayor, Dianne Feinstein, who addressed them briefly. Singer Joan Baez and the Gay Men's Chorus sang. The recorded voice of Harvey Milk spoke to them of the need for tolerance and understanding. Many in the crowd wept openly at the City's loss, at their own loss.

Dan White languished in a jail cell, held on bail set at $1,000,000. The City's newspapers wailed in pain and outrage, trying to understand the significance of the murders, trying to understand why they had happened. George Moscone and Harvey Milk were hailed everywhere as martyrs, and the City went into deep mourning. Officials asked the National Football League to cancel the 49ers game scheduled for that Sunday. The game was played anyway, and the team's loss seemed to fit the City's sad mood. The funerals of both Milk and Moscone set new records for attendance and for media coverage.

As the months passed with legal maneuvering and pre-trial jousting, Dan White was treated by his visitors, and even by his jailors, as a celebrity, if not a hero. People visited him outside of regular hours, he was given unlimited telephone time and extra medical treatment, and special meals were sent to him by friends.

Over the next months, the City settled back into some sense of normalcy. The tragic events of November began to fade into memory, as city government resumed its normal functions, city merchants enjoyed a thriving holiday season, and the New Year was celebrated with high hopes for the future. As the winter mellowed into spring, the City Hall murders seemed only an agonizing memory. But San Francisco and the nation were doomed to relive them yet again, this time in excruciating, and sometimes painful, detail. On May 1, 1988, Dan White went on trial for the murders of Mayor Moscone and Supervisor Milk.[33]

The prosecution was in the hands of a veteran city attorney, Tom Norman, and under the guidance of San Francisco District Attorney Joe Freites. White was to be defended by a transplanted Michigander, Doug Schmidt. Norman was basically a political creature, as anxious to preserve the reputation of Mayor Moscone as he was to prosecute White. Schmidt was determined, soft-spoken, with a sort of "aw-shucks" style that appealed to jurors. The first thing he did was to ensure that no homosexuals sat in the jury box.

The trial itself seemed to go White's way from the beginning. It was clear from the outset that Schmidt was trying for a "diminished capacity" defense.[34] The prosecution presented a clinical recitation of the facts, which were that Dan White killed George Moscone and Harvey Milk in cold blood. The prosecution's reasoning was that the circumstances of the case were so clear and so overwhelming that a first-degree murder verdict was all but certain.

Defense attorney Schmidt, while not challenging any of the facts of the murders, concentrated on White's state of mind. He called on witnesses who testified as to the alleged wrongs inflicted on White by the victims. Psychologists testified that White was clearly suffering from

Mayor Dianne Feinstein testifying that at first she thought White had killed himself.

deep depression, a recognized form of mental illness. Schmidt also called up friends of White, who testified that White's change in eating habits prior to the murders had affected his personality.

Denise Apcar, White's City Hall assistant, testified that White's health and mental state had, in her opinion, declined due to his strange diet. She said, "He would ask me to buy him candy during lunch breaks and at recess, and he ate a lot of candy, and he would eat donuts, junk food, sugar drinks."[35]

Schmidt knew a good thing when he heard it. Just a day later he called White's sister, a registered nurse, to the stand, and her testimony would inspire a new legal phrase that would have unexpected ramifications. "I noticed... during these periods (of depression) that he would go out and eat Cokes, Twinkies, candy bars, stuff like that."[36]

Norman, the prosecutor, was incredulous. He asked, "With respect to these foods that you have told us he ate—Twinkies, I think you said?"

"Especially chocolate cupcakes," the witness repeated.

"Are you equating his depression with the ingestion of chocolate cupcakes?" Norman demanded.[37]

White's sister could only nod. The prosecution was also speechless, and all too happy to dismiss the witness.

From that moment on, the "Twinkie defense" took its place in legal history. The most poignant moment of the trial, however, came when Schmidt played a tape of White's confession. White's voice, choked with emotion, floated over the courtroom like the wail of a victim, not a murderer. The emotion in his voice somehow seemed more important than the deeds he described. When the tape was finished, a number of jurors wept openly in the jury box. The main question now seemed to be not what he had done, but the circumstances and emotions that compelled him to do it.

Still, Norman, the reporters covering the trial, and San Franciscans who followed the progress of the trial in the City's newspapers, all felt that a first-degree murder verdict was inevitable. Almost no one was prepared for the verdict that came after five days of deliberation.

The jury verdict was a true shocker: Dan White was not found guilty of first-degree murder or even of second-degree murder. The jury decided on voluntary manslaughter, a verdict that carried with it a maximum sentence of seven and two-thirds years.[38] With time off for good behavior, Dan White could be a free man in five years. San Francisco was stunned. The residents of the Castro and of Harvey Milk's district simply went mad.

The verdict was announced on radio in the early evening. Within hours, a group of marchers left the Castro area for City Hall, swelling in

Jury foreman
George Mintzer
delivers the
astonishing verdict
to the bailiff.

numbers as it went. By the time it reached City Hall, it had turned into an angry mob of more than five thousand outraged citizens. They literally attacked the building in their rage, throwing rocks and bottles, overturning mailboxes, cars, anything they could find to express their fury.

The attack came so quickly that the police were short-handed and were barely able to keep any sense of order. The new mayor attempted to speak to the crowd, but it was to no avail. The attack lasted for more than two hours, and by the time the crowd's rage had abated, City Hall was a mess of broken windows and damaged walls. Eleven police cars had been overturned and burned. At one point, a small contingent of the crowd advanced toward the Hall of Justice, where Dan White paced his prison cell. However, the sight of police rifleman on the roof seemed to discourage them.[39]

The scars on City Hall reflected, in a very real sense, the damage to the psyche of the City itself. San Francisco had been wounded, and the effects of the murders, the verdict, and the riot would not soon dissipate. The aftermath of the City Hall murders seemed to continue on and on through the years that followed.

Dan White was sentenced to the maximum term of seven and two-thirds years and was sent to Soledad Prison, where he spent his time reading books, talking to friends, and dictating long, ponderous memoranda on his life and deeds. He worked out as often as his prison schedule permitted, and he frequently jogged on the prison track with Sirhan Sirhan, the assassin who had killed Robert Kennedy.[40]

Burning cars at City Hall give evidence of the city's outrage.

The state legislature reacted to widespread sentiment and subsequently passed a law that essentially eliminated the "Twinkie defense" from all future murder trials in California.

Dianne Feinstein, who had expected to leave politics after her term as supervisor, served two successful terms as mayor of the City of San Francisco, then went on to run for governor of California, eventually being elected a United States senator from California. At one point, she was seriously discussed as a candidate for vice-president of the United States.

The impact of Harvey Milk's life and death continues to this day. He had been the first openly gay, publicly elected office holder in the nation, and he was clearly more than a one-dimensional politician. Eulogized in death as he had never been praised in life, his fame inspired a whole generation of gay politicians to try for and achieve public office. The Milk legacy has been celebrated in song, in biography, in film, and even in an opera entitled, simply, *Harvey Milk*.

In 1984, Dan White was released from prison, having served his sentence with time off for good behavior. He returned to his family and tried to lead a quiet life, away from the public eye. Finally, unable to live with his own demons, Dan White issued his own verdict on the City Hall murders. One morning, he entered his garage, closed all the doors, turned on the engine of his car—and executed himself.

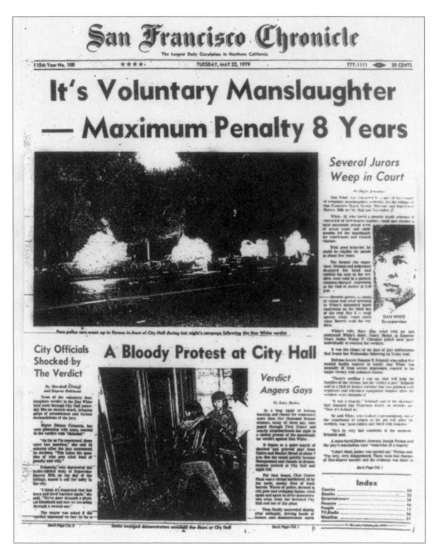

The San Francisco Chronicle announces the verdict—and shows the bloody aftermath.

Coda

The last murder described in this book took place more than two and a half decades ago. Since then, murder has, if anything, become more prevalent and commonplace. Following the City Hall crimes, there have been more than 10,000 murders in the greater San Francisco Bay Area, depending on how that territory is defined. There is no way of knowing how many of them, if any, will be remembered as having sufficient complexity and mystery or having created enough long-term public fascination or having sufficiently altered the course of jurisprudence to be deemed truly historic. Only the passage of time and the verdict of future historians can make that evaluation. But the odds are that, at some point in time, there will be another sixteen stories worth the writing and worth the reading. Let's all stick around and see!

Sources Cited

CHAPTER ONE: "THE DOOMED EDITOR—1856"

1. *San Francisco—A Pageant* by Charles Caldwell Dobie, Appleton-Century Company, Inc., New York, 1934, p. 127.

2. *Villains and Vigilantes* by Stanton A. Coblentz, Thomas Yoseloff, Inc., New York, 1936, p. 117.

3. *Vigilantes In the Gold Rush* by Robert J. Sukewicz, S.J., Stanford University Press, Stanford, CA, 1985, p. 157.

4. *A Pile, Listing of the Wealth of 600 Californians*, 1851.

5. *Vigilance Papers of the San Francisco Committee of Vigilance of 1851*, edited by Peter Garnett, University of California, Berkeley, CA, 1910, p. 22.

6. *San Francisco Bulletin*, May 21, 1856.

7. *Villains and Vigilantes*, p. 120.

8. *San Francisco Alta*, Mar. 2, 1855.

9. *Letter to Alta California*, July 26, 1855.

10. *San Francisco Bulletin*, Oct. 8, 1855.

11. Ibid.

12. *Villains and Vigilantes*, p. 139.

13. *A Short History of California* by Horace Campbell, Dorrance & Company, Philadelphia, 1949.

14. *San Francisco Bulletin*, May 14, 1856.

15. *History of San Francisco* by John S. Hittell, A.L. Bancroft & Co., San Francisco, 1878, p. 244.

16. *Villains and Vigilantes*, p. 163.

17. *Committee of Vigilance Manifesto, To The People of California*, June 9, 1855.

CHAPTER TWO: "THE SENATOR AND THE JUSTICE—1859"

1. *The Field of Honor* by Major Ben C. Truman, Ford, Howard & Hulbert, New York, 1884, p. 11.

2. *Tales of Love and Hate in Old San Francisco* by Millie Robbins, Chronicle Books, San Francisco, 1971, pp. 128-129.

3. *David C. Broderick, A Political Portrait* by David A. Williams, Huntington Library, San Marino, CA, 1969, p. 3.

4. *The Terry-Broderick Duel* by Carrol Douglas Hall, The Colt Press, San Francisco, 1939, p. 12.

5. *The Life of David C. Broderick* by Jeremiah Lynch, New York, 1911, p. 7-9.

6. Ibid., p. 12.

7. Ibid., p. 13.

8. *The Annals of San Francisco* by Frank Soulé, P. Appleton & Co., San Francisco, 1855, p. 823.

9. *David C. Broderick, A Political Portrait*, p. 57.

10. *The Terry-Broderick Duel*, p. 15.

11. *History of California* by Herbert H. Bancroft, San Francisco, 1888, p. 706.

12. *A Cast of Hawks* by Milton S. Gould, Copley Press, La Jolla, CA, 1985, p. 15.

13. *The Rise and Fall of the "Know-Nothings"* by Peyton Hurt, San Francisco, CA 1930, p. 37.

14. *David C. Broderick: A Political Portrait*, p. 109-112.

15. *A Cast of Hawks*, p. 65.

16. Ibid., p. 67.

17. *San Francisco Bulletin*, June 23, 1856.

18. *The Western Gate*, edited by Joseph Harry Jackson, Farrar, Straus & Young, New York, 1952, p. 212.

19. *The Terry-Broderick Duel*, p. 78.

20. Ibid., p. 51.

21. *The Field of Honor*, p. 407.

22. *Terry-Broderick Correspondence*, Society of California Pioneers Library, Terry to Broderick, Sept. 9, 1859.

23. *David C. Broderick: A Political Portrait*, p. 234.

24. *The Field of Honor*, p. 409.

25. *David C. Broderick: A Political Portrait*, p. 234.

26. *New York Times*, Apr. 17, 1852.

27. *The Terry-Broderick Duel*, p. 59.

28. *San Francisco Bulletin*, Nov. 2, 1895, p. 13.

29. *Harper's Weekly*, Sun., Oct. 22, 1859.

30. "The Terry-Broderick Duel", in *The Western Gate,* by Ben C. Truman, 1952, p. 219.

31. *The Terry-Broderick Duel*, p. 83.

32. Ibid., p. 86.

33. *Cincinnati Gazette*, Nov. 13, 1863.

34. *A Cast of Hawks*, p. 143.

CHAPTER THREE: "THE MISUSED MISTRESS—1870"

1. *San Francisco Chronicle*, "A Woman's Revenge—Assassination of A. P. Crittenden, Esq. By the Notorious Mrs. Fair," Fri., Nov. 4, 1870, p. 3.

2. *Who Killed Mr. Crittenden?* by Kenneth LaMott, Ballentine Books, New York, 1973, p. 137.

3. *The California Alta*, "Mrs. Fair's Performance Well-Received," June 23, 1863, p. 4.

4. *San Francisco Murders*, "Wolves In The Fold," by Robert O'Brien, Bantam Books, N.Y., 1948, p. 22.

5. Ibid., p. 25.

6. *San Francisco Chronicle*, "The Assassination—Love Letters of Crittenden Admitted on Evidence," Sun., Apr. 11, 1871, p. 3.

7. Ibid., "The Assassination—Cross-Examination of Mrs. Fair Concluded," Tues., Apr. 8, 1871, p. 3.

8. Ibid., "A Woman's Revenge," Fri., Nov. 4, 1870, p. 3.

9. *San Francisco Examiner*, "The Crittenden Tragedy—The Coroner's Inquest," Sat., Nov. 19, 1870, p. 3.

10. *The San Francisco Chronicle*, "The Assassination-Death of A.P. Crittenden," Mon., Nov. 7, 1870, p. 3.

11. *San Francisco Daily Call*, "Attempt to Murder," Fri., Nov. 4, 1870, p. 3.

12. *San Francisco Examiner*, "Death of A.P. Crittenden," Mon., Nov. 7, 1870, p. 3.

13. State of California Statute, "Act Defining Crimes and Punishments," Section 26.

14. *San Francisco Chronicle*, "The Fate of Mr. Crittenden," Sat., Nov. 5, 1870, p. 3.

15. *Who Killed Mr. Crittenden?*, pp. 129-130.

16. *San Francisco Chronicle*, "The Assassination—Mrs. Fair and Mr. Crittenden Born for Each Other," Thurs., Apr. 6, 1971, p. 3.

17. *San Francisco Chronicle*, "The Fatal Amour—Laura's Love Letters," Tuesay, Apr. 11, 1871, p. 1.

18. Ibid., "The Fatal Amour—Medical Testimony," Tues., Apr. 11, 1871, p. 1.

19. *Who Killed Mr. Crittenden?*, p. 132.

20. *San Francisco Chronicle*, "The Argument—Campbell Closes His Argument with A Brilliant Peroration," Sun., Apr. 16, 1871, p. 1.

21. Ibid., "Mr. Cook Continues His Argument for The Defense," Sat., Apr. 2, 1871, p. 3.

22. Ibid., "The Fatal Amour—Brilliant Oratorical Display by District Attorney Byrne," Wed., Apr. 16, 1871, p. 3.

23. *Who Killed Mr. Crittenden?*, p. 198.

24. Ibid., p. 199.

25. *San Francisco Murders*, p. 42.

26. *Daily Alta California*, "The Trial of Laura D. Fair—The Twelfth Juror Obtained," Wed., Sept. 18, 1872, p. 1.

27. *San Francisco Murders*, p. 43.

28. *Who Killed Mr. Crittenden?*, p. 209.

CHAPTER FOUR: "THE PUBLISHER AND THE PREACHER—1880"

1. *San Francisco Examiner & Chronicle*, California Living Section, "The Controversial Mayor Kalloch," Sun., Oct. 12, 1980, p. 47.

2. *The Other Writings of Richard Henry Dana, Jr.* by James D. Hart, Colophon— The Book Collector's Quarterly, 1937, p. 37.

3. *The Golden Voice* by M. M. Marberry, Ferrar, Straus and Co., New York, 1947, introduction, p. vii.

4. *The San Francisco Almanac* by Gladys Hansen, Chronicle Books, San Francisco, 1995, p. 119.

5. *The Story of Files* by Ella Sterling Cumming, published by the World's Fair Commission of California, San Francisco, CA, 1983, p. 427.

6. *San Francisco Chronicle*, Sept. 1, 1869, p. 1.

7. Ibid., Aug. 23, 1879, p. 3.

8. *The San Francisco Examiner & Chronicle*, California Living Section, "The Controversial Major Kalloch," Oct. 12, 1980, p. 49.

9. *The Golden Voice*, p. 250.

10. *The Golden Voice*, p. 299.

11. *San Francisco Magazine*, "The Chronicle Clan" by Richard Rappaport, Nov. 1987, p. 42.

12. Ibid., p. 42.

13. *The Golden Voice*, p. 248.

14. *The San Francisco Magazine*, "The Chronicle Clan," p. 43.

15. *San Francisco Examiner*, "The Controversial Major Kalloch", Oct. 12, 1980, p. 49.

16. *The Golden Voice*, p. 257.

17. *Pacific Magazine*, "Civilized Warfare," by Brian Garret, Dec., 1980, p. 14.

18. *San Francisco Examiner*, Aug. 23, 1879, p. 3.

19. *San Francisco Morning Call*, Aug. 24, 1879, p. 1.

20. *San Francisco Examiner*, Aug. 24, 1879, p. 4.

21. *The Golden Voice*, p. 261.

22. Ibid., p. 263.

23. Ibid., p. 274.

24. *Old San Francisco, Biography of a City* by Doris Muscatine, G. P. Putman's Sons, New York, 1975, p. 163.

25. *The Golden Voice*, p. 339.

26. Ibid., p. 339.

CHAPTER FIVE: "THE PHOSPHORESCENT BRIDES—1885"

1. *The Langley San Francisco Directory*, 1884-5, pp. 1250-1251.

2. Ibid., p. 262.

3. *San Francisco Morning Call*, Jan. 30, 1881, p. 5.

4. *Ambrose Bierce: A Sole Survivor* edited by T. S. Josln, University of Tennessee, Knoxville, 1998, p. 137.

5. *San Francisco Murders* edited by Joseph Harry Jackson, Duell, Sloan and Pearce, New York, p. 5.

6. *Daily Alta California*, "Her Recent Death Gives Rise to Unfounded Rumors," Tues., Nov. 3, 1885, p. 3.

7. *San Francisco Morning Call*, "Death of Dr. Bowers' Wife," Nov. 3, 1885, p. 2.

8. Ibid., "Testimony Given at Inquest Case," Nov. 4, 1885, p. 3.

9. Ibid.

10. *Daily Alta California*, "The Body of Mrs. Bowers Hurriedly Buried," Thurs., Nov. 3, 1885, p. 1.

11. *San Francisco Morning Call*, "Inquest Resumed—What the Autopsy Revealed," Sun., Nov. 6, p. 3.

12. Ibid., "Traces of Phospherous Found in His Late Wife's Stomach," Thurs., Nov. 10, 1885, p. 5.

13. *Daily Alta California*, "Grave Suspicions," Tues., Nov. 10, 1885, p. 1.

14. Ibid.

15. Ibid.

16. *San Francisco Chronicle*, "A Woman Who Was Treated Like a Dog," Sat., Mar. 13, 1886, p. 2.

17. *San Francisco Morning Call*, "Guilty of Murder," Sat., Apr. 24, 1886, p. 3.

18. Ibid.

19. *San Francisco Morning Call*, "Benhayon—Was His Death Murder or Suicide?" Tues., 25, 1887, p. 1.

20. Ibid.

21. *San Francisco Murders*, pp. 63-64.

22. *San Francisco Morning Call*, "A Lawyer's Theory," Sat., Mar. 13, p. 1.

23. *Great Crimes of the West* by Pete Fanning, San Francisco, 1929, pp. 142-143.

24. *San Francisco Morning Call*, "Free Once More," Sat., Aug. 17, p. 2.

25. Ibid., "A Talk with Bowers."

26. *San Francisco Morning Call*, "Dr. J. Milton Bowers Is Called to Render Account to Maker," Mar. 8, 1904, p. 16.

CHAPTER SIX: "THE REVENGE OF THE TONGS—1887"

1. *Annals of San Francisco* by Frank Soule, D. Appleton & Co., New York.

2. *A Short History of California* by Horace Campbell, Dorrance & Co., Philadelphia, 1949, p. 163.

3. *The Hatchet Men* by Richard H. Dillon, Coward, McCann, Inc., New York, 1962, p. 305.

4. *Tong War!* by Eng Ying Gong and Bruce Grant, Nicholas & Brown, New York, 1930, p. 10.

5. Ibid., p. 127.

6. *Celebrated Criminal Cases of America* by Thomas S. Duke, James H. Barry Co., San Francisco, 1910, p. 106.

7. *The Barbary Coast* by Herbert Asbury, Alfred A. Knopf, New York, 1933, p. 384.

8. *San Francisco: A Pageant* by Charles C. Dobie, Appleton-Century, New York, 1934, p. 206.

9. *Celebrated Criminal Cases of America*, p. 108.

10. *The Hatchet Men*, p. 314.

11. Ibid., p. 320.

12. *Tong War!*, p. 80-81.

13. *The Call Bulletin*, Sun., Jan. 24, 1897, p. 1.

14. *Tong War!*, p. 84.

15. *The San Francisco Call*, "Little Pete Has Passed," Wed., Jan. 27, 1897, p. 1.

16. Ibid., Jan. 24, 1897, p. 1.

17. *The Morning Call*, "Is Death Rampant?" Mon., Jan. 25, 1897, p. 1.

18. *The San Francisco Call*, "Terror In Chinatown," Tues., Jan. 26, 1897, p. 2.

19. *San Francisco Chronicle*, "Barbaric Pomp for Little Pete," Wed., Jan. 27, 1897, p. 3.

20. *Tong War!*, p. 90.

CHAPTER SEVEN: "THE BELLE IN THE BELFRY—1895"

1. *Thrillers* edited by John Miller and Tim Smith, Chronicle Books, San Francisco, 1995, p. 62.

2. *San Francisco Murders* by Marie F. Rodell, Duell, Sloan and Pearce, New York, 1947, p. 76.

3. Ibid., p. 77.

4. *Great Crimes of the West* by Pete Fanning, San Francisco, 1929, p. 31.

5. Ibid., p. 32

6. *Great Crimes of San Francisco* by Dean C. Dickensheet, Comstock Editors, Inc., Sausalito, CA, 1947, p. 67.

7. *San Francisco Call-Bulletin*, Wed., Apr. 10, 1895, p. 8.

8. *Great Crimes of the West*, p. 34.

9. *San Francisco Murders*, p. 83.

10. *Thrillers*, p. 73.

11. *San Francisco Murders*, p. 88.

12. *Thrillers*, p. 74.

13. *San Francisco Call-Bulletin*, Sun., Apr. 14, 1895, p. 6.

14. *San Francisco Murders*, p. 89.

15. *San Francisco Call-Bulletin*, Sun., Apr. 14, 1895, p. 6.

16. *San Francisco Chronicle*, Tues., Apr. 23, 1895, p. 1.

17. *San Francisco Call-Bulletin*, Mon., Apr. 15, 1985, p. 2.

18. *Celebrated Criminal Cases of America* by Thomas S. Duke, Barry Publishers, San Francisco, 1910, pp. 119-120.

19. *Great Crimes of San Francisco*, p. 73.

20. *San Francisco Murders*, p. 107.

21. *Great Murder Mysteries* by Guy B. H. Logan, Paul Publishers, London, 1931, p. 132.

22. *Great Crimes of San Francisco*, p. 72.

23. *Thrillers*, p. 64.

24. *Great Crimes of the West*, p. 35.

25. *San Francisco Murders*, p. 113.

26. Ibid., p. 113.

27. *San Francisco Chronicle*, Sat., Jan. 8, 1898, p. 1.

CHAPTER EIGHT: "THE STOCKTON TRUNK STUFFER—1906"

1. *History of the San Francisco Vigilance Committee* by Mary Floyd Williams, University of California Press, Berkeley, CA, 1921, p. 77.

2. *Historical Souvenir of El Dorado County*, 1882, p. 148.

3. *California Statutes, 1851*, chapter 95, p. 406.

4. *The Stockton Daily Evening Record*, "Ghastly Baggage Was Left At The S.P. Depot," Mon., Mar. 26, 1906, p. 1.

5. *The Stockton Evening Mail*, "Woman Confesses Part In Trunk Murder," Mon., Mar. 26, 1906, p. 1.

6. *The Stockton Daily Evening Record*, "A. N. McVicar Slugged to Death," Mon., Mar. 26, 1906, p. 1.

7. Ibid.

8. *San Francisco Murders*, "Other Than A Good One," by Joseph Henry Jackson, Duel, Sloan and Pearce, New York, p. 181.

9. *The Stockton Evening Mail*, "The Trunk Murder In A Minute," Mon., Mar. 26, 1906, p. 1.

10. *San Francisco Examiner*, "Trunk Murderess May Be Headed Here," Mon., Mar. 26, 1906, p. 3.

11. *San Francisco Murders*, p. 186.

12. *The Stockton Daily Evening Record*, "Murdered Man's Body on Exhibition at Morgue," Mon., Mar. 26, 1906, p. 1.

13. *The Stockton Evening Mail*, "McVicar Murdered By Mrs. Le Doux," Tues., Mar. 27, 1906, p. 1.

14. Ibid., "Woman Confesses Part In Trunk Murder," Mon., Mar. 26, 1906, p. 1.

15. *San Francisco Murders*, p. 186.

16. *The Stockton Daily Evening Record*, "Life Insurance Her Hobby," Thurs., Mar. 29, 1906, p. 1.

17. *The Stockton Evening Mail*, "Mrs. Le Doux Bought Deadly Cyanide of Potassium," Thurs., Mar. 29, 1906, p. 1.

18. Ibid., "The Facts Are Conclusive, But Officers Are Reticent," Thurs., Mar. 29, 1906,. p. 1.

19. *The Stockton Daily Evening Record*, "Le Doux Woman Faces Damaging Circumstances," Thurs., Mar. 29, 1906, p. 1.

20. *The Stockton Evening Mail*, "Coroner's Jury Charges Mrs. Le Doux with Murder," Fri., Mar. 20, 1906, p. 1.

21. *The Stockton Daily Evening Record*, "Mrs. Le Doux Arraigned," Wed., Apr. 4, 1906, p. 8.

22. Ibid., "Tomorrow, The Trial," Mon., June 4, 1906, p. 8.

23. *The Stockton Evening Mail*, "Self Destruction To Be The Defense of Mrs. Le Doux," Tues., June 5, 1906, p. 1.

24. Ibid., "Poisons and Their Effects The Main Topic In The Le Doux Case," Wed., June 13, 1906, p. 1.

25. *The Stockton Daily Evening Record*, "Mrs. Le Doux Has New Pair of Shoes," Tues., June 12, 1906, p. 8.

26. *The Stockton Daily Evening Record*, "Woman Doomed To Death On The Gallows," Mon., June 25, 1906, p. 1.

27. Ibid., "Emma Le Doux Is Sentenced," Tues., Aug. 7, 1906, p. 1.

28. *San Francisco Murders*, p. 201

29. Ibid., p. 201

CHAPTER NINE: "THE MOVIE STAR AND THE PARTY GIRL—1921"

1. *Roscoe "Fatty" Arbuckle: A Biography of the Silent Film Comedian, 1887-1933* by Stuart Oderman, McFarland & Company, Inc., Jefferson, N.C., 1994, pp. 3-10.

2. Ibid., pp. 27-18.

3. *King of Comedy* by Mack Sennet as told to Cameron Shipp, Doubleday, Garden City, N.Y., 1954, p. 156.

4. *Kops and Custards* by Kalton Lahue and Terry Brewer, University of Oklahoma Press, Norman, OK., 1967, p. 142.

5. *Roscoe "Fatty" Arbuckle*, p. 49.

6. *World of Laughter, The Motion Picture Comedy Short* by Kalton C. Lahue, University of Oklahoma Press, Norman, OK, 1966, p. 111.

7. *The Day The Laughter Stopped* by David Yallop, St. Martin's Press, New York, 1976, p. 84.

8. *Roscoe "Fatty" Arbuckle* by Paul H. Henry, website, p. 2 of 19.

9. *San Francisco Examiner*, "Miss Rappe Was Designer, Film Actress," Sun., Sept. 11, 1921, p. 3.

10. *The Day The Laughter Stopped*, p. 111.

11. *Roscoe "Fatty" Arbuckle*, pp. 181-182.

12. *Newsweek*, "Tales of Celebrity Babylon," June 27, 1994, p. 26.

13. *San Francisco Chronicle*, "Girl Dead After Wild Party In Hotel," Sat., Sept. 10, 1921, p. 1.

14. *San Francisco Telephone Directory,* 1923, p. 286.

15. *Roscoe "Fatty" Arbuckle*, p. 156.

16. Ibid., p. 156.

17. *San Francisco Examiner*, "Arbuckle Is Charged With Murder of Girl," Sun., Sept. 11, 1921, p. 1.

18. *Roscoe "Fatty" Arbuckle*, p. 153.

19. *The Fatty Arbuckle Case* by Leo Guild, Paperback Library, New York, 1962, p. 71.

20. *San Francisco Examiner*, "Girl Rational When She Named Actor," Sun., Sept. 11, 1921, p. 1.

21. Ibid., "Many Bruises Are Found By the Coroner On Girl's Body," Sun., Sept, 11, 1921, p. 3.

22. Ibid., "Los Angeles Actress Dies Here After Booze Party In Hotel," Sat. Sept, 10, 1921, p. 2.

23. *New York Times*, "Miss Rappe's Fiancé Threatens Vengeance," Tues., Sept. 13, 1921, p. 1.

24. *The Day The Laughter Stopped*, p. 190-191.

25. *Roscoe "Fatty" Arbuckle*, p. 152.

26. *The Day The Laughter Stopped*, p. 191.

27. *San Francisco Examiner*, "Arbuckle Dragged Girl to Room, Witness Says," Thurs., Sept. 15, 1921, p. 1.

28. *New York Times*, "Arbuckle Dragged Rappe Girl To Room, Woman Testified," Tues., Sept. 13, 1921, p. 1.

29. *San Francisco Examiner*, "Arbuckle Film Withdrawn From Two Theatres," Sun., Sept. 11, 1921, p. 3.

30. Ibid., "Comedian Is Charged With Girl's Death," Wed., Sept. 14, 1921, p. 2.

31. Ibid., "Arbuckle Will Be Tried for Murder," Sat., Sept., 17, 1921, p. 1.

32. Ibid., "Fatty Films Barred Out of Many Theatres," Tues., Sept. 13, 1921, p. 2.

33. *Roscoe "Fatty" Arbuckle*, p. 172

34. *San Francisco Examiner*, "Co-Authors of the Scenario of Arbuckle's Fate," Sat., Nov. 19, 1921, p. 2.

35. *The Fatty Arbuckle Case by Leo Guild, p. 107.*

36. *The Day The Laughter Stopped*, p. 248.

37. *San Francisco Chronicle*, "Arbuckle Quickly Acquitted," Thurs., Apr. 13, 1922, p. 1.

38. *The Day The Laughter Stopped*, p. 255.

39. Ibid., p. 254.

40. *Roscoe "Fatty" Arbuckle,* p. 193.

CHAPTER TEN: "MR. SCHWARTZ, MR. WARREN AND MR. BARBE—1925"

1. *Oakland Post-Inquirer*, "A Description of Schwartz Broadcast," Tues., Aug. 4, 1925, p. 8.

2. *Oakland Tribune*, "A Schwartz Case Inquest Set for Thurs.," Wed., Aug. 12, 1925, p. 2.

3. *Oakland Post-Inquirer*, "Identification of Schwartz Blast Victim Doubted," Sun., Aug. 9, 1925, p. 2.

4. *Oakland Tribune*, "Chemist Died in Explosion of Invention," Fri., July 31, 1925, p. 1.

5. *Great Crimes of San Francisco*, edited by Dean W. Dickensheet, Comstock Editions, Inc., Sausalito, CA, 1974, p. 88.

6. *Oakland Post-Inquirer*, "Exhaustive Probe Launched," Sat., Aug. 1, 1925, p. 2.

7. *Oakland Tribune*, "Dr. Schwartz Murdered By Hammer Blows on Head, Autopsy Reveals," Sun., Aug. 2, 1925, p. 1.

8. Ibid., "Blast Death Probed As Murder Plot," Sat., Aug. 1, 1925, p. 1.

9. *Oakland Post-Inquirer*, "Row Over Body of Slain Man," Mon., Aug. 3, 1925, p. 1.

10. Ibid., "Slayer-Suicide Danced, Played Cards as Police of Nation Tracked Him," Sun., Aug. 9, 1925, p. 2.

11. Ibid., "Mrs. Schwartz's Composure Astounds Walnut Creek People," Tues., Aug. 4, 1925, p. 8.

12. Ibid., "Schwartz Murdered Says Attorney, Blood Found in Cabin Proof," Sat., Aug. 7, 1925, p. 2.

13. *Eleven Days Wonder* by Lenore Glen Offord, Comstock Editions, Inc., Sausalito, CA, 1981, p. 79.

14. Ibid., p. 81.

15. *Oakland Tribune*, "Man in $50,000 Love Suit Tells of Friendship," Fri., July 24, 1925, p. 26.

16. Ibid., "Note Gives New Clue to Schwartz," Thurs., Aug. 6, 1925, p. 1.

17. *Oakland Post-Inquirer*, "Mrs. Schwartz Plays Mystery Role In Tragedy," Tues., Aug. 4, 1925, p. 8.

18. *Oakland Tribune*, "Schwartz Berkeley Home Found Stripped In Hunt for Suspected Chemist," Wed., Aug. 5, 1925, p. 1.

19. *Oakland Post-Inquirer*, "List of Missing Men Gives Clue," Sat., Aug. 8, 1925, p. 4.

20. *Oakland Tribune*, "Missing Portuguese Is Burned In Midnight Plot Declares Bay Area Sleuth," Sun., Aug. 9, 1925, p. 2.

21. Ibid., "Quick Finish of Slayer Expected By Crime Expert," Mon., Aug. 10, 1925.

22. *Oakland Post-Inquirer*, "Reporter Unearths Blast Victim Clue," Wed., Aug. 5, 1925, p. 1.

23. *Oakland Tribune*, "Schwartz Safety Deposit Box Taken Under Alias, Being Sought by Police," Fri., Aug. 7, 1925, p. 1.

24. Ibid., "Landlord Bares Blast Slayer's Hiding Place," Mon., Aug. 10, 1925, p. 2.

25. Ibid., "Schwartz Gay Life While Hiding Bared," Mon., Aug. 10, 1925, p. 1.

26. *Oakland Post-Inquirer*, "Chemist Denies Murder In Letter to Wife," Mon., Aug. 10, 1925, p. 2.

27. *Oakland Tribune*, "Self-Slain Chemist Stole Landlord's Paper in Plot to Kill Him," Sun., Aug. 10, 1925, p. 1.

28. Ibid., "Schwartz Widow Talks At Inquest," Thurs., Aug. 13, 1925, p. 1.

29. *Oakland Post-Inquirer*, "Probe of Murder Case Closes," Wed., Aug.12, 1925, p. 1.

30. *Oakland Tribune*, "Schwartz Wife Offers Help," Sun., Aug. 8, 1925, p. 20.

CHAPTER ELEVEN: "THE VENGEFUL VALET"

1. *This Was San Francisco* by Oscar Lewis, David McKay, New York, 1962, pp. 96-97.

2. *San Francisco Examiner*, "Young Actor, Victim's Friend, Released When Clued Traced." Wed., Dec. 10, 1930, p. 1.

3. Ibid., Tues., Dec. 9, 1920, p. 1.

4. *San Francisco Chronicle*, "Chinese Aids Shadow Actor In Strangling," Dec. 12, 1930, p. 1

5. San Francisco Pacific Bell Telephone Book, 1927.

6. *San Francisco Murders*, edited by Marie F. Rodell, Duell, Sloan and Pearce, New York, p. 282.

7. *San Francisco Chronicle*, "Slain Woman's Friend Tells of Last Evening," Tues., Dec. 9, 1930, p. 3.

8. Ibid.

9. *San Francisco Chronicle*, "Police Beat Him, Declares Aged Servant," Wed., Dec. 31, 1930, p. 1.

10. *San Francisco Murders*, p. 184.

11. *San Francisco Examiner*, "Truth Exposed Manned for Lui," Tues., Dec. 9, 1930, p. 2.

12. Ibid., "Skin Patch, Heel and Button at Killing Scene," Tues., Dec. 9, 1930, p. 1.

13. Ibid., "Servant Jailed in San Francisco Actress Slaying," Dec. 9, 1930, p. 1.

14. Ibid., "Young Actor Released When Clues Traced," Dec. 10, 1930, p. 1.

15. Ibid.

16. *San Francisco Chronicle*, "Servant Jailed in San Francisco Actress Strangling," Tues., Dec. 9, 1930, p. 1.

17. Ibid.

18. *San Francisco Chronicle*, "Real Strangler Held," Thurs., Dec. 18, 1930, p. 7.

19. Ibid., "California Cannot Believe Chinese Servant the Killer," Sat., Dec. 20, 1930, editorial page.

20. Ibid., "Real Strangler Trailed," Dec. 18, 1930, p. 7.

21. *San Francisco Examiner*, "Kin of Victim Appear for Lui Fook Trial," Wed., Feb. 25, 1931, p. 5.

22. *San Francisco Chronicle*, "Lui Fook Tells of Loyalty to 'Bossy-Missy,'" Thurs., Dec. 19, 1931, p. 7.

23. *San Francisco Murders*, p. 292.

24. *San Francisco Chronicle*, "Lui Fook Freed in 21 Minutes by Death Jury," Thurs., Mar. 19, 1931, p. 1.

25. Ibid.

26. Ibid.

27. *San Francisco Chronicle*, "Jury Acquits Lui Fook in Baker Murder," Thurs., Mar. 19, 1931, p. 6.

28. Ibid., "Police Reopen Case for Baker Killer," Fri., Mar. 20, 1931, p. 4.

29. Ibid., "Chinese Rally Hails Lui Fook," Mon., Mar. 31, 1931, p. 1, second section.

CHAPTER TWELVE: "THE LAST LYNCHINGS—1933"

1. *San Jose Mercury Herald*, "Brooke L. Hart Made Executive In Father's Firm," Tues., Sept. 2, 1933, p. 2.

2. *Swift Justice, Murder and Vengeance In A California Town* by Harry Farrell, St. Martin's Press, New York, 1992, p. 91.

3. *San Jose Mercury Herald*, "Brooke Hart, Son of Wealthy Merchant Kidnapped $40,000 Ransom Demand Is Received," Fri., Nov. 10, 1933, p. 1.

4. *Swift Justice*, p. 11.

5. *San Jose Mercury Herald*, Apr. 13, 1992, p. 3C.

6. Ibid., Fri., Nov. 10, 1933, p. 2.

7. *Swift Justice*, pp. 55-61.

8. *San Francisco Chronicle*, "Wealthy San Jose Youth Kidnapped," Fri., Nov. 10, 1933, p. 1.

9. *Swift Justice*, p. 77.

10. Ibid., p. 118.

11. *San Jose Mercury Herald*, "Full Confessions Bare Detail of Brooke Hart's Kidnapping," Fri., Nov. 17, 1933, p. 10.

12. *San Jose Mercury Herald*, Sat., Nov. 18, 1933, editorial page.

13. *San Jose Evening News*, Sat., Nov. 18, 1933, editorial page.

14. *San Jose Mercury Herald*, "Emotion the Trouble," Fri., Nov. 24, 1933, editorial page.

15. *San Francisco Chronicle*," "Holmes' Father Voices Fear of Jail Lynching," Thurs., Nov. 15, 1933, p. 2.

16. Ibid., "As Swift as Law Allows", Sat., Nov. 17, 1933, editorial page.

17. *Swift Justice*, p. 147.

18. Ibid., p. 146.

19. *San Francisco Examiner*, "Killers Secretly Moved to San Francisco for Safe-keeping," Fri., Sept. 17, 1933, p. 2.

20. *San Francisco Chronicle*, "Hart Kidnap Justice Aim of Vigilantes," Sat., Nov. 25, 1933, p. 1.

21. *San Jose Mercury Herald*, "Two Duck Hunters Who Found Body Relate Details," Mon., Nov. 27, 1933, p. 3.

22. *Swift Justice*, p. 203

23. Ibid., p. 193.

24. *San Francisco Chronicle*, "Hart's Kidnap Killers Hanged by Angry Mob of 10,000," Mon., Nov. 27, 1933, p. 2.

25. *New Stories of 1933*, edited by Frank Luther Mott, T.D. Publishing, New York, p. 91.

26. *Swift Justice*, p. 224.

27. *San Jose Mercury Herald*, "Thurmond and Holmes Taken From Jail, Hanged in Park," Mon., Nov. 27, 1933, p. 2.

28. Ibid.

29. *San Francisco Call-Bulletin*, "Lynchers Defy Tear Gas and Clubs in Storming Jail," Mon., Nov. 27, 1933, p. 2.

30. *Swift Justice*, p. 224.

31. *San Francisco Call-Bulletin*, Mon., Nov. 27, 1933, p. 2.

32. *San Francisco Chronicle*, "Hell Rips Loose, Women Laugh, Sob, Cheer in the Frenzied Mob," Mon., Nov. 27, 1933, p. ccc.

33. *New Stories of 1933*, p. 120.

34. *Oakland Post Inquirer*, "Gov. Rolph Hails Lynching as a Lesson," Mon., Nov. 27, 1933, p. 1.

CHAPTER THIRTEEN: "THE ALAMEDA ENIGMA—1955"

1. *Berkeley Daily Gazette*, "Statewide Search On for Daughter of Berkeley Family," Fri., Apr. 29, 1955, p. 1.

2. Ibid.

3. *Berkeley Daily Gazette*, "Hunt for Lost Girl Widens," Mon., May 1, 1995, p. 2.

4. *Alameda Times Star*, "Circling Buzzards No Clue to Missing Girl," Sat., May 21, 1955, p. 1.

5. Ibid., "Stephanie Bryan Clue Uncovered in Basement," Sat., July 16, 1955, p. 1.

6. *Berkeley Daily Gazette*, "Stephanie Clues Spur Intensive Quiz in Mystery," July 18, 1955, p. 11.

7. *Alameda Times Star*, "Abbott Showing Signs of Stress, Continues Lie Tests," Tues., July 19, 1955, p. 1.

8. Ibid., "Arrest Ends Happy Day For Abbott," Thurs., July 2, 1955, p. 1.

9. *Great Crimes of San Francisco*, "The Lingering Doubt" by Marian Allen de Ford, Comstock Publishers, Sausalito, CA, 1981.

10. *Alameda Times Star*, "Jury Indicts Abbott," Sat., July 30, 1955, p. 1.

11. *Berkeley Daly Gazette*, "Abbott Asks to Face Bryans," Fri., July 29, 1955, p. 1.

12. *Great Crimes of San Francisco*, p. 112.

13. Ibid., p. 109.

14. *Berkeley Daily Gazette*, "Abbott and Wife Take Stand: 'He's Innocent,' Says Georgia," Wed., Jan. 11, 1956, p. 1.

15. Ibid., "Prosecutor Says Suspect's Alibi All Imaginary," Thurs., Jan. 12, 1956, p. 1.

16. *Alameda Times Star*, "Time Table for Defense Draws Contradictions," Wed., Jan. 4, 1956, p. 1.

17. *Berkeley Daily Gazette*, "Abbott Defense Nears Final Stage," Fri., Jan. 13, 1956, p. 2.

18. Ibid.

19. *Berkeley Daily Gazette*, "2 Surprise Witnesses Blast Abbott's Alibi," Sat., Jan. 7, 1956, p. 1.

20. Ibid., "Abbott Case to Jury!", Tues., Jan. 19, 1956, p. 1.

21. Ibid., "Deliberations In Abbott Case Go Into Second Day," Fri., Jan. 20, 1956, p. 2.

22. *Alameda Times Star*, "Abbott Claims Frame," Fri., Jan. 27, 1956, p. 1.

23. Ibid., "Last Moments Electric with Legal Activity," Fri., Mar. 15, 1957, p. 1.

24. *Berkeley Daily Gazette*, "Knight Raps Stay Stunt," Sat., Mar. 16, 1957, p. 1.

25. *Alameda Times Star*, "Death Penalty Would Be Dropped if Pending Bill OK'd," Fri., Mar. 15, 1957.

CHAPTER FOURTEEN: "LABOR IN THE CROSSHAIRS—1966"

1. *San Francisco, 1865-1932* by William Issel and Robert W. Cherny, University of California Press, Berkeley, Ca., 1986.

2. *Barons of Labor* by Michael Kazin, Stanford University Press, Palo Alto, CA., 1983, p. 72.

3. "Industrial Associations" file, carton 10 of the Labor Council Manuscript Collection, Bancroft Library.

4. *San Francisco Chronicle*, "S.F. Union Leader Shot Dead," Wed., Apr. 6, 1966, p. 1.

5. Ibid., p. 16.

6. *Great Crimes of San Francisco*, edited by Dean W. Dickensheet, Comstock Editions, Inc., 1934, Sausalito, CA, p. 129.

7. *San Francisco Chronicle*, "Union Men Call It An Assassination," Wed., Apr. 6, 1966, p. 13.

8. *San Francisco Chronicle*, "A Possible Link to S.F. Slaying," Thurs., Apr. 7, 1966, p. 3.

9. Ibid., "A Possible Link, cont'd.," p. 16.

10. Ibid., "S.F. Union Boss Is Threatened," Sat., Apr. 9, 1966, p. 5.

11. Ibid., "A Possible Link to S.F. Slaying," Thurs., Apr. 7, 1966, p. 3.

12. Ibid., "S.F. Painter Boss Tangled With All Kinds," Wed., Apr. 6, 1966, p. 1.

13. *Great Crimes of San Francisco*, p. 135.

14. *San Francisco Examiner*, "Imported Hirelings Slew 2 Union Chiefs," Sun., May 8, 1966, p. 1.

15. *Great Crimes of San Francisco*, p. 131.

16. Ibid., p. 133.

17. *San Francisco Chronicle*, "Wilson Trial Jury Hears Tape of Plot," Fri., Aug. 26, 1966, p. 2.

18. *San Francisco Examiner*, "Painter Fund Theft, Suicide," Wed., May 18, 1966, p. 1.

19. *San Francisco Chronicle*, "Wilson Trial Jury Hears Tape of Plot," Fri., Aug. 26, 1966, p. 2.

20. Ibid., "Murder Case Opens On Heated Note," Tues., Aug. 9, 1966, p. 1.

21. *Great Crimes of San Francisco*, p. 138.

22. *San Francisco Chronicle*, "Wilson Trial Opens on Heated Note," Tues., Aug. 9, 1966, p. 12.

23. *San Francisco Examiner*, "Story of Painters Union Welfare Fund," Thurs., May 12, 1966.

24. *San Francisco Examiner and Chronicle*, "A Painters' Trial Playbacks," Sun., Aug. 29, 1966, p. 10.

25. *Great Crimes of San Francisco*, p. 134.

26. *San Francisco Chronicle*, "Charleston Unshaken as a Witness," Wed., Aug. 31, 1966, p. 2.

27. *Great Crimes of San Francisco*, p. 138.

28. *San Francisco Examiner*, "Murder for Love Hinted by Defense," Thurs., Nov. 17, 1966.

29. Ibid., "Wife Says Donna Asked for Bribe," Wed., Jan. 18, 1967.

CHAPTER FIFTEEN: "THE SIGN OF THE ZODIAC—1970s"

1. *The Encyclopedia of Serial Killers* by Michael Newton, Checkmark Books, New York, 2000, p. 224.

2. *Zodiac*, by Robert Graysmith, Berkeley Books, New York, 1976, pp. 1-6.

3. *San Francisco Examiner & Chronicle*, "Friends Quizzed in a Slaying of Teen Pair near Vallejo," page 1, Sun., Dec. 22, 1968.

4. *Zodiac*, pp. 25-30.

5. *San Francisco Examiner & Chronicle*, "Woman Slain, Friend Shot," Sun., July 6, 1969, p. 9.

6. *Zodiac*, p. 33.

7. *Times 17, The Amazing Story of the Zodiac Murders* by Gareth Penn, The Foxglove Press, 1987, pp. 392-376.

8. *San Francisco Chronicle*, "Coded Clue In Murders," Sat., Aug. 2, 1969, p. 4.

9. Ibid., "Vallejo Mass Murder Threat Fails," Sun., Aug. 3, 1969.

10. *The Great Crimes of San Francisco* by Dean H. Dickensheet, Comstock Editions Inc., Sausalito, CA, p. 152.

11. *Times 17*, pp. 372-374.

12. *Zodiac*, p. 66.

13. Ibid., p. 71.

14. Ibid., p. 71.

15. *The Great Crimes of San Francisco*, p. 156.

16. *San Francisco Chronicle*, "Stabbing Linked to Code Killer," Mon., Sept. 29, 1969, p. 31.

17. *Zodiac*, pp. 68-69.

18. *San Francisco Examiner & Chronicle*, "Cabbies Slain In Presidio Heights," Sun., Oct. 12, 1969, p. 1.

19. Ibid., "Letter Claims Writer Killed Cabbie, 4 Others," Wed., Oct. 15, 1969, p. 1.

20. *The Great Crimes of San Francisco*, p. 159.

21. Ibid., p. 160.

22. *San Francisco Chronicle*, "I've Killed Seven: The Zodiac Claims," Wed., Nov. 12, 1969, p. 1.

23. *Zodiac*, p. 122.

24. *Times 17*, p. 100.

25. *Zodiac*, pp. 127-128

26. Ibid., p. 129.

27. *The Great Crimes of San Francisco*, p. 168.

28. *Zodiac*, p. 140.

29. *San Francisco Chronicle*, "Zodiac Sends New Letter, Claims Ten," Wed., Apr. 22, 1970, pp. 1, 18.

30. Ibid.

31. *The Great Crimes of San Francisco*, p. 166.

32. *Zodiac*, p. 152, 153.

33. Ibid., pp. 153, 154.

34. *San Francisco Chronicle*, "Gilbert and Sullivan Clue to Zodiac," Mon., Oct. 12, 1970, p. 5.

35. Ibid., "Zodiac Halloween Threat," Sat., Oct. 31, 1970, p. 16.

36. *The Great Crimes of San Francisco*, p. 172.

37. *San Francisco Chronicle*, "New Evidence in Zodiac Killings, A Link to Murder in Riverside," Mon., Nov. 16, 1970, pp. 1, 4.

38. Ibid.

39. *The Great Crimes of San Francisco*, p. 172.

40. *Times 17*, p. 322.

41. Ibid.

42. *Zodiac*, p. 177.

43. *San Francisco Chronicle*, "Zodiac Mystery Letter----The First Since 1971," Thurs., Jan. 31, 1974, pp. 1, 18.

44. *Zodiac*, p. 304.

45. Ibid., pp. 309-311.

46. *The Zodiac Killer* by Henry Welshman, Pinnacle Books, Los Angeles, 1979.

47. *San Francisco Chronicle*, "The World" Section, Sun., Dec. 11, 1986, p. 2.

48. Ibid., "Detectives Still Hunting Zodiac," Mon., May 4, 1981, p. 4.

CHAPTER SIXTEEN: "THE CITY HALL MURDERS—1977"

1. *San Francisco Examiner*, "Supervisors Sworn In—Odd Numbered Districts Get Two Year Terms," Mon., Jan. 9, 1978, page 1.

2. *San Francisco Chronicle*, "George R. Moscone—A Quiet Leader," Tues., Nov. 28, 1978, p. D.

3. *Double Play* by Mike Weiss, Addison Wesley Publishing Co., Reading, Mass, 1985, p. 18.

4. *Dianne Feinstein: Never Let Them See You Cry* by Jerry Roberts, Harper Collins West, New York, 1994, p. 151.

5. *Double Play*, p. 138.

6. Ibid., p. 69.

7. *Gayslayer* by Warren Hinkle, Silver Dollar Books, Virginia City, Nevada, 1985, p. 5.

8. *San Francisco Chronicle*, "Candidate for Supervisor Saves Two Lives", Aug. 5, 1976, p. 6.

9. *Double Play*, p. 105.

10. *The Mayor of Castro Street* by Randy Shiltz, St. Martin's Press, N.Y.; 1982, p. 184.

11. *Gayslayer*, p. 5.

12. *Double Play*, p. 157.

13. *San Francisco Chronicle*, "A Close-Up Look at Dan White," Wed., Nov. 29, 1978, p. 14.

14. *Double Play*, p. 157.

15. Ibid., p. 148.

16. Ibid., p. 160.

17. Ibid., p. 186.

18. Ibid., p. 190.

19. Ibid., p. 191.

20. *The Mayor of Castro Street*, p. 250.

21. *San Francisco Chronicle*, "White Wants Old Job Back—City Attorney Not Sure," Thurs., Nov. 16, 1978, p. 4.

22. Ibid., "White Says Resignation Was Invalid," Sat., Nov. 25, 1978, p. 30.

23. Ibid., "The Trail of Dan White," Wed., Nov. 29, p. 5.

24. *San Francisco Examiner*, "Dan White's Confession," Thurs., May 3, 1979, p. 7.

25. *Double Play*, p. 251.

26. *Dianne Feinstein: Never Let Them See you Cry*, p. 169.

27. *Double Play*, p. 250.

28. Ibid., p. 253.

29. Ibid., p. 254.

30. *The Mayor of Castro Street*, p. 271.

31. *San Francisco Chronicle*, "Stunned Silence in San Francisco," Tues., Nov. 28, 1978, p. A.

32. Ibid., "White's Dramatic Confession," Fri., May 4, 1979, p. 16.

33. *San Francisco Chronicle*, "White Trial Testimony to Begin Today," Tues., May 1, 1979, p. 2.

34. *San Francisco Examiner*, "Defense—White Mentally Ill," Tues., May 1, 1979, p. 1

35. *Transcript of the trial of "The People of the City and County of San Francisco vs. Daniel White"* for the day of May 4, 1979.

36. Ibid., May 5.

37. *Double Play*, p. 343.

38. *San Francisco Chronicle,* "It's Voluntary Manslaughter," Tues., May 22, 1979, p. 1.

39. Ibid., "A Bloody Protest at City Hall," Tues., May 22, 1979, p. 1

40. *Double Play*, p. 422.

Index

Read, E. B. 69
Red Bluff, California 227
Ren, Milton U. 150
Rentzell, Captain 41
Republican Party 61
Reudy, Alfred H. 169, 172
Reuf, A. 85
Richardson, William 6, 12
Richmond 240
Richmond district 104
Riordan, T. B. 52, 53
Riverside 271, 274
Riverside City College 271
Rock, Richard 241, 245, 251
Rock Ridge Boulevard 176
Rockland, Maine 57
Rodriguez, Joseph 176, 177
Rogers, Roy R. 135
Rolph, James, Jr. 211, 216, 279, 280
Rood, Wallace 240
Rosenbaum's General Store 125
Ross Alley 99
Rossi, Angelo 280
Rumwell, M. E. 149
Russell, C. A. 57
Russian Hill 183

S

Sacramento 16, 30, 33, 34, 53, 121,
124, 177, 217, 223, 234, 239,
242-245, 248, 249
Sacramento Street 10, 11, 12, 108
Saint James Park 211
Saint Louis 59
Salinas 256
Sam Yup Company 93, 95, 103
San Bernardino 266
San Francisco 1-5, 7, 9, 12, 14, 16,
19, 23, 25, 26, 28-31, 33-39, 41,
43, 44, 52-54, 56, 57-59, 61, 62,
68, 69, 71, 72, 74-77, 80, 82, 84,
85, 89, 91, 93, 95, 98, 100, 105,
106, 109-112, 114, 115, 120, 121,
124, 126, 127, 130, 138, 140,
141, 145, 149, 150, 153, 155,
158, 161-163, 165, 173, 183, 184,
187, 190, 192, 195, 198, 199,
204, 208, 218, 236- 238, 240,
241, 245, 250, 252, 255, 256,
260-263, 266, 279, 280, 282, 283,
285-289, 292, 298, 299, 301-303
San Francisco Alta 3
San Francisco Bay 204, 210, 221
San Francisco Board of Supervisors 281
San Francisco Bulletin 56, 129. *See
also Bulletin*
San Francisco Call-Bulletin 110
San Francisco Chronicle 63, 81, 191,
255, 265. *See also Chronicle*
San Francisco City Hall 96
San Francisco County 273, 275
San Francisco Daily Evening Bulletin 4
San Francisco earthquake 132
San Francisco Examiner 111, 126,
130, 153, 210, 223, 255. *See also
Exam iner*
San Francisco Labor Council 239
San Francisco Morning Chronicle 72
San Francisco police 187, 260
San Francisco State College 261
San Francisco's "Big Four" 30
San Francisco's Midwinter Fair 98
San Jacinto 18
San Joaquin River 121
San Joaquin Valley 121
San Jose 34, 88, 89, 141, 174, 199,
200, 204, 207-211
San Jose Avenue 221, 222
San Jose Evening News 208
San Jose Mercury Herald 200, 209
San Mateo Bridge 205, 207, 210
San Quentin 116, 136, 138, 139,
210, 217, 232, 235, 251
San Rafael 220
San Yup cemetery 104
Sandeman, Frank 112
Sandlotters 70
Santa Clara 141
Santa Clara County 208, 209, 231
Santa Clara University 203
Santa Fe line 180
Santa Fe station 127, 163
Santa Rosa, California 277
Schmitz, Eugene 279
Schwartz, Alice 163, 166, 170, 172-
174, 176, 178, 181, 182

About the Author

Charles F. Adams, a twenty-year resident of San Francisco, is chairman of the Wajim Corporation and president of Adams Enterprises. He spent his work career in international marketing and was president and chief operating officer of D'Arcy,MacManus and Masius, Inc., one of the world's largest advertising agencies. He is also a former owner and general partner of the Pittsburgh Penguins of the National Hockey League. He has chaired a number of charitable and civic organizations.

Books by Charles F. Adams

Common Sense in Advertising
(McGraw-Hill, 1968)

Heroes of the Golden Gate
(Pacific Books, 1987)

California In The Year 2000
(Pacific Books, 1991)

The Magnificent Rogues
(Pacific Books, 1998)

Murder By The Bay
(Word Dancer Press, 2005)

Check out other great California titles
at WordDancerPress.com

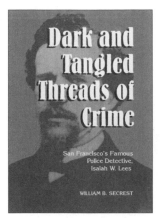

Dark and Tangled Threads of Crime

San Francisco's Famous Police Detective, Isaiah W. Lees

by William B. Secrest

$15.95
Scores of photographs and illustrations

Isaiah W. Lees came to California with the great Gold Rush, but instead of riches, he discovered he had a great talent for solving crimes and catching criminals.

In the 1850s, San Francisco was a city filled with adventurers, outlaws, con men, and desperadoes of every description. In 1853 Isaiah Lees was appointed the first chief of detectives on the new police force and over nearly fifty years he acquired an amazing record. An innovator of police methods, Lees' lifelong adventures easily eclipsed such legendary lawmen as Bat Masterson and Wyatt Earp. When he retired as police chief in 1900, the *San Francisco Chronicle* trumpeted "...in point of service, no one has ever equalled the record of Lees."

In his own time, Lees' career gained him an international reputation as one of the world's leading detectives, but somehow Lees has received short shrift in the annals of law enforcement. With this biography, master California historian William B. Secrest rescues Lees from an undeserved obscurity, fully recounting Lees' extraordinary tale for the first time.

Available at better bookstores or order Toll-Free: 800-497-4909
Or Visit WordDancerPress.com

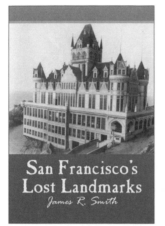